John Barth and the Anxiety of Continuance

Penn Studies in Contemporary American Fiction

A Series Edited by Emory Elliott, University of California at Riverside

A complete listing of the books in this series appears at the back of this volume

John Barth and the Anxiety of Continuance

Patricia Tobin

UNIVERSITY OF PENNSYLVANIA PRESS   *Philadelphia*

I wish to thank Rutgers, The State University of New Jersey, for the released time and the Rutgers University Research Council for the financial support that contributed to the timely completion of this book; Nancy Miller for her patient retypings; and Mindy Brown for her assiduous care to the editing.

Grateful acknowledgment is made to Harold Bloom and Oxford University Press for permission to quote from *The Anxiety of Influence, Agon: Towards a Theory of Revisionism*, and *A Map of Misreading*, and to Henry R. Schwab Publishers for permission to quote from Bloom, *Poetics of Influence*. Grateful acknowledgment is made to John Barth for permission to quote from *Lost in the Funhouse, Giles Goat-Boy, The End of the Road, the Sot-Weed Factor, The Floating Opera, and Chimera;* to The Putnam Publishing Group for permission to quote from Barth, *Sabbatical, A Romance, The Friday Book,* and *LETTERS;* and to Little, Brown and Company for permission to quote from Barth, *The Last Voyage of Somebody the Sailor.*

Library of Congress Cataloging-in-Publication Data
Tobin, Patricia Drechsel, 1935–
    John Barth and the anxiety of continuance / Patricia Tobin.
        p.   cm. — (Penn studies in contemporary American fiction)
    Includes bibliographical references and index.
    ISBN 0-8122-3093-0
    1. Barth, John—Criticism and interpretation.   I. Title.   II. Series.
PS3552.A75Z92   1992
813'.54—dc20   91-26900
                                                                          CIP

For my daughters,
SHANNON and CAYLYN,
who grew so beautifully
out from under the influence
during the course of
this book's writing.

Contents

Abbreviations

John Barth

FO   [1956] *The Floating Opera*. New York: Bantam, 1972.

ER   [1958] *The End of the Road*. New York: Grosset and Dunlap, 1971.

SWF   [1960] *The Sot-Weed Factor*. New York: Doubleday Anchor, 1987.

GGB   [1967] *Giles Goat-Boy or, The Revised New Syllabus*. Greenwich, CT: Fawcett Crest.

LF   [1968] *Lost in the Funhouse: Fiction for print, tape, live voice*. New York: Doubleday Anchor, 1988.

C   [1972] *Chimera*. Greenwich, CT: Fawcett Crest, 1973.

L   [1979] *LETTERS*. New York: G. P. Putnam's Sons.

S   [1982] *Sabbatical, A Romance*. New York: Penguin, 1983.

FB   [1984] *The Friday Book: Essays and Other Nonfiction*. New York: G. P. Putnam's Sons.

TT   [1987] *The Tidewater Tales: A Novel*. New York: Fawcett Columbine.

SS   [1991] *The Last Voyage of Somebody the Sailor*. Boston: Little, Brown.

Harold Bloom

AI   [1973] *The Anxiety of Influence: A Theory of Poetry*. New York: Oxford University Press.

MM   [1975] *A Map of Misreading*. New York: Oxford University Press.

BV   [1982] *The Breaking of the Vessels*. Chicago: University of Chicago Press.

AG   [1983] *Agon: Towards a Theory of Revisionism*. New York: Oxford University Press.

PI   [1988] *Poetics of Influence*. Ed. John Hollander. New Haven, CT: Henry R. Schwab.

The Map of Misprision

Dialectic of Revisionism	Images in the Poem	Rhetorical Trope	Psychic Defense	Revisionary Ratio
Limitation	Presence and Absence	Irony	Reaction-Formation	Clinamen
Substitution	↕	↕	↕	
Representation	Part for Whole or Whole for Part	Synecdoche	Turning against the self. Reversal	Tessera
Limitation	Fullness and Emptiness	Metonymy	Undoing, Isolation, Regression	Kenosis
Substitution	↕	↕	↕	↕
Representation	High and Low	Hyperbole, Litotes	Repression	Daemon-ization
Limitation	Inside and Outside	Metaphor	Sublimation	Askesis
Substitution	↕	↕	↕	↕
Representation	Early and Late	Metalepsis	Introjection, Projection	Apophrades

From Harold Bloom, *A Map of Misreading* (1975). By permission of Oxford University Press.

Chapter 1
Introduction: Creative Revisionism as Career

1967: "The Literature of Exhaustion"

John Barth's career as a comic novelist has now extended its course of writing over thirty-five years and ten mostly massive volumes of fiction. During this very long run, Barth has taught writing all but continuously at three major universities, given lectures and readings at numerous other campuses, stood up for literature at innumerable conferences and symposia, and on two notable occasions—in his *Atlantic* essays of 1967 and 1980—addressed himself cogently to the writing of narrative at the present time. The collection of his nonfictional pieces in *The Friday Book* (1984) testifies to the ardor that consistently placed Barth in the literary thick of things, and nothing has stuck to him with a more relentless adhesive than the sticky critical problem of defining the direction and import of "postmodernism."

Even before the term enjoyed any critical currency, Barth was sharing his intimations of its onslaught with the *Atlantic*'s educated readers. It was the American High Sixties, 1965–73, and Barth was right in the middle of them in Buffalo, at the state university center Nelson Rockefeller had built, now self-styled as the "Berkeley of the East" and housing an English faculty proudly self-designated as the "Ellis Island of Academia" (*FB*, 63). At the side of Barth, his esteemed colleague Leslie Fiedler was crying the death of the novel, and to the north of him, Marshall McLuhan was heralding the death of the whole Gutenberg galaxy in the wake of a new electronic culture. How is a writer in his mid-thirties to respond to such apocalyptic clamor? A writer who already has four novels behind him, work that has been sufficiently acclaimed and debated among critics of note to encourage his conviction that he's got the right stuff to become the foremost writer of his generation, and a writer who clearly intends making a career of it, thus one for whom knowing how to go on is of crucial if not sole significance? Barth responded reasonably and cheerfully, and to this day he probably does not comprehend what caused all the furor.

What Barth said in 1967 was that there was no cause for despair when, as can happen in the natural course of literary history, artists come to perceive certain forms as used up or worn out; rather, it is a time of opportunity for the interesting writer, who will move beyond refutation and repudiation to deploy these "felt ultimacies" as material and means for his own work, thereby creating new and original literature out of a literary heritage that is truly inexhaustible. After the silences of Beckett, Barth suggested, "It might be conceivable to rediscover validly the artifices of language and literature—such far-out notions as grammar, punctuation . . . even characterization! even *plot*!—if one goes about it the right way, aware of what one's predecessors have been up to" (*FB*, 68). Or a writer might take his cue from Borges' metaphysical parables of narrative production: from "Pierre Menard, Author of the Quixote," which applauds the originality of a twentieth-century French Symbolist's re-creation of Cervantes' seventeenth-century Spanish novel, from which it differs in nary a word; or from "Tlön, Uqbar, Orbius Tertius," which features an infinitely catalogued, imaginary world whose objects begin to appear in the real world as a lively inversion of the ancient mimetic contract between art and reality. For the alert visionary company of writers that Barth calls to his colors, the literature of exhaustion would quickly give way to a literature of replenishment, and in the conversion of disabling contradictions into enabling paradoxes, contemporary writers would be furthering a "positive artistic morality" while engaging in a "heroic enterprise, with salvation as its object" (*FB*, 75).

The geniality and optimism of Barth's remarks, however, could not offset the negative payload carried by his title word, "Exhaustion," which established the base note that would be heard throughout the high-pitched star wars over postmodernism in the years to come. We critics all have our hard-earned territories to sing, our well-considered agendas and affiliations to defend, and in the ensuing debates, postmodernism managed somehow always to hide its face while very much exposing our own. One could not enter the discussion without discovering one's preference between, say, repetition and difference, or between the tradition and the avant-garde, or between continuity and rupture; and in the process of drawing boundaries and discovering allies and foes, we critics, rare birds all, increasingly consolidated as birds of a feather.

So it was that some critics followed Jerome Klinkowitz down the road that privileges historical discontinuity, political adversariness, and absolute originality when, in his *Literary Disruptions* (1975), Professor Klinkowitz anathematized John Barth as a "regressive parodist," whose 1967 essay was a "literary suicide note" from a done-for author who, having exhausted his vein of originality, could now only stoop to parodying older stories and earlier forms. Any appreciative critic of Barth's fiction would want to take issue with any number of Klinkowitz's perverse pronouncements. The one I can't resist is his interpretation of Barth's essay as an "endorsement of those Sixties writers who had abandoned the Great American novel, and turned fiction—like poetry before it—into an elitist, academic diversion" (4). Reading this charge, I am reminded that elitism might better be laid at the feet of Klinkowitz's own surfictionists, and that not one of his disruptionists has ever made the grand bid for the Great American Novel that Barth made in 1960 with *The Sot-Weed Factor*. Local skirmishes aside, what will expose the weakness of Klinkowitz's position is the global assumption about originality and repetition that sustains his two terms of chastisement, parody and regression.

Parody is by no means a latecomer in the history of literary forms, nor is the writer of parody a figure besotted by belatedness. Quite the contrary, as Joseph Dane reminds us in his recent study of parody, *Critical Concepts versus Literary Practices, Aristophanes to Sterne* (1988), parody was a respectable option within classical poetics, and those who deployed it were among our most vital and original authors. Closer to modern times, as Barth himself is fond of repeating, the parodic anti-novel was born *as* the novel or *with* the novel, depending upon whether one is tracing the European line back to Cervantes' parody of Amadis de Gaul, or the English line back to its double origin in the twinned novels of Richardson and Fielding. Far from being a desperate and degraded phenomenon of literary secondariness, parody, in fact, has exhibited a shining virtue for bringing on the new by bringing out what has been ignored in the old, functioning as a fresh and robust, materialist airing of all that was smothered beneath the stale idealizations of Greek and Roman tragedy and bourgeois realism.

In the fifteen years since Klinkowitz's study, with the academic popularization of Mikhail Bakhtin's studies, parody has suffered critical inflation within the advocacies of both narrative theorists, who claim it as the backbone of narrative form and narrative history, and critics of the Left, who hear in the carnivalesque voicings of marginalities and minorities a democratizing force that encourages social hope. Such critical works as *The Politics of Transgression* (1986), by Allon White and Peter Stallybrass, and Linda Hutcheon's *A Theory of Parody: The Teachings of Twentieth-Century Art Forms* (1985) celebrate parody's generalization and amelioration on the world's historical stage and within our theoretical endeavors; but one might also suspect, with the wide circulation of parody as a wild card, that the whole critical enterprise has turned into a political crapshoot and that after the game is played out, the concept in its literary specialization will once again be consigned to pejoration.

I tend to concur with Joseph Dane's sobering suggestions that parody now requires some purification and deflation, and that perhaps, given its present entanglements, its study should be shifted from the realm of artistic production to that of critical reception. Consider, for instance, the scrupulous care with which semiotician and reception theorist Umberto Eco handles parody. In "Innovation and Repetition: Between Modern and Post-Modern Aesthetics" (1985), Eco identifies parody as but one type of the intertextuality so pervasive in our contemporary art forms, as a single instance of intertextual dialogue that includes ironic retakes and playful remakes, burlesques and travesties, quotation, citation, and plagiarism. Although such repetitions can appear in high or popular art and although neither their excellence nor banality can be guaranteed or ruled out, Eco argues that for the sophisticated postmodern receiver, whose critical intelligence precludes naive reception, repetition has become the source of a continuing pleasure at least as great as that accorded innovation in the past. Very much aware of the debasement that repetition has suffered within our Platonic theory of representation—which recognizes no copy, imitation, or replication that is not debased—Eco offers the interesting hypothesis that our current fascination with repetition, as opposed to the old idealization of innovation, may represent a divide between modern and postmodern aesthetics.

Yet even at the very origins of modernism, in T. S. Eliot's "Tradition and the Individual Talent" (1919), we encounter the same plaint against the privilege accorded originality and a similar plea for a proper respect for repetition. Eliot's well-known assault upon the Romantics opens with a severe call to critics to become self-reflective about the act of criticism:

> One of the facts that might come to light in this process is our tendency to insist, when we praise a poet, upon those aspects in his work in which he least resembles anyone else. In these aspects or parts of his work we pretend to find what is individual, what is the particular essence of the man. We dwell with satisfaction upon the poet's difference from his predecessors; we endeavor to find something that can be isolated in order to be enjoyed. Whereas if we approach a poet without this prejudice we shall often find that not only the best, but the most individual parts of his work may be those in which the dead poets, his ancestors, assert their immortality most vigorously. And I do not mean the impressionable period of adolescence, but the period of full maturity. (71)

Eliot's passage is a useful reminder that postmodernism has yet a Romantic heritage to deal with, and that it was the Romantics who reintroduced the concept of absolute originality, glorifying as its source the self-affirming Poetic Soul and esemplastic Imagination. It seems that to be a postmodernist one must be resolutely post-Romantic on this matter of repetition and innovation. The critical mistaking of John Barth, which attributes a state of literary decadence to parody in particular and intertextuality in general, would then be properly understood as the proceeding of a modernist sensibility yet entangled in this Romantic prejudice.

Elsewhere, the postmodernist critical practice has proven itself decisively post-Romantic. The structuralists and semioticians, in their foregrounding of language and literature as rule-governed structures with built-in limits and constraints, have fenced in the free range of the Romantic imagination; and the deconstructionists, with their teasing out of the play of textuality at the linguistic surface, have thoroughly demolished the Romantic notion of the poem as a fading ember dropped from the white-hot and ineffable I-am. However, alone among the theorists, only Harold Bloom has come up directly against the Romantic peril, with his strong revision of literary history that grounds the creative process in the antithetical poetic will of desperate poets who must wrest their patrimony from their predecessors within the tradition—a revision that scotches both the Romantics' originary imagination and Eliot's benign tradition. Anyone reading Bloom's mythopoeic *The Anxiety of Influence* in 1973 knew that literary history had suddenly become a psychodrama of compelling interest.

1973: *The Anxiety of Influence*

The Anxiety of Influence is Harold Bloom's melancholic anatomy of poetic melancholy. For Bloom, poetic influence since the Renaissance has been a scene of catastrophic creation, agonistic strife, and ambivalent transference, and the creativity of our strongest poets has necessarily been grounded in an antithetical and revisionary stance toward their precursors that involves negation, evasion, and extravagance:

Poetic Influence—when it involves two strong, authentic poets—always proceeds by a misreading of the prior poet, an act of creative correction that is actually and necessarily a misinterpretation. The history of fruitful poetic influence, which is to say the main tradition of Western poetry since the Renaissance, is a history of anxiety and self-saving caricature, of distortion, of perverse, willful revisionism without which modern poetry as such could not exist. (*AI*, 30)

It was Bloom's genius to recognize the parallel between the ephebe poet and the oedipal son in Freud's "family romance": The form-making of the poetic will, like the self-making of the defensive ego, seeks an impossible identification away from the father, and makes audacious and anxious attempts at self-begetting in willful revisions that vitalize the quest for independent identity and authority while confirming the compulsion by which we are condemned to repeat the father. Bloom's brilliantly selective trajectory through Freud's meta-psychology follows the late, dark Freud who, beyond the pleasure principle, affirms that no happy substitutions for the father are possible:

> This is the Freud who establishes the priority of anxiety over its stimuli, and who both imagines the origins of consciousness as a catastrophe and then relates that catastrophe to repetition-compulsion, to the drive-toward-death, and to the defense of life as a drive toward agonistic achievement, an agon directed not only against death, but against the achievements of anteriority, of others, and even of one's own earlier self. (*AG*, 97)

Poetic art thus ultimately arises from the oedipalized poet's phantasies of the precursor's omnipotence, of an Imaginary and Symbolic father whom he cannot deny but must not worship and therefore is condemned to magnify, in the creative acts of falsifying, mis-taking, and misreading that shake him every which way but loose. Fixated upon his predecessor, at once identifying with and repressing his un-matchable achievements, traumatized by his own belatedness, yet avid to become the self-engendering father of himself, and finally slammed into the compulsions to repeat of the death-drive—this is Bloom's anxiety-ridden and aggressive young poet destined for greatness, whose quest for literary authority, like the child's quest for unique identity, can proceed only through resilient protestations against influence.

This creative wherewithal of the strong poet, which can nevertheless not succeed in killing the father, Bloom charts as six *revisionary ratios* available to the poet as stances, acts, and turns against the poetic father: The ephebe can swerve from the precursor (*clinamen*), antithetically complete him (*tessera*), reduce and empty him out (*kenosis*), bring him low (*daemonization*), curtail and exile him (*askesis*), and call him back from the dead (*apophrades*). The story of poetic "success" that Bloom tells is thus radically ambiguous even more so because it is belatedness itself that condemns the poet to take his revenge against Time's "it was," and to try to escape and refute the fate of a latecomer. Freud may be Bloom's main man, but Nietzsche is Bloom's first prophet of anti-thetical revisionism, and his deconstruction of culture in *A Genealogy of*

Morals is the model for Bloom's own de-idealization of literary history in *The Anxiety of Influence*.

Two studies on specific authors, appearing since the publication of Bloom's book, instruct us in the kinds of slippage that can occur when the oedipal agon is translated by interpretive critics into the drama of a literary career. In *Prodigal Sons: A Study in Authorship and Authority* (1980), David Wyatt deploys the biblical parable of departure and happy homecoming as a frame tale that encompasses the literary careers of various American modernists—except that their successful cyclical completion of the pattern of the mythic heroes is directly contrary to the lyrical unsuccess of Bloom's strong poet and to Freud's own view of the oedipal conflict as the "nucleus of the neuroses." In *Doubling and Incest/Repetition and Revenge* (1975), John Irwin argues much more closely to the spirit of Bloom, but then in Nietzschean fashion generalizes the theme of belatedness into a revenge on deeds through words intended by all creative users of language. Wyatt's chapter on Faulkner is, in fact, a revision of Irwin's book on Faulkner, and considering them together, we come to comprehend that Bloom's theory of anxious influence, without further implementation, is neither complex nor persuasive enough in its own right to cover the extensions of a real-life career.

Both critics, but especially Wyatt, rely heavily upon the evidence in Joseph Blotner's biography of the "problem of unconsummated revenge" that plagued the male members of Faulkner's family line, and upon the same expressed theme that informs the dynastic families in Faulkner's Yoknapatawpha novels. Moreover, each makes his own selective and incomplete trajectory through Faulkner's works which stops far short of the oeuvre that constitutes his career: Irwin focuses on the Compson and Sutpen families in *The Sound and the Fury* (1932) and *Absalom, Absalom!* (1936), whereas Wyatt follows the Sartoris family in *Sartoris* (1929) and *The Unvanquished* (1938). My point is not that these two critical practices have somehow failed Bloom's theory—they are indeed compelling interpretations in their own right; it is rather that Bloom's theory has yet to undergo a development sufficiently comprehensive to float the vast ship of a career. What is lacking is the diachronic and synchronic articulation of the antithetical creative process.

Without handing the critic the biographical and themative evidence so generously supplied by Faulkner to his critics, how could Barth, in his self-becomings and form creatings, be accommodated by Bloom's theory? His line of descent from hard-working German immigrants claims no locally famous great-grandfather to make Barth feel that he's at the diminished tail end of dynastic distinction, nor do his novels

feature anything but affectionate portraits of real and imaginary predecessors. More to the point, Barth's pronouncements of opportunistic
delight, in "The Literature of Exhaustion," at finding himself the
belated son of a long literary line mark a comic vision wholly contrary
to Bloom's gloomy insistence on the "melancholy of the creative mind's
insistence on priority" (*AI*, 13). Barth is happy to be a latecomer and
grateful to the tradition for its treasure trove that can be raided for new
fabulation. Like the chambered nautilus, which carries its personal
history on its back, literary history for the writer, says Barth, is "his
Personal Flotation device, not a dead weight carrying him under" (*FB*,
170). Nor, argues Barth, should the contemporary writer feel any
anxiety about his immediate or near predecessors: "My ideal postmodernist neither merely repudiates nor merely imitates either his twentieth-century modernist parents or his nineteenth-century premod-
ernist grandparents. He has the first half of our century under his belt,
but not on his back" (*FB*, 203).

Barth's doubled modification of "repudiates" and "imitates" with a
twice-told "merely" in this pronouncement should alert us to the im-
plication that he knows some poetic maneuvers between these oedipal
extremes that are more conducive to productive displacements of the
father. For Barth *is* an agonist, no doubt about it. In a clear reference to
his own practice, he affirms that "any gutsy writer who happens to be
afflicted with a formalist imagination would . . . feel compelled to go the
existing corpus one better, or two or three better . . . in order to
actualize an attractive possibility in the ancient art of storytelling that
one's distinguished predecessors have barely suggested" (*FB*, 234).
Barth is a competitor then, and very antithetical and revisionary in the
bargain, but the enterprise is a buoyant one, unburdened by any cloud
of anxiety or unconscious revenge or bad conscience.

More telling than his direct negation of literary influence is Barth's
tone—affectionate and playful, but finally just plain casual—whenever
he finds himself in the vicinity of precursordom. Nowhere is this more
evident than in the graceful and humorous address Barth delivered on
Walt Whitman Day, 1976, in the Good Gray Poet's house in Camden,
New Jersey. It is patently clear that, prior to his invitation as a guest
speaker, Barth had given no thought whatsoever to Whitman as a
potential precursor, but under the gun now, he discovers a connection—and proceeds to run amok with Bloom's theory of influence:

Whitman's project of going forward by going *back*, beyond the immediate
European conventions of verse and their American imitations, to something
older, looser, freer, more epical and rough—there were surely some resemblances there to *my* project of returning to the inventors of the English novel
for my long story of Ebenezer Cooke, the misfortunate poet laureate of Mary-

land, in order as it were to make an end run around Flaubert and the modernist novel. So I discovered in Walt Whitman not a lost father, for better or worse, but a kind of mislaid literary uncle, who seemed to me to ratify, after the fact— benignly, avuncularly—my own project. (*FB*, 154)

The absurdist tilt toward influence—benign, avuncular, and mislaid literary uncles!—is quintessential Barth. Yet one also notices that, were Bloom looking for it, Barth has supplied him with a superbly anxious motive for writing the kinds of books that Barth writes. If the precursor problem seems always to recede from Barth, it is because, as a post-oedipal postmodernist, Barth reaches back down the far-away centuries to a pre-oedipal and non-oedipal past—for Homer, Scheherazade, Cervantes, Fielding—to cultures in which the conflictual drama between fathers and sons does not occur. What stronger revision/ greater evasion could Bloom hope for, from a poetic will determined "to make an end run around Flaubert and the modernist novel"? It is all of oedipal culture, and not just the twentieth century, that Barth has deliberatively put under his belt and off his back: It's a canny, comic child who doesn't know his own father, Harold.

In the closing lines of the Whitman address—as if he hadn't taunted Bloom enough—Barth mentions him by name, the only time in *The Friday Book* that he does so, but merely to hedge in the theory of influence with two much more tantalizing alternatives offered by Borges:

Well. Jorge Luis Borges says in his essay on Kafka that every writer creates his own precursors. This is the opposite of Harold Bloom's argument that great writers as it were were created *by* their precursors—by their struggles against and pacts with their spiritual fathers. Borges also says, in an essay on Walt Whitman, that Whitman, who *had* no immediate precursors, invented himself. (*FB*, 157)

However, Barth and Borges only apparently have the last word on Bloom in this passage.

My argument is essentially this. John Barth has indeed chosen the Whitman option from the three above, but he conducts his self-inventions within the Bloomian schema of oedipal conflict—not inventing himself, like Whitman, once and for all in a miraculous conception aimed at public consumption, but rather *re*inventing himself with each new work of art, as new ephebe to his own precursor, in order that the career might go on. In taking himself as precursor, Barth has potently revised Bloom on two counts: With no diminishment in the agonistic strife, he has realized at the *core* of both the creative process and the life cycle of the poet the antithetical revisionism which Bloom had theorized as their *context*; and he has rendered poetic anxiety much more conscious and urgent in his retirement of the anxiety of influence for an *anxiety of continuance*. Such a threefold shift in focus—from context to core, from influence to continuance, and from the poem to the career—is not explicitly countermanded by Bloom's theory. Rather, it is more like an outside option that infrequently presents itself while Bloom concentrates on how poems are influenced by other poems in his oedipalized literary history. In fact, in his own critical practice, especially when he interprets his own strong poets, Bloom can swerve in this Barthian direction; reading Bloom across his books, on Emerson or Whitman or Stevens, one begins to recognize an individual career emerging, one that is self-contained and self-regulated by a one-on-one antitheticalism. As Bloom acknowledges concerning Freud, the strongest of modern revisionists (*AG*, 129), the stronger the poet, the more likely he is to reinvent himself as his own precursor. Barth, I am arguing, is such a poet.

There occurs a distinct escalation and extension of motivation once the outside is brought in, when the Bloomian context is moved to the Barthian core and Barth, self-divided into eternal precursor and eternal ephebe, goes after himself, Barth-on-Barth. For the writer, the anxiety of influence tends to recede (Who can really care about precursor priority when he is his own pa, grandpa, and great-grandpa?), while the anxiety over continuance increases and sustains itself, the view through time continually growing less retrospective and more prospective ("What to do for yet another and yet another encore? How to save and save again one's narrative neck?" [*FB*, 219]). Poetic anxiety becomes positively creative and life-affirming when, aimed at continuance, it directs itself against any danger that would terminate the career; and in the poetic misreading of his work, the poet discovers that a miss is often better than a hit and that failure can open up many more options than success. With no modernist distinction between the man who suffers and the mind that creates, such a doubled postmodernist is constantly engaging his life in the creative process, making the self as he makes a career, and each ongoing project is crucially involved with the other.

Nevertheless, as Barth tropes Barth with each new novel, temporarily banishing himself as Covering Cherub and re-marking himself as ephebe, his antithetical turns are not those unpredictable spasms of intuition imagined by the Romantics as the poetic imagination. Rather, Barth's creative revisions of his previous work will follow precisely the sequence of revisionary ratios predicated for the strong poet by Bloom in *A Map of Misreading* (1975). But before we turn to this expert retooling by Bloom of his theory of influence, let us hear Barth on the self-reinventions that ground his creative process and the anxiety of continuance that fuels it:

If the writer is not going to repeat himself (which isn't always a bad thing to do), he has to keep changing, more or less reinventing himself. He hopes that the changes are "developments"; that his "stages," like a rocket's, are all pushing the same payload to heaven, in their different ways. He hopes too—since some legs of the trip are liable to be rougher than others—that his audience will stay with him across the troll-bridges and that they'll reach the happy cabbage fields together. (*FB*, 78)

1975: "The Map of Misprision"

Two years after *The Anxiety of Influence*, Bloom had completed the appropriations—from Freud, from classical rhetoric, from negative theology—that culminated in the comprehensive and potent paradigm of the creative process that is his "Map of Misprision," the document that summarizes Bloom's analogical thinking in *A Map of Misreading*. For this second development of his thought, Bloom put his radical reinterpretation of the poetic tradition in the background, and brought to the foreground the creative process through which the poetic will moves, once the strong poet has committed himself to an antithetically revisionist stance toward his precursor. The central creative act of misprision, or misreading or misinterpretation, is broken down into its synchronic and diachronic articulations in the map, which charts the recurring pattern Bloom discovered in the great poems of the Western tradition, culminating in Wordsworth's grand crisis-poem, the *Intimations* ode. Bloom intended his map for single poems, in which the becomings of the self and the creatings of artistic form take place in an intense, analogous domain—a domain where the poet-as-poet mobilizes his *revisionary ratio* against the blocking agent, effectuates the *dialectic of revisionism* that mandates a self-contraction prior to any representation, assembles the *psychic defense* that stabilizes the ego and directs itself against change, deploys the *rhetorical trope* that turns defensively against literal meaning in willful error, and creates the *poetic image* that is the masked imitation within space and time of our makings and becomings.

My own revisionary move is to use the map to chart the course of John Barth's long literary career as a diachronic progress in creative self-revision that receives its synchronic punctuation with his ten volumes of fiction. Bloom's map provides excellent accommodations for that career through Barth's seventh volume, after which the mature and major poet recommences the second half of his life and career in a Second Reenactment. Barth's Second Revolution remains true enough in its fashion to the spirit of Bloom's map, yet just unfaithful enough to its letter—in swerves that only a post-Romantic, postmodernist novelist with a comic vision could have dreamed up—that Barth's critic, comically belated as she is to Bloom the Father, must extract from her author's latter three novels such ratios, defenses, tropes, and images as were undreamt of in Bloom's modernist philosophy. The current stage or stance from the map that Barth is assuming in the ongoing process of the career is reprinted for easy reference beneath the heading of each chapter, which will consider the book (or books) produced at this particular point of armistice in the battles of Barth against Barth. For the moment, however, the reader may want to turn to the reprint of Bloom's entire map at the front of this book, since I shall now follow Bloom, much too summarily, through his own explanations of its diachronic successions down the vertical columns and its analogical relations across the horizontal.

Misprision. "The term can refer to anything from treason, malfeasance in office, wrongful capture, through mistake to scorn or misprizing. These all mean being wrong. The larger sense is mistaking" (*PI*, xxix). This is John Hollander speaking, as editor of the volume of Bloom's excerpted pieces and essays entitled *Poetics of Influence* (1988), and he urges Bloom's readers to take this central act of the antithetical imagination for the dynamic and violent poetic revision that it is—*mistaking*, says Hollander, that rhymes with *breaking, shaking, faking, waking* as well as *making*, and that collects such aggressive meanings as taking in and on, taking up, over, and out, undertaking and overtaking. We must evade the trivial in every case of misprision, if we are to understand the force that is necessarily and deliberately exerted by the poetic will in the creation of the antithetical new.

Revisionary ratio. Carried over from *The Anxiety of Influence*, Bloom's six revisionary ratios parade down the fifth column(!) of his map as "relations between unequal terms, because the later poet always magnifies the precursor in the very act of falsifying ('interpreting') him" (*MM*, 95). Bloom derived their number and sequence from his model of the Romantic crisis-poem. Designating the poet's present revisionary task, they are also the forms within which analogous tropes and defenses can be interchanged by the practicing antithetical critic. As ratios of revision against a blocking agent, they work in matched or dialectical pairs, each one following the pattern of the dialectic of revisionism, represented vertically as the map's first column.

Dialectic of revisionism. This is the pattern of limitation/substitution/ representation that Bloom discovered in Isaac Luria's strong misreading in the sixteenth century of the Genesis Creation story, a radical reinterpretation that identified the Creator as the source of violence and chaos in the world. Bloom's anxiety book, it has been suggested, was written in a large sense against the illusory freedom of the Romantic imagination; the map book, via Luria's argument for Creation as God's contractive self-limitation, is written against the poet's fullness of being. Luria's heretical myth of antithetical Creation is at once more catastrophic and more creative than Freud's family romance. Bloom finds its basic rhythm of contraction, filling and breaking, and restitution to be more commensurate with the violent limitation/substitution/ representation by which poetic meaning is produced—limitation is the strong poet's re-seeing, substitution is his re-estimating, and representation is his re-aiming (*MM*, 4–5). Like the revisionary ratios that Bloom named from the Greek, the Lurianic appropriation reinforces the connection between trope and poetic defense. John Hollander, referring to the book in which Bloom argues for the appropriateness of his Lurianic theft, describes succinctly the functioning of Luria's dialectic:

> *Kabbalah and Criticism* provides a genetic link between the exemplary phenomenon of Kabbalah as a *model* for all neoteric, or modern (as opposed to classical) literatures, and a theory of the poetic imagination which employs Kabbalah's own concepts of withdrawing from linguistic signification (or, indeed, from truth), filling it with meaning (as an effusion of will, of intending to utter) to overflowing, and a final restitution of meaning in a transformed significance. (*PI*, xxvi)

Poetic trope. "Tropes are necessary errors about language, defending ultimately against the deathly dangers of literal meaning, and more immediately against all other tropes that intervene between literal meaning and the fresh opening of discourse" (*MM*, 94). Bloom's notion of the motive for metaphor follows Vico, for whom the metaphoric logic of the ancient giants of the "first human nature" was a willed error and a turn from literal meaning by which they defended themselves against any given that interfered with the sacred divination of the poetic nature (*MM*, 93–94). Each new tropological divination must defend against interference from prior givens; thus, we have the troping-against-trope in a diachronic rhetoric that proceeds vertically down the map. Unlike the "two-dimensional and paradigmatic at best" readings of the trope at the surface of the text by formalists and structuralists, for Bloom, as Hollander poetically explains,

> A trope is a twisted strand of transformational process, anchored deep in the rock of expressive need, and stretched upward, taut, to a connection at the surface with a flat sheet of text. . . . Bloom is concerned with the length of the rope, the layers of whatever it is through which it passes, the ways in which, at any particular level, the strands may seem in their twisting to be pointing away from the determined direction upward, the relative degrees of tension and slackness and so forth. (*PI*, xxxi)

Psychic defense. Bloom argues that what presents itself to the critic as a trope of the poetic will directed against influence likewise presents itself to the psychoanalyst as a defense of the ego directed against the drive. For Bloom, the drive in its fundamental modifications is a defense, the defense is a fantasy (and not a mechanism), and "fantasies are always tropes, in which so-called 'deep structures,' like desires, become transformed into 'surface structures,' like symptoms" (*AG*, 93). Bloom has reduced Anna Freud's basic ten ego defenses to his primary six, by reasonably bunching those that are so closely allied that they are quite difficult to distinguish separately (*MM*, 92); and he has appropriated Freud's concept of the ego's defenses for his own "poetic will," which he defines as the "ego of the poet not as a man, but of the poet as poet" (*AG*, 120). Defenses serve the cause of self-preservation and the life-instincts because they trope against death—as the trope defends against literal meaning—in their formation, protection, and enhancement of the ego.

Poetic image. The images come in polar pairs, and are imitations of the alternations possible in the phenomenal world of space and time. They are also maskings or coverings that befall the mind as it takes in the world of things, and are thus, like the trope and the defense, "forms of a ratio between human ignorance making things out of itself, and human self-identification moving to transform us into the things we have made" (*PI*, 125). Read vertically and diachronically, they trope against one another directly, with each stage representing a renewal of the mis-taking in different spatial or temporal guises.

To my knowledge, no existent studies use Bloom's map to chart a career, although some studies of poetic careers suggest the need for such a fully articulated model. Lawrence Lipking's *The Life of the Poet: Beginning and Ending Poetic Careers* (1981) concentrates on initiation and summation and thus does not set itself the task of uncovering a consistent internal logic informing the artist's augmentation and prolongation of the career. Indeed Lipking, who seems to like his middles muddy, is inclined to celebrate his poets' creative freedom and the arbitrariness of the direction it may take: "A major author may go through many stages, sometimes as often as every few years, and his career may seem to shift direction with every passing wind" (ix). Moreover, his poets are much more inclined than Barth to sacrifice their lives to poetry, submit to the refining fire, welcome dismemberment and dispersal, and squelch the authorial personality; in short, Lipking brings to his poets (Vergil to Mallarmé) an entire tragic, Romantic, and modernist pathos that would be wholly inappropriate for John Barth's career as a comic postmodernist.

A second critic of careers, more given to writerly ordeals and their structuralist description, is Edward Said, whose *Beginnings: Intention and Method* (1975) proffers a model that demonstrates his basic conviction of the unity between career and text, "a unity between an intelligible pattern of events and for the most part their increasingly conscious transformation into writing" (196). The star that Said steers by is Jean Piaget, whose broad definition of structure as a dynamic process (a system of transformations, a totality, and something capable of self-regulation) promotes the definition of a career as a *developing structure*, the regulated plasticity of a flexible subject (191–97). In considering the literary careers of Conrad, Wilde, and Proust, Said brilliantly deploys Piaget's particularizations of the developing structure and their implications—for the simultaneous gradation, conservation, and formation within a career, for the idea of a movement leading toward something, for an intensified concentration upon the achievement of completeness.

A third career-critic, Gary Lee Stonum, takes a tack similar to Said's in *Faulkner's Career: An Internal Literary History* (1979), a study very unlike the two studies that chart Faulkner's anxieties of influence. Similar to Piaget's developing structure, Stonum develops the concept of a "disciplined mobility," and for his theoretical model he appeals to what I take to be the current homology to Piaget's transformational structure, the cybernetic study of open systems. Contrary to closed systems, Stonum explains, open systems engage in goal-seeking behavior: "Such a system is capable of 'reprogramming' itself at any point, capable, that is, of remembering its own past, perceiving a present environment, and using information derived from both sources to plot a future course" (31). This is strikingly similar to Barth's description of his own method of "reprogramming": "The themes of my work, I suppose, are regression, reenactment, and reorientation. Like an ex-cart driver in monsoon season or the skipper of a grounded ship, one must sometimes go forward by going back. As an amateur sailor and navigator myself, I like the metaphor of dead reckoning: deciding where to go by determining where you are by reviewing where you've been" (*FB*, 132). With the Yoknapatawpha novels, Faulkner's career generated a vast bulk of intentional continuity, and Stonum engages in some delicate tracings of the continuous feedback loop which guided that very unified career. Faulkner impinges upon Barth's antitheticalism, nevertheless, in his own negative evaluation of each successive work as a failure in the order of perfection that he is reaching for; by this criterion, his also is a career achieved within the anxiety of continuance.

I am not prepared to argue, nor is it my desire to, for any wholesale applicability of the map of misprision to individual literary careers. It may not be a model that can be all-inclusive by virtue of its comprehensive mapping of our mental operations in relation to the physical world, although I admit to being intrigued by this possibility—more so, I suspect, than Bloom himself, who mentions only in passing the two theoreticians I have in mind. The fact is that the number and sequence of revisionary ratios on Bloom's map exhibit an extreme goodness of fit both with Piaget's six stages of the child's mental development in the construction of reality and with C. S. Peirce's sixfold progression in the semiotics of the sign (signal, index, icon, symbol, sign, allegory). My sole concern, nonetheless, is Bloom's fit with a "gutsy writer who happens to be afflicted with a formalist imagination" and typically feels "compelled . . . to actualize an attractive possibility in the ancient art of storytelling" (*FB*, 234). It is because Barth's structuralist imagination seeks greater efficiency and strength in the process of creation, and is also intensely aimed at an achievement of completeness, that the course of his career can be mapped by Bloom's schema. Returning one final time to "The Literature of Exhaustion," and retrieving some Barth that has been overlooked, we will better understand the adequation between Barth and Bloom, which is to say, Barth a-Bloom.

Barth's unflagging pursuit of Borges in that essay is a strategy cunningly designed to refute the negative connotations associated with "to exhaust"—to consume, wear out, use up, expend the whole of; to drain of strength and energy; to deprive and destroy—and to promote in their place the positive meaning of "exhaustion" as a comprehensive and thorough, even righteous, *completion*. Quoting Borges' definition of the Baroque as "that style which deliberately exhausts (or tries to exhaust) its possibilities and borders on its own caricature," Barth pursues Borges' remark down to a footnote, which contains his own italicized emphasis: "his remark about the Baroque includes the *attempt* to exhaust as well as the hypothetical achievement of exhaustion. What's more, his cardinal themes and images rather contradict that passing optimism—a state of affairs reminiscent of the aesthetics of Tlön, where no book is regarded as complete which doesn't contain its counterbook, or refutation" (*FB*, 74). Here, Barth is clearly re-tuning Borges' piano to play along with his own orchestrations of the "*attempt to exhaust*," the unending beginning-again that is Barth's best insurance against the anxiety of continuance.

Absolutely pertinent to Barth's positive version of the literature of exhaustion are Borges' two favorite images of the infinite library, where "every possible combination of alphabetical characters and spaces, and thus every possible book" are housed, and the labyrinth, where "ideally, all the possibilities of choice (of direction, in this case) are embodied" (*FB*, 75). For Barth, the appetite-for-the-all gets its heart from

Homer's story of Menelaus on the beach tackling Proteus, an episode from the *Odyssey* that also had profound appeal for Borges. Menelaus has got to hold fast to the Old Man of the Sea while he exhausts reality's frightening guises, says Barth, "so that he may extort direction from him when Proteus returns to his 'true' self" (*FB*, 75). The ephebe, as played by Barth to his "true" precursor-self, is genuinely Baroque in the Borgesian spirit, for unlike Proteus, he does not need to enact all the possible combinations, but needs only to be aware of their existence in order, like the hero Theseus, to "go straight through the maze to the accomplishment of his work" (*FB*, 76). It is when the poet affirms the literature of exhaustion as completion, without wearing out or depleting the possibilities, that the writing of such literature becomes a "heroic enterprise" with a "positive artistic morality."

Barth thus depicts Bloom's poetic will as a *scanner*, as a surveyor, examiner, and scrutinizer of the available possibilities, all of which will be fictive or false creations, turns from the true. Barth's view of creativity as a scansion aids and abets Bloom in one of his major theoretical aims, the demystification of the Romantic Imagination as the source of *ab ovo* creation. Not a gossamer web, then, spun out of the inspired and intuitive Poetic Soul that scarcely knows what it is about, but a choice made after scanning the various disguises of Proteus or the volumes in the infinite library, and a path tried among the many options of the labyrinth. Indeed, the poetic will as scanner sounds very much like the Fancy which Coleridge sought to exorcise in the thirteenth chapter of the *Biographia Litteraria*: "Fancy, on the contrary, has no other counters to play with, but fixities and definites. The fancy is indeed no other than a mode of memory emancipated from the order of time and space; while it is blended with, and modified by the empirical phenomenon of the will, which we express by the word *choice*." An emancipated memory permits the poet to scan, in Eliot's words, the "simultaneous order of literature," liberates him from his bondage to the present, and opens his eyes not only to the Symbolic representations of the literary tradition, but also to the Imaginary phantasies within his own past productions.

As the poetic will becomes increasingly conscious, the poet becomes the active reader of himself and others; he takes to playing with and shuffling, rearranging and revising the fixities and definites, trying out and trying on the possibilities unrealized but inherent in them. The essentialist Imagination *pre*formed the work of art; Fancy, more existentialist and materialist, *per*forms it. The true Fancy Man would have to be a postmodernist, beyond the tragic sublime of the Romantics and the elitist ironies of the modernists, with a poetic will that knows the joy of antithetical creation. With John Barth, Fancy is back in business, with a new kind of poetic freedom that thrives on the constraints presented by the conventions of the always already done.

1980: "The Literature of Replenishment"

The dialectic between freedom and constraint is explicitly resolved in the rule-governed methods of a postmodern Fancy, that revels in the freedom of constraint. This notion of agonistic triumph can only be implicit in Bloom's map, for his melancholic meditations on priority and belatedness tend to overwhelm the challenge to self-sufficiency actually presented by the revisionary ratios. Bloom's argument, that the poem or career commences in a primal fixation and continues through an elaboration of defensive processes, grounds poetic creation in the context of repression. And what the poetic will represses is its own freedom. Bloom's term for the poetic will, in his essay on "Poetry, Revisionism, Repression," is in fact "repressed freedom." As Bloom explains, "It is only by repressing creative 'freedom,' through the initial fixation of influence, that a person can be reborn as a poet. And only by revising that repression can a poet become and remain strong" (*PI*, 141–42). This study supports Bloom's explanation of a constrained artistic freedom, but for his "initial fixation of influence," it substitutes the scanner's awareness of fixities and definites.

It is his editor John Hollander, and not Bloom himself, who constantly reminds the readers of Bloom's works of the joy of being antithetical and self-affirming, the joy of mis-taking and willfully inheriting prior texts, and the joy of imaginative and self-creating quests beyond the labor of the negative. Hollander takes Bloom's story of the creative process to be one of victory, not failure, and Bloom's ratios, far from signaling a mechanistic determinism, to be the poet's "varied positions of freedom" (*PI*, xxi). Hollander's sunny version of revisionism is much closer to Barth's own. Indeed it is difficult not to get the impression that Barth loves his secondariness *because* he has inherited literary "fixities and definites" and loves the literary game *because* it has built-in constraints. Listen to Barth's praise for the writer's "proper adversity," as he speaks to Smollett's *Roderick Random*:

Adventure and adversity—hazarding forth and overcoming. . . . Those ancient, most profoundly lifelike human sports, *the obstacle race and the scavenger hunt*, are also the oldest, appealingest matter for the storyteller. Of painful searching and futile running around, our literature is avoidably full, as of despair in all its Kierkegaardian varieties, including the comic; but not of proper adversity, for the obstacle race implies obstacles not regarded as insurmountable, and the scavenger hunt presumes an ultimately findable treasure. They also imply a racer, a hunter—that is, a hero, scapegrace or otherwise, not an antihero; and heroes, for good and obvious reason, are hard to come by in the age of antimatter and the anti-novel. (*FB*, 40)

The writing of fiction as obstacle race and scavenger hunt? These are the revisions Barth makes upon the revisionary ratios themselves, which for the artist-as-hero are not a fate he must accede to as a victim of priority, but rather the adversities and opportunities proper to antithetical creation. One hazards forth and overcomes: "Disabling contradiction," Barth had proclaimed in his 1967 essay, "can be escalated or exacerbated into enabling paradoxes" (*FB*, 79). The givens of language and literature that precede the player are at once the hurdles to be negotiated, and the treasure to be found only along the way and in the doing. In Barth's comic revision of Harold Bloom, the initial yielding to repression is wholly strategic for the literary gamesman of hearty verve and consummate skill; what earns the laurel are the transformations performed and the possibilities activated beyond the contractions of the poetic self.

This revisionary emphasis is evident in Barth's choice of two new artist-heroes of the obstacle race and scavenger hunt in his 1980 essay on "The Literature of Replenishment." Here, Barth redefines his earlier essay as having been about the "effective 'exhaustion' not of language or of literature, but of the aesthetic of high modernism" (*FB*, 206), and he retires Borges as a "*dernier cri* modernist" in favor of Italo Calvino and Gabriel García Márquez as his exemplary postmodernists. Calvino is congratulated for keeping one foot in the Italian narrative past and the other in the Parisian structuralist present, and for providing "along with the nebulae and black holes and lyricism . . . a nourishing supply of pasta, bambini, and good-looking women"—all of which contribute to a postmodernist fiction that is "both delicious and high in protein" (*FB*, 204). García Márquez is saluted for his "synthesis of straightforwardness and artifice, realism and magic and myth, political passion and nonpolitical artistry, characterization and character, humor and terror"—the proper recipe for a "masterpiece not only artistically admirable, but humanly wise, lovable, literally marvelous." And, pertinently, Barth adds: "One had almost forgotten that new fiction could be so *wonderful* as well as so merely important." (*FB*, 204).

What becomes apparent, with this last statement and throughout the entire essay, is that Barth-the-critic has become weary with the aesthetics of production and is now enthusiastically turning toward the aesthetics of consumption. Having surveyed the mess surrounding "postmodernism" by way of the critics yet woefully debating the term, Barth writes off the whole project, asserting that, for the critic-as-reader, "a truly splendid specimen in whatever aesthetic mode will pull critical ideology along behind it, like an ocean liner trailing seagulls" (*FB*, 200). He then argues that the "relative unpopularity of modernist fiction" was due to its famous "difficulty of access," which notoriously engendered a "necessary priestly industry of explicators, annotators, allusion-chasers" (*FB*, 201). Postmodernist literature will be democratic in its appeal, unlike modernist works, and—as the fictions of Calvino and García Márquez testify—with no sacrifice of high artistry. Barth's vision of a postmodernist literature that might someday be called the "literature of replenishment," is delivered in an analogy: "My own analogy would be with good jazz or classical music: One finds much on successive listenings or close examination of the score that one didn't catch the first time through; but the first time through should be so ravishing—and not just to specialists—that one delights in the replay" (*FB*, 203–204).

Nothing replenishes like wonder. I share John Barth's partisan concern for readers, for their ravishments and delights, and would hope that this postmodern critic might extend to her readers the same gift bestowed upon them by a replenishing novelist. As I commence now to replay Barth a-Blooming, to follow the career that is Barth's triumph over the anxiety of continuance, I offer a passage that I have ever before me as something like a critic's prayer:

My ideal, when I write about an author, would be to write nothing that would cause him sadness, or if he is dead, that might make him weep in his grave. Think of the author you are writing about. Think of him so hard that he can no longer be an object, and equally so that you cannot identify with him. Avoid the double shame of the scholar and the familiar. Give back to an author a little of the joy, the energy, the life of love and politics that he knew how to give and invent. (Gilles Deleuze, *Dialogues* [1987], 119)

Chapter 2
The Floating Opera (1956): Beginning with Almost-Death

Image	*Trope*	*Defense*	*Ratio*
Presence and Absence	Irony	Reaction-formation	Clinamen

In 1983, having just apprised his writing students of the dismal statistics concerning their chances of eventual publication, Barth then advises them to forget the odds because talent, with a little help from cockiness, will always win out, and that if the muse had told *him* at their age that there would be only three great writers in his generation, Barth would have shot back, "Who needs the other two?" (*FB*, 109).

John Barth wrote his first novel at twenty-four, and nothing about it bespoke the journeyman or apprentice. In the confidence of his immodesty he intended to come on the literary scene strong and swinging, independent and fully launched. Not for him that staple first novel of the modernists, the autobiographical *Bildungsroman* or *Künstlerroman*. Not for him the tentative and waffling ephebe who doesn't manage to get his piano tuned until the very last pages: no Frederick Henry going through his baptismals of love and war to walk out finally into the hard rain, no Paul Morel swimming upstream against the oedipal current to liberation from Mom, no Stephen Daedalus surviving an untender Irish acculturation to test his Icarian wings in a short flight across the Channel.

Barth is going to imitate neither the formal beginnings of his modernist predecessors nor the existential beginnings of his own life in *The Floating Opera*, an autobiographical fiction which is not about the preparation for life of a young novelist but the preparations for death of a mature bachelor-lawyer in no way traceable to his newly married, twenty-four-year-old creator. Barth's narrator-protagonist, Todd Andrews, likes to reflect upon the Germanic root hidden in his name:

"Todd is almost *Tod*—that is almost death—and this book, if it gets written, has very much to do with almost-death" (3). Todd moved into his solitary room at the Hotel Dorset in Cambridge, Maryland, upon the event of his father's suicide in 1930, and he has spent some part of every day in the intervening twenty-four years on his interminable works-in-progress—his inquiries into the possible causes of Thomas Andrews' self-hanging, into Todd's memories of the two of them as father and son, into the reasons for their imperfect communication. Todd's only completed work, the novel we are reading, is his story of that one June day in 1937 when he woke up having decided to commit suicide and went to bed that night having decided not to.

It sounds like Camus, but ultimately it isn't. In the early 1950s Camus and Sartre were everywhere in the air, and even young John Barth, holed up with Scheherazade in the Hopkins library stacks, could not have avoided hearing the prevailing wisdom, via Heidegger, that if one wanted truly to live, one must face the reality of one's own death. Barth made Todd's meditations on death so pervasive and persuasive that the reviewers rushed to acclaim *The Floating Opera* as the existentialist small masterpiece of a young author embroiled in the *Zeitgeist* and *Weltanschauung* of a dire new age of uncertainty. And as recently as 1983, the critic Charles Harris was arguing, from R. D. Laing's existentialist generalization in the 1960s of the psychoanalytic entity, that Todd Andrews was a schizophrenic, a suffering child of the century born at its beginning and now heir to the ontological insecurity that is its tragic legacy. Barth's protagonist, nevertheless, is not the glum and sulking existentialist who resents his non-mastery in life and passes it off as "authenticity." He is a "mean rationalizer" who demonstrates an excessive and mordant reliance on rational control of himself and of others. No existentialist would, and no schizophrenic could, use intellectual objectivity as such a successful shield against every variety of human commitment, investment, communality, and union. Todd Andrews is too firmed up in his identity to lose the self, and too ironic in his consciousness to be playing any serious endgame while waiting for Godot.

Todd, in fact, can be wholly comprehended through concepts developed within traditional psychoanalysis. Freud has not been silent about the effects of the death of a parent upon the surviving child. His "Mourning and Melancholia" might be taken as a strong revision of Heideggerian existentialism: If you want life, prepare for the death of the other. Freud argues that since the unconscious cannot know its own death, only through the death of a loved one can there arise the intuition of one's own mortality. Todd was informed of his a whole decade before his father's suicide, when his doctor told him of his heart condition, but it is Todd's improper mourning for his father that yanks him out of life and into bondage to the dead. Proper mourning is intended not only to liberate our grief and assuage our guilt for the normal love/hate ambivalence in all human relations, but to detach us from the deceased.

Nonetheless, Thomas Andrews is hardly in his grave when, with no time given to grieving, Todd is sitting down to his *Inquiry* and searching for reasons why. Thereafter, his psychic life in all its ambivalence is fixed on the absent father he has identified with and internalized as a foreign object; and his existence, glutted with the father, is all dead time—a life of almost-death. Freud's bad mourner then becomes Freud's Rat Man, or even better, Serge Leclaire's Jerome. The obsessional neurotic of Leclaire's Lacanian case study dominates and defends his death-in-life by packing it full of busyness—with projects, rituals, intellectual questings, the more interminable the better—in order to forestall the intrusion of anything so messy, amorphous, and chancy as real life. Everything and everyone outside his tomb is met with disinterested curiosity and unenthusiastic excitement, precisely the oxymoronic appeals attractive to a mournful obsessional who doesn't know whether he's dead or alive (Schneiderman 1980, 94–109).

This posing of the obsessional's question, and the investigation into the compulsive structure generated by that question, are typical of a first swerve, or *clinamen*, away from Freud taken by Lacanian analysts in dealing with obsessional neurosis. Freud's primary emphasis had been placed on the *theme* of death operating in the life of the obsessional—how identification with the dead father escalates the obsessional's own fear of death, how internalization, the eating of the father, reflects the wish to be rid of him, and how guilt for that desire motivates all solicitous inquiries into the father's death. Although Freud judiciously enumerated the symbolic equivalencies of death adopted by his Rat Man—silence, immobility, sleep—his main interest, as always, was upon the oedipal conflict, in this instance as it proceeds beyond the grave. Lacanian analyst Serge Leclaire, on the other hand, views the obsessional as Oedipus at the crossroads—if Oedipus were to play the part of the Sphinx.

In "Jerome, or Death in the Life of the Obsessional," which appears in Stuart Schneiderman's collection of clinical psychoanalysis done by French Lacanians (1980, 94–129), Leclaire focuses on the protection afforded by the obsessional's return to the stability of the inorganic, as a busy non-actor on the far side of life: His false acceptance of himself as already finished is equivalent to the refusal of the possibility of his own death, and a life already ended, one with absolutely no future, can nevertheless be filled with many back tasks that require completion—

"files to classify, affairs to liquidate, problems to bring up to date." Like Todd, Jerome lives to organize, provided that he doesn't participate in the event itself. The worst atrocity that either can imagine is being surprised outside his tomb by someone else before he can name him or her "corpse." The obsessional's privileged nightmare is of the perfectly conserved mummy, the very image of a human form saved from the ravages of time, which proceeds horrifyingly to liquefy, as its solid armor gives way to formless putrefaction. The obsessional, therefore, must give constant attention to his wrappings and must resist all temptations to throw open the coffin lid, while repressing the desire most fervent in the obsessional unconscious: his directly antithetical yearning to broach the distance between two bodies and accede to communication.

Leclaire, speaking of Jerome, has set the Lacanian scene for Todd Andrews, as an unmobilized and immobile Oedipus at the crossroads. Unlike Jerome, however, who passes by the German who surprised him on his evening walk, Todd enjoyed with his German, a frightened sergeant who inadvertently stumbled into Todd's foxhole in the Argonne, the most "intense intimacy" and "clear communication" that he will ever know with another human being. Yet the coffin can stay open only briefly before it is slammed violently shut again, and almost at once Todd cancels the sexualized emotional intimacy with a lethal bayonet through the man's throat. Todd's way with language is similarly defensive, as can be seen in the fore and aft statements that he self-righteously appends to his account of the affair:

> Now read this paragraph with an open mind; I can't warn you too often not to make the quickest, easiest judgments of me, if you're interested in being accurate. The thing I did was lay aside my rifle, bayonet and all, lie in the mud beside this animal whom I'd reduced to paralysis, and embrace him as fiercely as any man ever embraced his mistress. I covered his dirty stubbled face with kisses: his staring eyes, his shuddering neck. Incredibly, now that I look back on it, he responded in kind! The fear left him, as it had me, and for an hour, I'm sure, we clung to each other.
>
> If the notion of homosexuality enters your head, you're normal, I think. If you judge either the German sergeant or myself to have been homosexual, you're stupid. (64)

In his opening and closing demands for his readers' objective, rational judgment, Todd manifests the obsessional's first line of defense against the instincts, his hyper-rationality. In normal development, our rationality serves culture and the ego in the erection of that monolithic defense against instinctual behavior that is *reaction-formation*. Diametrically opposed to the repressed wish but equal to it in strength and working in the directly contrary direction, reaction-formation depends upon the child's moral review of his sexual wishes, the subjection of them to the painful emotions of shame, disgust, and revulsion, and the subsequent development in the child of such culturally desirable traits as cleanliness, orderliness, and conscientiousness. Our personality traits are thus constituted, in Freud's term, as "countersymptoms" in an extremely powerful countersystem that blankets a suffering unconscious and at the same time strengthens one's sense of an integrated identity. If reaction-formation is the ego defense especially preferred by the obsessional neurotic, who is firmly installed within all of his character traits and deathly fearful of change or novelty, it is because reaction-formation is permanent and polar enough to stifle instinctual danger whenever it may arise (Laplanche 1973, 376–77).

Barth knows well enough about the death-in-life that is the obsessional's lot. His protagonist's single room, where he lives and writes, is impeccably organized, his clothes sorted into drawers and his works-in-progress into peach baskets. Todd leaves that room every morning at the same time (6:15 to 6:45) for coffee with his ancient hotel neighbors, Captain Osborn and Mister Haecker. He goes to his office where, gazing at his "staring wall," he fabricates the legal intricacies that will complicate and prolong his cases at law. When he works on his terminally unfinished boat, as he has done every week for many years, Todd labors in his dress clothes just as his orderly father did. Generally, Todd Andrews floats above the content of his life on the wings of rationality, classifying, categorizing, and quantifying experience rather than having it—how many times the heart has beaten since its death sentence, how many adulterous copulations he has enjoyed with Jane Mack, how his impotency rate is progressing (up from one-in-four to one-in-two). When emotional trauma does come to him unexpectedly, Todd's typical response is to beat an immediate retreat into the rigid behavior of "on-the-contrary": With the news of his bad heart, he becomes a rake; nearly murdered by the prostitute Betty June, he becomes a saint; having cut his father down from the rope, he becomes a cynic. Once the world has forced Todd into a new position, he "can philosophize (or rationalize) like two Kants, like seven Philadelphia lawyers" (167), and he is not unaware of how rationality has opposed his instinctual life: "I know for certain that all the major mind changes in my life have been the result not of deliberate, creative thinking on my part, but rather of pure accidents—events outside myself impinging forcibly upon my attention—which I afterwards rationalized into new masks" (21).

Todd's masks, in their stolid stability, are death masks. They are not those masks on the side of life, described by Laing and Harris, with which the schizophrenic frantically disperses his identity and multiplies his possibilities of escape; the obsessional, driven by fear to a continuing consolidation of the self, seeks but a single mask that will preserve his fragile bag of skin. Nor are Todd's masks in the service of art, as Thomas LeClair has argued (1973). Todd's aesthetic values do indeed correspond with Barth's at several points, but Todd does not fit LeClair's description of him as "the first of Barth's protean fictiona- lizers" (a line that truly begins with Henry Burlingame III in Barth's third novel), who adopt masks more frequently than they change underwear in their comic boosting of a kaleidoscopic world. Todd's masks, on the contrary, are defenses *against* the world's variety, which leave his dispassionate mind free to conduct its experiments on a less stable humanity. Nevertheless, Todd is never far from the psychic pain that his masks cannot sufficiently distance, and he compulsively re- hearses over and over the gory details of his every trauma—the "tiny horrible puncturing sound" of his bayonet, the grim grin on Betty June's face as she reached for the jagged bottle, his father's bulging eyes and blackened flesh. In his first book, Barth shows himself to be an astute psychoanalyst in the Lacanian field, and he gives his protagonist precisely the domineering trope most suitable as a co-defender with reaction-formation.

Rhetorical figures of speech are also masks. Tropes are disguises and defenses against literal meaning, and in their alternative turns from truth, they peel off like Proteus and reel off like the schizophrenic one creative possibility after another. Irony is the single exception. As the trope full of thought, irony is a promoter of the intellectual dogfight and an inhibitor of the other creative figures—the trope most vulner- able to reason's use and abuse, and the trope that kills its own. Vico was the first to locate irony as the highest development of matured thought, a latter-day demon that comes to dominance in an age of decadence, when judiciousness has paralyzed the will to act and the ironic mind instead conducts its intellectual witch-hunts for the lie, the error, the ideology. Socrates meant his irony to close the gap between imperfect opinion and perfect fact, but the Western mind, developing Platonic dualism into the cold war of consciousness, ends by deploying irony as a trope of negation that sets the wedge between intention and act, pre- tense and fact, expectation and fulfillment. As a trope, irony is always a winner, an assertion of the speaker's intellectual mastery and self- superiority; but as a mode of consciousness, it achieves its pyrrhic victories at the expense of emotion, imagination, attitude, the senses, and subjective self-affirmation. "That rank analytical impulse," Nietz- sche called it, "that makes the present into a desert"—and a desert, of course, is just what the obsessional takes and wants his life to be.

Beyond their cultivation for legal argument, Todd's ironies are never fertile for himself, although they are superbly machined to show up others. His irony exposes Mister Haecker's "visionary false face," and demolishes his pretense of a beautiful death, but also thereby drives the old man to his first attempt at suicide. His irony wises up Harrison and Jane Mack about their specious liberality and objectivity, but preserves himself so well from any emotional participation in the five-year affair with his best friend's wife that he can say, at the end of it, "I scarcely regarded myself as involved." Nor is Todd any more involved when he determines to decide Harrison's $3-million lawsuit on the flip of a coin, or when he plans to take along with him on his suicide trip the 699 other townspeople, including the Macks and the daughter possibly his own, aboard the showboat.

Barth's depiction of his first protagonist shows nothing but the existential abuses of supra-rational irony as a mode of consciousness. Author and narrator agree only on the aesthetic abuses of irony as a trope—that irony is trite, easy, and heavy-handed when it merely imitates "life's elephantine ironies," as when Stephen Crane couldn't resist letting the cash register display its zeroes over the corpse of his Swede (107), or when Haecker can't resist dramatizing his suicide by dressing all in black and underlining the passage in *Hamlet* as his final rebuttal to Todd. But Barth knows, and Todd does not, that ironic laughter is as much a reaction-formation against the fear of the flesh's mortality as is severe asceticism: When Todd the mature narrator makes such ironic hay out of two dogs copulating in the path of pallbearers exiting a funeral parlor, the reader with a nose for suspicion should look back to Todd the protagonist at age seventeen who— catching himself and Betty June in the mirror, going at it like dogs— hooted himself out of an erection his first time out, and Betty June into a lifetime of prostitution thereafter.

On his map Bloom aligns the trope of irony with the defense of reaction-formation because both plant themselves in direct opposition to emotional disorder. Bloom, however—friend to Vico and Nietzsche, but an even greater friend to the aspiring ephebe—will not countenance irony as the endgame of a dying culture. In *Agon: Towards a Theory of Revisionism* (*AG*, 1982), he explicitly objects to those literary critics who assume irony as a final position and pretend to a discourse of non-mastery: "Increasingly I suspect that Abrams and Hillis Miller, when they debate interpretive modes, truly dispute only degrees of irony. . . . Beware the rhetorical or ironic impersonalist, whether traditionalist or deconstructionist, whose cool tone is a reaction-formation defense of a private quest for power" (*AG*, 31, 41). Irony for Bloom is a preparatory trope, the first swerve on the poet's path to mastery, the first occasion for the strong ephebe to roll up his sleeves and make the present precursor absent, the birthing place of antithetical artistic novelty. This ironic swerve from the father is basic to all the tropes that follow it in Bloom's schema, just as the *clinamen* of Lucretius, from whom Bloom borrowed the term for his first revisionary ratio, is the primal swerve into disorder that accounts ultimately for the creation of the universe. Had the rain of atoms remained steady and parallel, Lucretius argued, there never would have been a universe; only collisions between atoms, perturbations to that perfect order, could have initiated the creation of complex structures and new forms. This is Bloom's positive affirmation of all figurative meaning, including irony: that it is part of Eros, of the life-drives. Most rhetoricians and aestheticians would follow Bloom in this direction, but perhaps not in the other direction when Bloom—reading Freud's darkest book of pain, *Beyond the Pleasure Principle*—equates literal meaning with the death-drive: "Literal meaning equals anteriority equals an earlier state of meaning equals an earlier state of things equals death" (*AG*, 136).

Not only has Todd Andrews not caught on to Lucretius—his typical anti-*clinamen* being a precipitate rationalization of chance, caprice, and freedom into the straightjackets of order, destiny, and authority—but he is also Bloom's death-driving literalist. As obsessively tied as he is to his deceased father through his writings, Todd Andrews may not be, after all, the most weakly belated son in all of postmodern fiction; surely the children of the dead father in Barthelme's book of that title deserve the palm. But just as surely, in his inability to swerve from the literal letter of the law, Todd is the weakest of ephebe poets. As a writer, he cannot even achieve the symbolic overcoming of the literal engineered by Freud's five-year-old grandson who, no less oppressed by parental absence than Todd, mastered his loss with a spool of twine and the *Fort/Da!* game, the figurative creation that returns little Ernst's mother to him again and again (Freud 1920, 8–11). It is not for Todd, however, to depart from literal fact for the play of any trope except the true/false of irony; like any good obsessional, he is reactively consumed with playing the dogged ratiocinator, the laborious researcher, the pedestrian recorder. For good and obvious reasons of dramatic and lyrical interest, Barth has spared his readers any excerpts from Todd's dreary documentation. It is conceivable that Todd might have written Kafka's *Letter to His Father*—but Kafka's "Hunger Artist"? Never. Nor could he have written—to get to the crux of the matter—Barth's *Floating Opera*.

We really like the way Todd tells his story, or better, we like the way Todd tells *a* story, dressing and jazzing it up with all kinds of passing irrelevancies and comic symbolisms. But if we think about it—and it is to Barth's supreme credit that as ravished readers we don't think about it—this compulsive neatener-up and hellbent literalist of a protagonist could not have made up the book we are reading, not on the most figurally propitious day of his wan and dogged life. Were Barth's *Floating Opera* truly Todd Andrews's autobiography, what a sad trip would have been our ephebe's first voyage out: on a ship whose only cargo was a wholly undramatic and anti-climactic plot of dismal heritage, flat love affair, and aborted suicide attempt as narrated by Almost-Death himself. Todd the protagonist we can understand, if not appreciate; Todd the narrator we very much appreciate, but cannot, I think, understand. Let us grant that someone as distanced from his life as Todd, someone as enamored of patterns that delay order as of order itself, could be matched to this narrator who remains aloof from the scenes he writes and calls attention to his means and methods of composition.

Beyond this initial adequation, however (adequate also to Barth's own aesthetic preferences), the discrepancies begin to multiply through the book, writ large and small. When in the course of narration we hear Fielding fussing over us like guests and Tristram Shandy trying his darndest to keep on the straight and narrow, this eighteenth-century comic affability begins to sound alien to a protagonist whose irony wishes nobody well. And wouldn't Todd, having abjured clichéd irony, be too squeamish about self-contradiction to have singled out for mention Cap'n Osborn and his cronies on their loafers' bench, parked in front of a "Men Working" sign and beneath a movie marquee flaunting *Life Begins at Forty* and *Captains Courageous*? Wouldn't he be too hidebound to have begun his twentieth chapter, "Calliope Music," with the creatively stylish trick *à la* Derrida of double-voiced double columns? Trapped in his fear and loathing of the flesh, Todd could not have conjured up Colonel Morton's wife as Morton's Most Marvelous Tomato, and could not have conceived of a huge lawsuit won by a stray fart and seventy-two jars of pickled human excrement. With his impoverished fancy, Todd could not have written the five-page handbill for "Adam's Original & Unparalleled Floating Opera," or given "impish Tambo, irrepressible Bones" their lines for the opera's minstrel show. But most emphatically, as suffering protagonist, Todd Andrews would not have created Cap'n Adam's Opera as a comic parallel and scathing parody of his own existentialist soap opera.

Other critics have been troubled by these and other inconsistencies and have tried to make orderly sense of them, perhaps too often sacrificing the book to the oeuvre and a fictional life to authorial art. Thomas LeClair (1973) associates Todd's unreliability as a narrator with strictly aesthetic values held by Barth, and extolling Todd's imaginative idiosyncracy (where I would not), he takes the metaphor of the floating opera as a justification of art and of life as "a fiction to be created" (719). Jan Gorak (1987) charges LeClair (as I would), with settling for "a kind of minstrel-show Faust who bought his imaginative virtuosity at the cost of becoming a moral idiot" (150). Gorak himself argues that Todd trades in his control as "a matter of pure power" and is reborn as the proper *deus artifex* who writes this book, *after* he has attended Cap'n Adam's performance and learned to celebrate "the human capacity for change rather than the will to power" (151). Taking *The Floating Opera* itself as his post-facto evidence, Gorak assumes that its movement "from mastery to wonder" is Todd's.

Heide Ziegler (1987) massively ignores the comedy, takes the book as a mistake arising out of Todd's nihilistic despair—his overliteralization of the showboat metaphor that makes art a substitute for life—and argues that such overapplication is Barth's way of "liberating contemporary literature from the existentialist predicament: the necessity that any protagonist find his own essence as the pre-condition of his life" (25). For Ziegler, apparently anything poetically creative that goes beyond the negative task of exhausting existentialism goes without saying. Charles Harris (1983) is especially wary of the inconsistencies between Todd as narrator and Todd as protagonist. He catches him out of character when Todd, "who forces distinctions and thrives on dualisms," blesses with his biscuit a copulating "doubler crab," and when Todd, with his suffocating disgust of the body, "having picked his toenails, sniffs his fingers in secret glee" (25–26). Harris declares the opera as Todd's "most implausible fabrication of all" (24), but goes on to account for it with the somewhat lame conclusion, *pace* Borges, that "desperation, it seems, begets the baroque" (29).

The extended metaphor that has given so much trouble to Barth's critics, who take it as the metaphoric center of Todd's book as well as Todd's life, I offer below—as Barth's own:

It always seemed to me a fine idea to build a showboat with just one big flat open deck on it, and to keep a play going continuously. The boat wouldn't be moored, but would drift up and down the river on the tide, and the audience would sit along both banks. They could catch whatever part of the plot happened to unfold as the boat floated past, and then they'd have to wait till the tide ran back again to catch another snatch of it, if they still happened to be sitting there. To fill in the gaps they'd have to use their imaginations, or ask more attentive neighbors, or hear the word passed along from upriver or down river. Most times they wouldn't understand what was going on at all, or they'd think they knew, when actually they didn't. Lots of times they'd be able to see the actors, but not hear them. I needn't explain that that's how much of life works. . . . And that's how this book will work. (7)

This passage certainly coincides with Barth's aesthetic principles (one might even see a *career* floating by out there), but it does not correspond to Todd's life or to his book. The plot is fragmented, but poses no problem for the sense-making reader, thanks to Todd's reliance upon a linear logic that connects event to cause and motive to consequence, and to his ongoing disclosures about his artistic ways and means. Todd would not himself have presented the floating showboat as an exemplary metaphor, however, for it is a perfect figure of the "imperfect communication" that plagues his life and is escaped only in those rare, traumatic moments when his reactive and ironic defenses have been caught unaware. If the metaphor in any way repeats Todd's paralyzed existence, it does so as Barth's parody of his living, loving, thinking, and writing. For the strong young poet who is going to be nobody's weakly belated son, "imperfect communication" should be a positive phrase that beckons to the possibilities of tropological transformation beyond minimal transmission and reception. Barth would have his readers realize how mediocre are Todd's literalist and traditionalist choices for life and art: that to live one's life in a tragic-ironic mode and to write one's autobiography in a linear, confessional form are relatively unimaginative, even adolescent, options; and that a more adventurous and mature choice—one that would free art from life, and life from death—might be to frame tragic vision and autobiographical realism with a grown-up comic wisdom gained in reflecting upon their worth and their arbitrariness.

This, I think, is one of the tasks that Barth set himself in his first novel. That this framing of the tragic by the comic does not entirely succeed, that Barth's floating opera remains a sideshow to Todd's main show, is evidenced in the interpretive confusion surrounding the book. It is no easy task, perhaps an impossible one, for an author to seize the helm from a rationalizing and ironic first-person narrator telling his own life and steering his own ship; therefore, on his own first voyage out, we catch Barth's act only at port and starboard, like the Cheshire Cat appearing and disappearing and grinning through the grim.

But this sideshow in *The Floating Opera* is to become Barth's main show by the time of his third novel, and thus it is important to comprehend Barth's authorial intention even if it was not fully realized in his first effort. To do so, we return to Harold Bloom and his basis for antithetical creation, the precursor. My argument throughout this study—that Barth has sustained his literary career mainly by choosing himself as his own precursor—necessitates an exception, of course, for his initial publication; furthermore, the answer to the question, "If Barth had chosen a precursor, who would it have been?" yields too many interesting signposts to that career to be ignored. Aiming for a contemporary beyond, Barth would have chosen the greatest modernist of them all, and the particular piece of his distinguished predecessor's work that he would choose in his "creative unfreedom" to "resee" would have been the autobiographical fiction with which this precursor launched his own novelistic career: Barth's temporary and well-chosen precursor is James Joyce, and the book that is re-seen in *The Floating Opera* is *A Portrait of the Artist as a Young Man* (1964 [1916]).

Stephen Daedalus at every age is as mature as Todd Andrews, which is to say, old before his time and condemned to live life as a poor substitute for art. Like Almost-Death himself, Daedalus has discovered reaction-formation and irony to be his surest defenses against instinctual living. As a sickly, sensitive boy at boarding school, Stephen is always afraid, afraid of the ghostly figure with the deathwound in his side who haunts the halls at night, and afraid also of the bigger boys who physically bully him and upon whom he achieves a perfectly passive revenge by imagining their remorse during the requiem mass delivered over his own corpse. During his painful adolescence, Stephen converts his instinctual fear to the reactive emotions of shame and guilt (defiling Emma with his whores) and disgust and self-loathing (his gross body, fat with grease, being borne to judgment); and when these negative self-assessments are exacerbated by the horrific sermon preached at the Retreat, Stephen is driven to the confessional and thereafter slammed into the reaction-formation of laying his life out in devotional areas of intellectual questioning and bodily mortification. In late adolescence he calls irony to his rescue, only to discover that what makes him invulnerable to others not only makes him opaque to himself, but does not spare him emotional pain. At the close of *A Portrait*, in the penultimate image and ultimate event that Stephen records in his diary, we see that Stephen's endgame is still reaction-formation and irony.

In a fashion similar to Todd's presentation of his encounter with the German sergeant, Stephen frames his image of the Gaelic spirit he fears and hates with introductory ironic distancing and a final reactive disclaimer:

14 *April*: John Alphonsus Mulrennan has just returned from the west of Ireland. (European and Asiatic papers please copy.) He told us he met an old man there in a mountain cabin. Old man had red eyes and short pipe. Old man spoke Irish. Mulrennan spoke Irish. Then old man and Mulrennan spoke English. Mulrennan spoke to him about universe and stars. Old man sat, listened, smoked, spat. Then said:

—Ah, there must be terrible queer creatures at the latter end of the world.

I fear him. I fear his redrimmed horny eyes. It is with him I must struggle all through this night till day come, till he or I lie dead, gripping him by the sinewy throat till . . . Till what? Till he yield to me? No. I mean him no harm. (251)

The shorthand conventions of diary writing are exceeded here in the terse sentences with their dropped articles and mocking repetition, by which Stephen brings on his imaginary scene of real, violent emotion and its immediate, equally violent repression. Stephen's emotions run the gamut from abject fear to murderous rage before he brings them to a halt with his ellipsis, after which a reaction-formation announces itself as perfect, cold, void and null indifference. One hears the thud of Stephen's conscious negation, his *Verneinung* in "No. I mean him no harm," without believing it; it is repression knocking at the only door through which the strong psyche will let it enter. Once again, a reaction-formation accomplishes its success story. Stephen's last encounter with Emma, like Todd's entire affair with Jane Mack, is an "imperfect communication," brought on by the ironic stance he assumes toward her and toward his own sexual feelings, and by his reactive refusal to reflect upon them:

> 15 *April*: Met her today pointblank in Grafton Street. The crowd brought us together. We both stopped. She asked me why I never came, said she had heard all sorts of stories about me. This was only to gain time. Asked me, was I writing poems? About whom? I asked her. This confused her more and I felt sorry and mean. Turned off that valve at once and opened the spiritual-heroic refrigerating apparatus, invented and patented in all countries by Dante Alighieri. Talked rapidly of myself and my plans. In the midst of it unluckily I made a sudden gesture of a revolutionary nature. I must have looked like a fellow throwing a handful of peas into the air. People began to look at us. She shook hands a moment after and, in going away, said she hoped I would do what I said.
>
> Now I call that friendly, don't you?
>
> Yes, I liked her today. A little or much? Don't know. I liked her and it seems a new feeling to me. Then in that case, all the rest, all that I thought I thought and all that I felt I felt, all the rest before now, in fact . . . O, give it up, old chap! Sleep it off! (252)

Stephen is here very far from his adolescent ideal of the masterful black avenger who vanquished the woman that scorned his love with his own suave scorn. Instead, confronted by Emma, Stephen's psychic valves are sent banging on their hinges, as longing and enthusiasm battle shame and irony, and Stephen's resultant self-disgust will slam the lid on self-analysis when he climbs back into his coffin at bedtime. At the end of Joyce's line of irony, the "spiritual-heroic refrigerating apparatus" has frozen everything over.

Passages such as the two quoted above from Joyce's first book might well have impelled Ihab Hassan, in the "Postamble" of his *Paracriticisms* (1984), to the two pointed rhetorical questions with which he pins Joyce to the wall: "Did the lapsarian irony of this sensualist sometimes turn into final despair and thus turn into a kind of malice? In fact, how much malice lies in the mocking multiplicity of *Finnegans Wake* and how much delight in the fullness of being?"

No more than the postmodernist Barth does the postmodernist Hassan believe the modernist critics who tried to drive an ironic wedge between Joyce and his narrator-protagonist. When Joyce threw *Stephen Hero* into the fire as despised juvenalia, he destroyed the only Stephen, closest to the non-heroic and non-ironic Joyce, who might have stood between himself and his projection of an ironic Stephen Daedalus. Thereafter, with *A Portrait of the Artist as a Young Man*, the autobiography became an autobiographical fiction in which Joyce substituted his symbolic child, Stephen Daedalus, for his biological child, Stephen Hero—very much as Stephen will substitute the Greek artisan as his symbolic progenitor for his literal father Simon, that Irish farce. Stephen's willful choice to descend from on high, and not from a failed father and a "race of clodhopppers," had direct consequences for Joyce's aesthetic theories regarding the artist's aloof impersonality and the work of art's radiant stasis, and grew from deep roots in Joyce's own existential evasions of act by means of words—a double hindrance to active, creative freedom not likely to go unnoticed by a comic story-teller, who can freely delight in artful multiplicity because he owes no debt to and bears no malice toward the biological father.

Daedalus cannot discharge in action the image of the red-eyed Gaelic progenitor he fears and hates; he can merely dismiss him in lying words that mask the emotional self. Although Todd Andrews remains bonded to his biological father, these ties of puzzlement and deliberation dictate the low-level, unswerving kind of tale Todd tells but do not prevent him from putting a bayonet to his own nemesis and discharging his hate. Reaction-formation is not usually followed by the physical taking of revenge, and irony's taking of revenge in words is an unsatisfying substitute for the real thing—this is the lesson of literature's unhappiest non-avenger, Hamlet. By following the fortunes of Hamlet in Barth's first and Joyce's second book, we can understand more fully how tragedy, like modernist irony, lends itself to the circumscriptions of postmodernist comedy.

Captive to the ghost of the dead father, wrapped in the crepe of mourning, given to speculations on mortality, adept at multiplying obstacles in his path—Todd Andrews bears many intended resemblances to Shakespeare's tragic hero, but their dissimilarities count for more in Barth's replay of *Hamlet*. The stage will not be littered with bodies as the curtain falls because Hamlet's "To be or not to be" is found by Todd to be absolutely meaningless, without a first premise that would support either being or non-being (246). Todd thus writes himself out of his role as an existential Hamlet, as Barth all along has been writing off the tragic *Hamlet*. Barth riddles with comic holes Todd's Prufrockian meditations on his bad heart: "Having heard tick, will I hear tock? Having served, will I volley? Having sugared, will I cream?" (49). He aligns the tragic view with unadroit irony (and comedifies them both) in Todd's discovery of Mister Haecker, all laid out in his black pajamas and beside him, next to the sleeping pills, his copy of *Hamlet* with "believe it or not, the words *not all* noted in the margin opposite *Thus conscience does make cowards of us all*" (243). He gives us the showboat star T. Wallace Whitaker, blustering through his declamations of Shakespeare's deathliest soliloquies, and his audience, Todd among them, rewarding him with sneers and jeers and a hailstorm of pennies (230–33).

Moreover, in a depletion of tragic form itself, Barth deprives his hero of both his *anagnorsis* and *peripateia*. Todd's life will go limping along much as it did before his nonrecognition of any value in values, "much like a rabbit shot on the run keeps running in the same direction till death overtakes him" (251). The comic difference between the *pre-* and the *post-* of tragedy's scene of recognition may but be—says Barth in the comic wisdom of his 1960 lecture on "How to Make a Universe"—the same difference experienced by Kierkegaard's man-who-has-come-through: "He goes about his daily rounds as always, but he 'is every moment leaping perfectly and surely into the infinite, the absurd, and every moment falling smoothly and surely back into the finite.' Similarly, that which is attained by the final enlightenment of certain Buddhists is called *wu-shih*, a term that means 'nothing special'" (*FB*, 25). In *The Floating Opera* Barth has demonstrated that *Hamlet* is "nothing special" to a comic storyteller, and has suggested that enlightenment is not, after all, the exclusive property of tragedy.

But while Barth can play with Hamlet in his book, popping him up like a jack-in-the-box, the return of the repressed allows Joyce no such blithe spirit in *Ulysses* (1961). The ghostly father of Clongowes who so terrified Stephen and the black Count who was to enact his revenge return again, this time as father and son, in the Cave of the Winds chapter (187–213), where the young literary rebel, ever more exhibitionist in advancing his intellectual singularity, is holding forth on *Hamlet* to a mature Irish audience panting for enlightenment. In his lecture on the tragic showpiece of the single English precursor whom Joyce would have admired and feared, we hear Stephen answering, as it were, Hassan's question about the quality of despair and malice in Joyce. Onto Shakespeare—who, most scholars would agree, has no biography, and therefore no history upon which to build a psychoanalytic case study—Joyce, with definite malice and forethought, has displaced the psychoanalysis that he himself ever refused. Stephen's malicious interpretation is of the boldfaced Stratford wench who seduced the boy Adonis, then made the beast with two backs with a local yokel, thus driving her young husband out of virgin Stratford with "its conjugal love and chaste delights" into a corrupt Elizabethan London of "scortatory love and its foul pleasures." Anne Hathaway is the guilty Queen Gertrude, who makes Shakespeare at once the murdered father and dispossessed son of (Hamnet) Hamlet. Hers was the original sin that victimized Shakespeare, "darkened his understanding, weakened his will, and left in him a strong inclination to evil."

Thus Stephen pours into the porches of his elders' ears the poison that is working in him. Still "waiting to be wooed and won" so that he may be taken up among the stars, like the Shakespeare who found his initial in Cassiopeia, Stephen is all too despairingly aware that his first Icarian flight took him by steerage merely to Paris, and then only briefly, before he was summoned back to that "old sow who eats her farrow" and to his mother's "squalid deathlair." Stephen tells us more about Joyce than he does about Shakespeare, in an unwitting confession that may well be the psychoanalytical fate of those sons, biological and literary, who protest too much that "paternity is a legal fiction."

Autobiographical fiction, more than any other, risks a psychoanalytic response from the reader, thus detracting from what the book *is* to what it is *for* its author. Similarly, the novel of realism imitates the familiar world of contemporary reality at the risk of the reader losing the sense of the text as a work of art. From very early on, John Barth was determined to evade both these eventualities. In 1965 he was disclaiming his membership among the current black humorists, whose comedy was directed at the socio-historical scene, and proclaiming his own irresponsibility in that area: "Your teller of stories will likely be responsive to his time; he needn't be responsible to it." (*FB*, 55). However, he admits to having been tempted once in this direction by a muse now firmly abandoned, who was to him as Faust was to Mann and Daedalus was to Joyce: "My own favorite image in this line used to be Cassandra—a madly *laughing* Cassandra, of course—the darling of many a young writer convinced he has unhappy truth by the tail, or on his back, and that no one's getting the message" (*FB*, 56). As if his comic conversion of "darling Daedalus" as the tragic prophetess of personal doom were not already sufficiently pointed, Barth puts another finger to Joyce's ribs: "Joyce's Daedalus calls history a nightmare from which he's trying to awake. . . . For me, also, the past is a dream—but I laugh in my sleep" (*FB*, 59).

The suggestion is that the strong ephebe knows precisely who the covering cherub is, and whose shadow he must lose. Nowhere is Barth's antithetical target more anxiously apparent than in the earliest pieces

collected by Barth in *The Friday Book*, his maiden public lecture at
Hiram College and the seminar that followed it, delivered four years
after the publication of *The Floating Opera*. Barth begins by disavowing
any interest "in the question of what sort of person an artist should be
and what sort of life he ought to lead," and goes on to assert his partial
belief in, but distinct dislike for, "the pearl/oyster theory of artistic
creation," that is, art as the product of neurosis. The novelist himself,
Barth continues, "may be out to forge racial conscience in the smithy of
his soul . . . On the other hand, he may aim for nothing more or less
than aesthetic bliss—that's what Vladimir Nabokov says *his* pure and
total aim is" (*FB*, 15, 28). Knowing Barth's lifelong admiration for
Nabokov, one must assume he stands with him for "aesthetic bliss," and
not with Stephen Daedalus's unspoken conviction that "I am the fire
upon the altar. I am the sacrificial butter." Whatever self-magnification
accrues to the artist's ego in so construing itself as humanity's victim
and savior, and whatever irony or pathos resides in that thought, the
writing of much autobiographical fiction does proceed from it. But
Barth resolutely turns his back on the fictional self-analysis and self-
revelation, as if, himself now the new prophet of a comic vision, he
could see all the way to the bad end of tragic and ironic elevations—
which terminate in Hamlet and Joyce: "Socrates bids us know ourselves, but Shakespeare shows that at the end of the road of self-
examination and insight may very well lie paralysis of the will like
Hamlet's, and abdication of one's personality" (*FB*, 16).

The final phrase in Barth's Cassandra-like prediction, which may or
may not have been intended for Hamlet, is nonetheless central, as
Barth well knew, to Joyce's aesthetic theory. Here is Joyce's notorious
passage on the impersonality of the artist, which occurs in *A Portrait* as
Stephen is playing Socrates to his friend Lynch:

> The personality of the artist, at first a cry or cadence or a mood and then a
> fluid and lambent narrative, finally refines itself out of existence, impersonal-
> izes itself, so to speak. The esthetic image in the dramatic form is life purified in
> and reprojected from the human imagination. The mystery of the esthetic, like
> that of material creation, is accomplished. The artist, like the God of creation,
> remains within or behind or beyond or above his handiwork, invisible, refined
> out of existence, indifferent, paring his fingernails. (215)

Joyce's striking portrait of the artist as a detached and idle god
was picked up gratefully by the critics, who were in need of some kind
of conceptual image that would organize the practice of modernist
fiction just as the monolithic trope of irony would organize modernist
poetry. Authorial impersonality and poetic irony hold in common a
basic literary strategy, by which mastery is achieved through dis-

tancing. This is also the psychic strategy of reaction-formation, which not only detaches consciousness from the instincts but also promotes disgust for their primitive barbarism. Modernism forms a perfect economy of defensive definition through the alliance of these three literary and psychological factors, a definition that is much enhanced by the cultural preference for a history of the species modeled upon a gradual evolutionism. Stephen's first sentence, therefore, states not a universal or revolutionary law, but rather a conservative and orderly view of literary history in civilized progression through the three modes deployed by European scholarship ever since Aristotle—the lyrical ("at first a cry or cadence or a mood"), the epical ("then a fluid and lambent narrative"), and ultimately the dramatic ("life purified in and reprojected from the human imagination"). This progression, it will be noted, places modern man further and further away from his unconscious, and increasingly spiritualizes the author in relation to his creation. Joyce's civilized choice for the dramatic mode, which is at the zenith of these purification proceedings, involves a massive repression of the instinctual that will necessarily call upon reaction-formation as a primary ego defense. Stephen's pronouncements upon art and the artist, as Joyce acknowledges, are "applied Aquinas," and they can be seen as implicating modernism in a monkish, medieval choice for dramatic "imagination" over the epical "narrative" of Homer.

In adhering to the epical inflection rather than the dramatic, choosing Homer over Aquinas, Barth is in effect honoring narrative before poetry, the structuralist imagination before the Romantic imagination, and the working storyteller before a musing god. And he means to insist on the distinction that results from this choice "literally and rigorously."

At Hiram, when Barth moved the literary question over to the proper realm of what a work of art *is*, he introduced a surprising contrast between himself and Joyce as "makers":

> My contention . . . is that a novel is not essentially a view of this universe (though it may reflect one), but a universe itself; that the novelist is not finally a spectator, an imitator, or a purger of the public psyche, but a maker of universes: a demiurge. At least a semidemiurge. I don't mean this frivolously or sentimentally. I don't mean it even as a figure of speech (as Joyce does, elsewhere in the *Portrait*, when he speaks of the artist as God, standing in the wings of his creation, paring his fingernails). I mean it literally and rigorously: The heavy universe we sit in here in Hiram, Ohio, and the two-pound universe of *The Sot-Weed Factor*, say, are cousins, because the maker of this one and the maker of that one are siblings.
>
> This contention will strike you as immodest. It is. (*FB*, 29)

Barth's distinction is between the literal artist and the metaphorical Artist, between a god doing and God viewing, between the hands-on creator and the Heavenly Host. It requires no great leap to close the distance between Stephen's concept, out of Aquinas, of the finished poetic product (exhibiting wholeness, harmony, and radiance) and Joyce's metaphor of the artist-as-God transcendent above his accomplished creation. Nor would it be psychoanalytically aberrant to suspect that both Stephen's choice for the stasis of the aesthetic emotion and Joyce's investment in impersonality were traceable ultimately to a reaction-formation defending against the body-rendering and mind-blowing *kinesis* of lust and loathing. Of a *Weltenschaung* or a psychoanalytic history for Barth, to the contrary, we are not enabled to speak: He appears only in the present of the creative process, as an immodest, blue-collar god making a weighty *Welt*, a chunk of universe every bit equal to God's. What could John Barth learn or steal from a precursor who is out of action and up there high and dry with only a view, from the novelist-as-God resting on his metaphorical laurels and calling it good? It is Barth, as brother of Homer, god of the epic, who scorns the Joyce that refuses to tell a story and wants the novel "purified in and reprojected from" his own refining-it-out-of-existence flame. Barth is here announcing the dynastic line he can live with, the honorable literary line from which he is proud to descend—that of the storyteller.

It also might be argued, I suppose, that Barth has set up his own strong line of defense against the invasion of his person and privacy by his insistence that the distance of his art from the real and the autobiographical shall be absolute. As long as that distance is relative, it can be crossed by the author to his protagonist, and in reverse, by sociological and psychoanalytic critics from the protagonist to his author. Yet Barth's stance is finally more an offensive than a defensive strategy, for his aesthetic distance will ultimately allow him the "opportunity for counterrealism" (*FB*, 59) and the free use of historical and autobiographical material in the comic spirit. What shines forth most brightly in Barth's skirmishes with Joyce on autobiography and aesthetics is how marvelously relieved Barth is of the usual burdens of the past, whether the past of history or of his own life. It is when Barth finally springs his notion of the artist's psychological genesis on his Hiram audience that one realizes how genuinely alien are Bloom's theory of influence and Freud's theory of neurosis to Barth the artist: "It seems to me that it is insight into the blind arbitrariness of physical fact, together with the gross finality of it, that upsets the thoughtful young person and sometimes makes of him or her an artist. One doesn't mind, really, but why must that be the only way it is?" (*FB*, 20–21).

Barth, who always eludes Bloom's notions of anxious influence, never eludes Bloom's map of misprision, and in this instance, it is his artist's sense of the arbitrariness of things that brings him back to it. This antithetical notion of the arbitrary, Bloom agrees with Barth, must be present if the *clinamen*, the central strategy of the antithetical poetic act, is to take place at all. For Bloom, the ephebe's sense of the arbitrary in the precursor's work motivates his re-seeing, re-aiming, and re-representing of a piece of that work—the antithetical process that I have been arguing is Barth's swerve from Joyce's *Portrait*. Even more pertinent to Barth's comic technique, however, is Bloom's description of the poet's re-representation as a *framing* structure, which I take to be comedy's way with the tragic and ironic views in all of Barth's books. In the following passage from Bloom, I read Barth's framing of not only Joyce the precursor but also Todd the narrator-protagonist:

> The clinamen stems always from a "Pataphysical sense of the arbitrary. The poet so stations his precursor that the visionary objects, with their higher intensity, fade into the continuum. The poet has, in regard to the precursor's heterocosm, a shuddering sense of the arbitrary—of the equality, or equal haphazardness of all objects. This sense is *not reductive*, for it is the continuum, the stationing context, that is reseen, and shaped into the visionary, it is brought up to the intensity of the crucial objects, which then "fade" into it. (*AI*, 42)

This is the point at which Barth accedes to sole ownership of his floating opera metaphor, where he loosens the stationing context of tragedy and irony from their moorings, and sets afloat, in the current of comedy, the visionary objects of Todd Andrews and James Joyce. The strategic aim of Barth's comic framing is not reduction but inclusion, the lifting up of Joyce's whole show and Todd's main show in the comic continuum of his sideshow. The "higher intensity" assumed by tragedy, the angst of existentialism, and the superior defenses of irony are all seen to be equally haphazard and are equally destabilized aboard comedy's floating opera; and the posted property, of a potential candidate for precursordom or of one's own created narrator, is now simply one passing show among many that emerge and fade in our lives and our books. That the comic vision is to be a re-seeing and comic action a re-representing of the tragic-ironic real is surely this new ephebe's artistic goal, and if the intention was imperfectly realized in his first voyage out, we should nonetheless let Barth bring us home to harbor now, telling us in hindsight what he meant to achieve in setting out as an original and unparalleled, comic Adam:

I had begun to find my general subject matter, but it took me two years beyond that—of imitating Faulkner, imitating Joyce, imitating Boccaccio imitating the *Arabian Nights*—to get a bona fide handle on it: to book Ulysses and Scheherazade aboard a tidewater showboat with Yours Truly at the helm and the steam calliope. . . . (*FB*, 10)

Chapter 3
The End of the Road (1958):
At the Nihilist Terminal

Image	*Trope*	*Defense*	*Ratio*
Part for the whole, Whole for the part	Synecdoche	Turning round on the self, Reversal into the opposite	Tessera

Doubleday considered *The End of the Road*, written in the last three months of 1955, to be so similar to Barth's first novel, written in the first three months of that year, that Barth's first publisher delayed the publication of his second book for another two years. For the editor looking for it, there is some repetition of content—another adulterous triangle, another pregnancy with the father indeterminable, another decision for suicide. But no strong beginner is about to make a weak repetition, and in the world according to young Barth, the "nihilist tragedy" of Novel #2 takes a very different form from that of the "nihilist comedy" of Novel #1. This is Barth's grimmest book, claustrophobic and catastrophic, with no comic opera aboard to float it home free. Harold Bloom provides the term that most accurately describes the relation between Barth's pair of novels: *The End of the Road* is neither repetition nor difference, but the *antithetical completion* of *The Floating Opera*.

Antithetical completion is Barth's first ticket to continuance, and the imaginative strategy that achieves completion is conspicuously synecdochic. Not only is *The Floating Opera* taken up as the passive part of a much more aggressive whole, but its narrator-protagonist is dismembered, as it were, and divided up between the protagonist Joe Morgan, a resolute man of the whole, and the narrator Jacob Horner, a very irresolute man of parts. Bloom's revisionary ratio for this part-taking is appropriately the *tessera* or "token of recognition," used by ancient cultists as the password that effects an entrance, and by more recent potters as the piece of tile that will complete the mosaic. Bloom was attracted to the term by Jacques Lacan's potent deployment of it in his 1953 *Discours de Rome* (Wilden 1981) as a metaphor for the well-worn word—the effaced coin that retains its value as an effigy of the past and yet is the completing link that enlarges and fulfills the present word (*AI*, 66–67).

Barth's second book, then, will enlarge upon and go farther than his originary word, which he re-sees now as truncated and incomplete unless it can be redeemed by its successor. To redeem comedy by tragedy is the most antithetical of completions, demanding a catastrophic termination made even more terrible in this horrific novel of ideas—where the Hegelian triad of thesis/antithesis/synthesis lays heavy on the adulterous triangle of Joe Morgan, his wife Rennie, and Jake Horner—where the dialectic proceeds over someone's dead body: Todd's aborted suicide is "redeemed" by Rennie's suicidal abortion. Bloom's formulation of the ephebe's stance toward the precursor work—that he has not dared enough, that he has erred on the side of idealization, that he must reduce all idealisms to a pragmatic tough-mindedness (*AI*, 68–69)—pales by comparison with Barth's ruthless achievement. Nor do the turning-and-reversal defenses assumed by all three characters enhance or protect the self; rather, they confirm the primordial suffering that inheres in this affair of adultery, and mirrors, as microcosm to macrocosm, the function of nihilistic thought at the present time.

So the book is not pretty. The whole of Barth's theme, in the words of his friend, the novelist John Hawkes, is the "threatening irrationality of total consciousness" (Hawkes 1974, 20). To draw the parameter of this totality, Barth splits Todd's hyperrationality between Joe, who takes it to its virulent end in the pursuit of intellectual objectivity and moral certitude, and Jake, who abdicates personality and the will to act in the face of the doubt cast upon them by the incertitudes generated in rational thought. Similar but antagonistic, warring look-alikes, together they demonstrate the different but equally despotic conclusions that follow from wholly rational premises. The existential difference between them is a consequence of the very good possibility that any active drive, in the face of the world's vicissitudes, may revert in its aim to an opposite passivity. Joe's intellectual mastery is actively vicious; Jake's is more vacuously so. Joe Morgan forces ideas and persons to pass muster before him and come up to his mark; Little Jake Horner sits in his corner and passively awaits their appearance in order to put them down. The antithetical difference by which Jake completes Joe, however, lies in the means by which synecdoche tropes irony and *The End of the Road* turns on *The Floating Opera*. Irony, Joe's inheritance from Todd, depends upon a solid sense of self and a steadied determinacy in the identity and opposition of ideas in order to produce a dualistic mental universe where contradiction is eliminated and ambiguity is intolerable; therefore, Joe's logic of the undistributed middle deals only in *either/or* judgments and is lethal to both indecision and error. Synecdoche, taking the self as a bit of the world, sees the cosmos as a chaos of successive, multiplicitous, and heterogeneous parts and, protected in its logical impoverishment from making any judgments whatsoever, finds everything adequate rather than ironically inadequate; nevertheless, the metaphysical and ethical toleration of synecdoche, which recommends it over irony's polarities, is also liable to the overkill of *both/and* that preys upon Jake and leaves him paralyzed whenever he must make any choice at all. Total consciousness, as it is encompassed by these two enemy brothers, terminates in no good end.

As might be anticipated in a world reduced to abstractions, both men take others as specimens to be examined or manipulated or taught; and where kindness and emotional empathy play no part, victimization is inevitable. Partly because she is so little loved by the two men in her life and partly because she is so little loved by herself, Rennie Morgan, wife to Joe and mistress to Jake, is as antithetically complete a victim as is to be found in postmodern fiction. But if she drops out of their concern and serves only as a pretense for their intellectual battles, it is because the author intended his heartless rationalists and her suffering self for a Hegelian ménage à trois. As Barth confirms in an interview,

> A probable reason for the recurrence in my stories of the triangle, that takes the form of one woman and two men instead of the other way around, is that if you have for thematic reasons a character who represents single-mindedly some position, then the dictates of drama suggest that you're likely to have another character who's his antithesis—these are likely to be male characters if they're embodiments of ideas—then you need a woman between to be the catalyst for the reaction between the two males so that you can work out your dialectic. (Prince 1968, 46)

Barth's metaphorical use of "catalyst" is chemically correct and atrociously appropriate as regards Rennie: She *is* that energizing substance that causes activity between two forces without itself being essentially affected. Rennie's adultery is unlike Emma Bovary's or Anna Karenina's because it is not motivated by male desire that flows toward the woman. Sexual desire is but a poor player in the scenes of signifying sound and fury that dominate the lives of Joe and Jake. It makes no appearance in the college bedroom where, in a nonsexual courtship,

Joe woos his wife-to-be with his principles and plans for them, and it is scarcely apparent in his study where, shouting executive commands and making parade turns in his scoutmaster's uniform, Joe picks his nose with one hand and absentmindedly masturbates with the other (*ER*, 70). Jake does not desire Rennie so much as identify with her ("She had peered deeply into herself—and found *nothing*" [62])—and he falls into bed with her just as absentmindedly, his initial attraction to her physicality already aimed toward her denigration as "a clumsy animal," a minimalizing of desire already anticipated by Jake's synecdochic disgust at the female bodies stretched out on a public beach: "Only a forest of legs ruined by childbirth; fallen breasts, potbellies, haggard faces, and strident voices" (21).

There is little male lust in this affair of three, but much male identification, which makes it an affair of two. This is the focus of René Girard's strong revision of Freud's oedipal triangle, in which the son's initial desire for the mother is countermanded by the father, and after an unsuccessful rivalry with this much larger force, the child forgoes his desire, takes the father as his model, and accedes to an identification with him. Girard argues in *Deceit, Desire, and the Novel* (1965) that there is no desire that is not mediated or "triangulated" by identification, no desire that is not in the first instance mimetic; it is identification, and not desire, that is primary. Thus in Girard's Hegelian re-thinking of Freud, as in Barth's Hegelian re-formation of adultery, the woman drops out, an object that has served its purpose of bringing together two men in conflictual violence and mimetic identification. Joe Morgan, who has always been a tutor to his wife, in fact masterminds Rennie and Jake's affair through a first attraction to Jake's intellect, an identification which encourages him to foist Jake upon Rennie as a second tutor. Admiring Joe's rational control and flattered by his attention, Jake only later challenges Joe's perfected will by undermining Rennie's faith in him as her bulwark against the world. Yet in the almost continuous intellectual combat that ensues—Joe browbeating Jake to come forth with his nonexistent reasons, and Jake mocking Joe for holding so tenaciously to his existent ones—Joe consistently seeks to win Jake over rather than vanquish him, and Jake finds himself emulating Joe's gestures, arguments, and brutal ways with women. Each acting the model and obstacle for the other, Barth's hyperconscious protagonist and antagonist constantly interact as "enemy brothers," the phrase coined by Girard in deference to Freud's *Totem and Taboo*, the only place in his theory, in Girard's estimate, where Freud got it absolutely right—in the mimetic violence of the adult males in the primal horde.

At one point in *The Ego and Its Mechanisms of Defense* (1967 [1936],

120–21), Anna Freud likewise hearkens back to her father's speculations on the anthropological source of the oedipal conflict. It happens during her discussion of a special instance of identification, "identification with the aggressor," which occurs only in dual relationships that are also duels. This antithetical bonding leads her to consider two psychic defenses that are always found together and cannot be extricated for analysis, *turning round on the self* and *reversal into the opposite*. Turning round on the self is the process whereby the instinct replaces an independent *object* with the subject's own self, while reversal into the opposite occurs when the instinct transforms its *aim* from activity to passivity (Laplanche 1973, 399). Anna Freud then suggests that turning-and-reversal may be the most primitive and ancient of the ego's defenses, vestigial tokens of the entire process in which the young males murdered the all-powerful leader of the horde (active aim with an independent object), partook of his power through incorporating his body during the totemic feast (identification with the aggressor), and ultimately established the prohibitions against aggression and sexuality to which they themselves would have to submit (passive aim with the self as object).

These matters are pursued even further in another return to Freud, that of Lacanian analyst Jean Laplanche. In *Life and Death in Psychoanalysis* (1976), Laplanche establishes a continuity, in the light of Freud's revision of the economics of sadism and masochism, between Freud's early work in 1905 on the pre-genital development of the child in the oral and anal stages, and Freud's revelation in 1920 of primordial masochism as the source of the death-instinct. Using Freud's texts, Laplanche argues that the sexual pleasure of sadomasochism associated with the inflicting or receiving of pain is but a later development of two nonsexual instincts, also inextricably entwined, that predate and generate infantile sexuality, the instinct to suffer and the instinct for mastery. The nursing infant has already, in phantasy, lost the breast, and the subsequent sexual excitation (autoeroticism, primary narcissism) that rises from this reflexive moment of making oneself suffer is in truth a secondary phenomenon. Likewise, the instinct for mastery is the origin of the "sadistic" child's cruelty, which in fact is wholly independent of sexuality and rises instead from his own mastery over his limbs and sphincter muscles, another instance of the self as passive sufferer (Laplanche 1976, 91–92). All mastery, of self or other, is thus grounded in self-suffering, and these two nonsexual instincts will appear in *Beyond the Pleasure Principle* much aggrandized as the primary masochism and the heteroaggression of human behavior in the individual microcosm that reflects Freud's ultimate macrocosm, where the noisily aggressive life-instincts are subordinated to a quietly passive but primary death-instinct (1961 [1920], 97–102). In Freud's theory, then, the instinct to suffer claims precedence, and aggression turned round on the self as suffering is prior to aggression turned outward toward others as mastery. We dominate others after submitting to ourselves; we are homicidal so that we might not be suicidal.

Sigmund Freud's end of the road—a vision so dark that few of his successors prior to Lacan have been inclined to share it—is the same terminal resting point, I would argue, that John Barth envisions in his anatomy of nihilism. The thought that concludes, in the senselessness of the world, Reason's pact with absurdity, turns back on the self in a movement of reflexivity; and whether the reversal into passivity occurs late (as with Rennie) or early (as with Joe), nihilistic thought produces the human evidence of primordial masochism, as the self that submits to auto-aggression and heteroaggression, or as the self that submits to self-mastery in order to master others.

In marriage as in courtship, Joe and Rennie Morgan are bound to each other in this complementary complicity of the instinct for mastery and the instinct to suffer. When Joe wins Rennie by recounting his history of painful self-conquest and demanding that as his wife she must also whip herself into shape, he already knows his woman. But thereafter, when he contemptuously dismisses her opinions or hits her for apologizing or insists on her freedom to kill herself, we are to understand that Joe receives no pleasure from Rennie's pain and is, in truth, completely without concern for it. "We shouldn't have to make allowances for each other," Joe is fond of saying, his mastery now actively homicidal rather than passively suicidal. Rennie, on the other hand, rises to her wooer's challenge, but her active aim of mastery ends in the reflexivity of a self-inventory, whereby she re-views her happy childhood as unhappy history, discards her friends, cancels her so-ciality, throws out all of her own ideas, and altogether satisfies her instinct to suffer. Self-afflicted and self-effaced, Rennie then reverses the aim into the passive mode, now a suffering object desiring her husband as the active subject of aggressive domination. As grisly as her end may be, and as contemptible a role as Joe and Jake have played in it, it becomes increasingly difficult to picture Rennie only as a victim and not also as a self-victimizer, especially when we comprehend that the decision of this mother of two to kill herself is motivated by her husband's crazed distraction and not by her own suffering. Of the three characters that dominate this novel, the death-instinct is most alive and well in Rennie Morgan.

This is not an argument brought forth, to my knowledge, by any of Barth's critics. I could perhaps understand if they had singled out Joe as the villain, since Barth has situated both Joe and Rennie—unlike

Jake, so far removed from the instincts—at Freud's terminal, where nihilism is neither intellectual nor moral, but terrifyingly instinctual. Compared to the deep roots and long history Barth gives to Joe's wife-battering, Jake's own offhanded brutality seems that of a minor actor who has walked into the fifth act of an ongoing tragedy and merely hastens its already fated end by fumbling through identification for a drive toward mastery that is nowhere instinctually rooted in him. Nonetheless, it is Jake Horner whom some of Barth's critics (Kerner 1959; Ziegler 1987; Gorak 1987) have summoned forth as the book's personification of evil, as the Horned One who has put horns on Joe and a horn to Rennie, as the serpent in the garden of this psycho-drama, as the torturer of Adam and the destroyer of Eve.

Yet the Morgans' Eden is already rank with original sin, and if Jake enters into it, it is at their individual insistences, each instinctually driven—Joe needs an admiring son/student/disciple, Rennie needs another man made in the image of her domineering god, and both Morgans have long been adept at getting what they need, if not what they want. Jake plays neither the heavy nor the hero, and to view him as anything huge enough to be a principle of Evil is deliberately to ignore Barth's qualifying humor, which keeps Jake at his mediocre size, sometimes partially exonerating him, sometimes hilariously mocking him, sometimes even lending his non-positionality some credence. In addition to his contribution to the tragedy that all three bring about, Jacob Horner also serves as the comic counter to this tragic couple. What they fear the most, Rennie tells Jake, is that "anybody could grant all of Joe's premises—our premises—understand them and grant them and then *laugh* at us" (60). Much of the time this mocking laugh-ter is precisely Jake's response, and some of the time Jake's laughter is therapeutically intended to lighten them up: "Maybe the guy who fools himself least is the one who admits that we're all just kidding" (131).

Yet Jake the kidder is also liable to highly intense fear and guilt, which at one crucial and laudable point are strong enough to rouse him to act: When Joe's principles do not prevent him from interfering in his wife's decision to kill herself, Jake's feelings impel him, with one frantic ploy after another, to secure Rennie an abortionist, an abortion being the single condition on which she will consent to continue living. Jake's "mastery," in this instance as in others, is severely and comically quali-fied, assuring the reader that the boy in the corner has no instinct for it. More typically, Barth is making comic hay of the pathological hospi-tality Jake extends to indecisiveness. A hapless buffoon of indecision, the only answer that Jake can give to the college president pressing him for an interview hour is, "Either Monday or Tuesday is okay, sir." So utterly passive, so customarily "weatherless," so placidly depressive is

Jake that when he is hit by a brief and infrequent manic high, he does his antic best to nurse it along. And when an unflappable landlady agrees right off to rent Jake a room, he tries to ward off the finality with fictional roadblocks—I play the clarinet, I might buy a Doberman, etc. Charles Harris, who missed the obsessional in Todd, errs, I think, in finding him belatedly in Jake; Jake's "compulsive need for incertitude and doubt" is not rooted instinctually in this character, but rather tied to the author's need for a comic butt as comic relief, and to the author's current view of the cosmos as genuinely and pervasively ambivalent.

Much of the humor of the book, all of its sanity, and most of its metaphysical affirmations are attached to the somewhat illicit, wholly unorthodox, and otherwise anonymous doctor who helps Jake toward a modicum of good health. Barth planned originally to title his book "What To Do until the Doctor Comes," and his doctor's therapeutic emphasis is fixed unwaveringly upon such "doing." A no-nonsense superpragmatist and behavior modifier, Barth's doctor puts to passive shame the psychoanalyst puling about a "talking cure" or the "Absolute Genital." Having discovered Jake four years back, stuck to his seat in the Baltimore train station and doubly incapacitated by having found no reason to leave and by being unable to leave without a reason, the doctor does not care what caused Jake's cosmopsis, the pathology associated in this book with a cosmic view of things; instead, he wants his patient to stop moping and get himself a life by making a choice among the almost infinite and relative possibilities for action. As an alternative to the couch, which in his passivity Jake would find much too comfortable, the good doctor puts him through an array of action therapies: informational therapy (memorizing the 1951 World Almanac), to comprehend the world in its facticity; mythotherapy (assuming various roles and masks), to learn how all action must result from partial worldviews; occupational therapy (teaching prescriptive grammar at Wilcomico State), to welcome home and feed an instinct for mastery; and finally scriptotherapy (the post-Rennie writing of the book we are reading), to force an absolute choice among purely relative values.

The doctor's cosmology betrays a distinct preference for *synecdoche* over irony in the cosmic view of things, a preference that allows the reader ultimately to privilege one enemy brother over the other. The macrocosm, the doctor informs Jake, is neither paradoxical (a term invented by logic) nor contradictory (a term invented for language), but rather purely ambivalent. Like the Roman god Janus, the universe faces both ways, all its objects held in an equilibrium of permanence and change, a world in "charming equipoise" (130). A cosmos of loosely assembled and easily separable parts should encourage a human appreciation of heterogeneity and should not discourage the choosing of partial values in the face of the failure of the absolute to sustain its arguments. A cosmos of such gracious ambivalence would gaze back at the pseudo-constructs of a human reason that has ironized itself out of sync with the universe, and would scorn both the rationalized position-taking of Joe Morgan and the rationalized inaction of Jacob Horner. The stance of sanity, it is to be understood, is that of a man of parts in a universe of parts, not all of them agreeing but none of them warring, who chooses one quality, one value, one action that inheres somewhere in the generous totality as his own unique and independent variable. The doctor, in other words, is prescribing a switch in tropes.

When Jake finally does choose his one-among-the-many, his choice has Barth's blessing:

> Articulation! There, by Joe was *my* absolute, if I could be said to have one. . . . To turn experience into speech—that is, to classify, to categorize, to conceptualize, to grammarize, to syntactify it—is always a betrayal of experience, a falsification of it: but only so betrayed can it be dealt with at all, and only in so dealing with it did I ever feel a man, alive and kicking. It is therefore that, when I had cause to think about it at all, I responded to this precise falsification, this adroit, careful myth-making, with all the upsetting exhilaration of any artist at his work. When my mythoplastic razors were sharply honed, it was unparalleled sport to lay about with them, to have at reality.
>
> In other senses, of course, I don't believe this at all. (112–13)

Jake's concluding sentence recalls the book's opening sentence, "In a sense, I am Jacob Horner," and the reader has come to recognize this voice that has no weather to it. Between the two, a progress has certainly taken place since "articulation" is indeed Jake's invested choice, but the rest of the passage is not spoken by his weatherless voice. The vigorous inflections heard in "by Joe," "have at," "man, alive and kicking," and "mythoplastic razors" belong to the author, as do the "precise falsification" and "adroit, careful myth-making" that will become John Barth's trademark.

The critics implicitly acknowledge Barth's complicity in this passage when, like Charles Harris, they worry over the ethical implications of the choice for the "paradigmatic aesthetic act" as Barth's relative absolute. But Jake's narrative, they may or may not have noticed, is already implicitly ethical. Over the ghastly scene of Rennie's abortion, where she aspirates her dinner into her lungs and strangles to death on her own vomit, the doctor pronounces the ultimate moral position of every tragedy: "This thing was everybody's fault, Horner. Let it be everybody's lesson" (183). And no more than Todd can ever forget his father will Jake ever forget "Rennie dead there now, face mottled, eyes wide, mouth agape; the vomitus running from a pool in her mouth to a pool under her head; the great black belt lying finally unbuckled across the sheet over her chest and stomach; the lower part of her body nude and bloody, her legs trailing limply and clumsily off the end of the examination table" (181–82). A person in pieces, viewed hopelessly by a man of parts. Yet even the brutal physicality of Rennie's death and the full assumption of his responsibility for it cannot lift Jake out of his abjection, for when Joe asks him afterward, "What do you think about things?" Jake can only answer, despite flooding tears and violent chills, "God, Joe—I don't know where to start or what to do" (188).

Nothing has changed for the male protagonists in their existential positionings; Barth the novelist appears to be a doctor who sees only terminal cases. He has accomplished the "undoing" which was the intention of this second book: "I deliberately had him (Todd Andrews) end up with that brave ethical subjectivism in order that Jacob Horner might undo that position in #2 and carry all non-mystical value thinking to the end of the road" (Bluestone 1960, 584). Rational thought, even when raised to the highest level of ethical responsibility, concludes in a nihilist terminal, with a horribly mutilated body that no longer suffers, one survivor locked into abject helplessness, the other into dogged questioning.

If Barth's own choice is for the aesthetic act, that choice does not leave him any less ethically implicated in his fictions. His readers should never forget that, by his own repeated and forceful admission, John Barth subscribes unjokingly to the tragic vision of the universe; yet he believes that although there is no way for humankind to win, there are nevertheless "more or less noble and spectacular ways to go down" (*FB*, 52–53). Comic fiction is going to be Barth's noble and spectacular way of framing the tragic and ironic within a wiser and more humane vision that makes life and art an adventure rather than a substitute for death. Because Barth's first book was so preoccupied with death and his second so sodden with it, his later critics have tended to follow his earlier ones, John Stark (1974) and David Morrell (1976), in dismissing the pair from Barth's postmodern canon as exercises in realism and false starts. Barth himself contributed to that conclusion with an early statement he made to his interviewer, Leslie Fiedler: "I thought I had invented nihilism; when I found out I hadn't, I lost interest" (Fiedler 1961, 47). But Barth does not suffer from secondariness, originality is not a major priority for him. And although with his first two efforts he may well be tuning the piano before he gets into the main orchestration of his career, I think there is an explanation that cuts much closer to the bone.

John Hawkes points in this direction when in public conversation he tells Barth, "You take risks when you reverse the thoughts closest to you" (Hawkes and Barth 1979, 32). Barth is bold in *The End of the Road*, so bold that I have temporarily had to separate him from Bloom, who treats the violent defenses of turning-and-reversal with surprisingly prim idealization, as representing "a lost wholeness of instinct" and a "bewilderment . . . profoundly analogous to the 'Where is it now?' question" (*AI*, 98). Replaying these defenses against himself, the young Barth risks much more than the vague longings of an *ubi sunt*. He explores his first theme of the "threatening irrationality of total consciousness" through a turning round on the authorial self and a reversal into passivity; then, taking his own mind as his object, he suffers the possible paths down which it might take him. In his mid-twenties, already the novelist as man-thinking and a thinking man's novelist, Barth holds at arm's length his own post-Romantic consciousness, in which rationality and reflexivity are major stockholders, and stares down his own mental tunnel, making himself suffer the mind's potential for anathema and nemesis—an act of active masochism that was cannily prophetic, since it is precisely for his infamous cerebration that Barth's negative critics will chastise him throughout his career.

Barth's first two novels were his psychically self-aggressive attempts at discerning and experiencing the ultimate consequences of rational thought, and he ceased making himself suffer only when he was able to separate the destructive negatives of rationality from its positively creative potential. The light at the end of the tunnel shines through for Barth with the realization that rational mentality also fosters the formal imagination and feeds the encyclopedic appetite required for the wholesale invention of fictional universes. Borges and his *Encyclopedia of Tlön* are yet ahead for Barth, but he will be ready for them because his painful turning-and-reversal has disclosed a rational ideal for art whereby the mind can exhaustively and meticulously articulate an entire universe. Barth first had to find the good conscience of rationality—and Novels #1 and #2 are testimony to how aggressively he can reverse his own good thoughts about it—before he could proceed, ethically, to seize literate mastery for the making of myth. In the Bloomian sense of the strongly self-revisionary poet, John Barth was capable of whatever self-affliction was required to put himself on the road.

"Terminal," Jake's last word in *The End of the Road*, points to the termination of Barth's inward auto-aggression, and to his relief at discovering that a *both/and* ethics need not impede the aesthetic project but can actually sustain it—that Jake's last word need not be his own. *The Sot-Weed Factor* would receive prominent publication in 1960, and it would represent Barth's best chance at the great American novel—a fictional universe re-conceptualized, re-categorized, re-grammarized, and re-syntactified far beyond Jake Horner's power of articulation. To quote e e cummings not so very much out of context: "There's a helluva universe nextdoor—let's go."

Chapter 4
The Sot-Weed Factor (1960): Discontinuity Through Repetition

Image	*Trope*	*Defense*	*Ratio*
Fullness/Emptiness	Metonymy	Undoing, Isolation, Regression	Kenosis

As Bloom explains the third phase of antithetical creation, the poet's problem is repetition and his solution is discontinuity. The ephebe has become disheartened by his repetition of self and others, and now needs a strong breaking device to cut off the past definitively and to polish off the illusion of a fresh start. "He who lives with continuity alone cannot be a poet," and a repetition that is meekly respectful of the original will put the ephebe into an enfeebled relation of secondariness with his precursor; a strong repetition, however, "repetition dialectically raised to re-creation," repetition that is in fact re-invention, is "the ephebe's road to excess, leading away from the horror of finding himself only a copy or replica" (*AI*, 80).

With his third book Barth thus intends a "recollecting forward"—in Bloom's happy translation of Kierkegaard's phrase, "a breaking forth into a freshening that yet repeats his precursor's achievements" (*AI*, 83), but because Barth means to write his signature across the genre of the novel, he must take into account not only himself as precursor but also many others. This is how the twice-published, thirty-year-old author envisioned his problem: "By the time I began to compose *The Sot-Weed Factor* . . . I was more acquainted with the history of literature than I'd been when I began to write fiction. And so I set about to untie my hands; I presumptuously felt them tied by the history of the genre, and less presumptuously, by the kinds of things I had written before" (Bellamy 1974, 6). Young Barth thus puts a terminal punctuation mark after his first two books, that "little duet" on the rationalist ironies and tragedy of the existential predicament in our time, and determines to write something big, excessive, wildly comic, and not of our times: "When I started on *The Sot-Weed Factor* . . . I had two intentions. One was to write a large book, something that the publisher could print the title on across the spine. . . . The second was to see if I couldn't make up a plot that was fancier than *Tom Jones*" (Enck 1965, 7).

The first universe that John Barth is going to re-invent is that of the eighteenth-century English novel. Barth's novel will "imitate the form of the Novel, by an author who imitates the role of Author" (*FB*, 72)— an imitation, then, not of the world directly, but of a certain historical and formal representation of life, an imitation of an imitation; and with this twice-removed imitation, this wily repetition of his literary precursors, Barth expects—some would say, perversely—to effect a discontinuity with his predecessors. The comically antithetical Barth is showing himself for the first time, and depending upon whether they were appalled or beguiled by his act of magical repetition in Novel #3, Barth's fans and detractors would line up for life.

Bloom will not follow Barth down his path to an active repetition designed to gain mastery and individuation. Although all the instruments of his map of misprision agree that Barth achieves with *The Sot-Weed Factor* an economy of excellence unsurpassed anywhere in his subsequent career, Bloom's theory of anxious influence can lend no credence to a wholly conscious and canny decision to repeat. Bloom does not believe in any successful repetition, nor in any repetition that is not under the gun of compulsion. He mentions Freud's positive interpretation of the *Fort/Da!* as the symbolic restoration of absence by his little-artist grandson, as well as Lacan's elaboration of this scene as "the past which reveals itself reversed in repetition" (*AI*, 80), but Bloom's own focus is upon repetition in its hyphenated form as Freud's repetition-compulsion, the negative repetition in the compulsive mode that is appropriate to Bloom's darkest chapter in *The Anxiety of Influence*, "Kenosis, or Repetition and Discontinuity" (77–92). In his description of the agonistic combat at this stage, the ephebe is emptied out of everything that is his own, for the precursor himself has chosen the young poet and has returned unbidden to haunt him as his unconscious double, a haunting whose essential horror is the uncanny déjà vu. Whenever such a shudder occurs in Bloom, we can assume that Barth is not sharing it.

Nevertheless, Freud and Bloom are not alone in considering repetition a dire phenomenon. All of Western culture has looked at it askance ever since Plato demoted art to the third-best bed, an imitation of an imitation of an ideal Form. Imitation, copy, replica, reproduction—all are anathematized as the shame of repetition and the poverty of artistic indebtedness. For Barth and Borges, on the other hand, repetition is an "intellectually serious" literary idea that gains "intellectual validity" through its thorough historicization of the author and his time within the new re-creation. In "The Literature of Exhaustion" (*FB*, 68–69), Barth approaches the notion of a perfect reinvention through Borges' short story, "Pierre Menard, Author of the Quixote" (Borges 1962, 54–55). One cannot imagine Plato exclaiming with delight, as Borges' narrator does, over the rich sophistication and intellectual subtlety achieved by Menard in his exact re-creation in the twentieth century of Cervantes' novel written in the seventeenth. The deliberately anachronistic repetition in the cause of comic high seriousness, which would have been an aberrant artistic choice for Plato, is equally alien to the modernisms that descend from him. Of those contemporary critical voices that speak with Plato against repetition, none has shouted "Foul!" more loudly than Jerome Klinkowitz, who attempted to throw Barth out of the current literary game for being a "regressive parodist." Klinkowitz was especially incensed with *The Sot-Weed Factor*, one gathers from his *Literary Disruptions*, in which his own preference is for a conventional avant-gardism that is notoriously contemporary with its time and noisily advertises its novelty with formalist innovation and authorial reflexivity. That such individual experimentation, so often herded into a collective movement behind a manifesto, is likely to be appreciated only by the pedant-reader and is liable to make but a minor footnote in literary history does not deflate Klinkowitz's literary boosterism, which gets its puritanical edge from his chastisement of any author who would deliberately turn away from the life and literature of his own historical period.

"Regressive" John Barth deliberately is, but a parody his *Sot-Weed Factor* is not. Barth's book is a pastiche, not a parody, and Klinkowitz has mistaken a superbly orchestrated echo for a reliably reversing mirror. Unlike parody, pastiche does not take as its source an individual author or a particular piece of work, and its mode in the main is neither critical nor satirical; rather, it is a comic mélange of motifs and techniques borrowed from multiple sources by an author who has the highest respect for them. It is not that Barth's book does not have its bits of parody and satire—two pertinent targets being the Cambridge Platonists and the Socratic dialogue—but that, as a whole, Barth's repetition is not what Klinkowitz claims it to be. *Pace* both Klinkowitz and Bloom, *Sot-Weed* is an echo of the multiple—of Fielding's foundlings and male virgins, of Smollett's pirate ships and his gentleman with valet, of Defoe's shipwreck and Crusoe's fortunate find in Friday, of Tristram's abbreviated member and Uncle Toby's wound, not to mention extra-English borrowings belonging to Voltaire, Cervantes, and

Rabelais. And it echoes the forms of the eighteenth century as shame-lessly as its materials—the quest for the father, the rogue narrative, the sentimental romance of the virgin, the captivity tale, the found and fictive historical document. Pastiche, like parody, is also unfortunately weighed down with negative connotation, derided as a hodgepodge or incongruous combination of materials. But "incongruity" itself is a concept forged in the crucible of culture and tempered by the novel of realism in its ascendancy; and Barth's pastiche, I would argue, seizes the advantage of amplitude within "incongruity" in order implicitly to critique the more shaped fictional creations of realism, and thereby to create a hiatus in the Anglo-American novel's dynastic line of descent.

So Barth is playing a much larger game than cutting his present poesy loose from his own past by abandoning Todd Andrews to his staring wall and Jacob Horner to his corner, in order to take on a whole parade of fast-stepping mummers on the road, donning their masks and rattling on with their stories. The "novel" he chooses to repeat is that form of the genre which conveys the formal illusion that reality is too chaotic to accept any authorial patterning beyond the narrative recording of it. The eighteenth-century novel, compared with the neat housekeeping of its nineteenth-century heir, is the house of fiction before the maid arrives. Modern novelists as different as Joyce, Woolf, and Faulkner have repeatedly proclaimed their admiration for it, and the New Critics appreciated the reality effects of its circumstantial realism, which flaunted the colorful and wayward detail. Nevertheless, modernist literary history, following the Victorians, has consigned De-foe, Fielding, Smollett, and Sterne to the "infancy" of the English novel. They were the new kids on the block who hadn't quite got the hang of it, the truant boys who engaged in detour and digression to the endangerment of relevancy, manufactured elaborate plots only to ter-minate them in unpersuasive coincidence, and cooked up prose con-fections that generally botched the recipe for organic fictional form. New Critical literary historians, in other words, were Aristotelian: Aristotle's formulation of tragic representation as "an imitation of life" could be safely transported to realistic fiction just so long as it man-ifested the kind of "magnitude and order" approved by the proper Victorians and their modernist direct descendants; the outlaw organi-zation of picaresque, peripatetic, and panoramic narratives of the eigh-teenth century was not to be encouraged.

By 1960 no alternative history of the genre had come forward to challenge Ian Watt's emplotment in *The Rise of the Novel*. However, Barth's regression to the eighteenth-century novel can be considered an early preview of Mikhail Bakhtin's arguments (1987, 366–415) for the precedence of the parodic or anti-novel, the Second Stylistic Line, in that history. In Freud's theory "regression" is a general descriptive term rather than a theoretical and pragmatic concept like the other ego defenses, and it can be manifested differentially in existence and in thought. Under its first aspect, temporal regression goes back to an earlier period in a course of evolutionary development that has already taken place—to the pre-genital phases of infancy, to the womb, ultimately to the inertia of death. Secondly, there is formal regression (much favored by the Gestalt psychologists), which evades an established hierarchy of ordered forms and functions by choosing more primitive methods of expression or representation (Laplanche 1973, 386). By regressing directly to the comic prose epic, thereby temporally eliding the nineteenth century's formal development of the novel of realism, and by identifying with the eighteenth-century novel as closely as a son with his father, Barth seeks to legitimize a literary descent that has been consigned by Bakhtin's First Stylistic Line to bastardy. The novel, Barth is reminding us, had a double origin; it was born twinned. By promoting the regressive conceit that two centuries of literary realism and modernism had not intervened between him and the origin, that it was those prodigal sons who had abandoned the father and wandered from home, Barth announces his comic heritage as the more legitimate history of the brother who stayed close to his origins.

Simultaneously, Barth locates in the metaphysics of the eighteenth-century novel a certain contemporaneity with postmodern science, which confirms the randomized and mutable cosmos of that century, while relegating Newton's physics of formal order to a parenthesis. Barth's fictional universe is a repetition of that early Heraclitean flux which preceded Plato's and Socrates' ordering of it—a regression, in Jan Gorak's words, to "a universe constructed as a field of force rather than an image of ideal forms . . . a philosophy of energy, by which everyman becomes his own godly artist" (170). This is the metaphysics posited by Barth's protean protagonist, Henry Burlingame III: "The world's indeed a flux, as Heraclitus declared; the very universe is naught but change and motion. . . . Your true and constant Burlingame lives only in your fancy, as doth the pointed order of the world" (*SWF*, 125–26, 330). Burlingame is chastising the novel of realism in the nineteenth century for the "pointed order" it deployed to stabilize and hierarchize the formless world it found and misrepresented, and realism's complacent "triumph" is severely curtailed. Moreover, the very undecidability of subgenre considerations for Barth's readers—Is the *Sot-Weed Factor* parody, travesty, satire, or farce? Is it an imitation or a debunking of history?—occurs partially because Barth exercises all these available options, and partially because he has given his novel the kind of universe that is the ground for all future metaphors of form and can thus absorb all interpretations. As itself a repetition of the multiple, the Heraclitean flux is the cosmological equivalent of Barth's formal method of pastiche and Freud's formal regression.

Like the twin defenses of turning and reversal, isolation and undoing are often found together in obsessional behavior. Isolation is the act that inserts a hiatus in a temporal line of thought or action so that the connecting links are broken. It separates an incompatible ideal from its affect by depriving it of context, and thus allows the subject to give his concerted attention, otherwise, to the object at hand. In the light of the novel-making of the realists and the evolutionary construct of the genre's historians, and in support of Barth's aesthetic illusion of letting the world be in all its becomings, it is interesting to note that the clinical weapon that works against and exposes this defense of isolation is the rule of free association (Laplanche 1973, 232–33). With the high value they place on free association in the practice of the cure, the psychoanalysts appear to be affirming the Heraclitean flux of the unconscious, and to be disaffirming the congruities constructed by the analysand's narratives. From the other side, the subject's isolating defense—often acted out in washing rituals, that is, "washing myself clean of"—is impinged upon also by the prohibition against touching, and both uses could well be in play for the strong poet dedicated to carving out his own place in literary history through a withdrawal from its pallid continuity and a consequent localization of his own work. No one has ever accused John Barth of a lack of ambition, and we should not assume anything capricious about his scissoring of the history of the novel; it is designed to settle several hashes, while drawing a circle around himself as a holy untouchable.

Like isolating, undoing (what has been done) serves authorial and historical discontinuity. Undoing is a direct aggression against an act that has preceded it, by a second act that is supposed magically to undo or cancel it out. A magical procedure for the obsessional who incorporates it into his rituals and formulas, it is also magical for the comic novelist, whose own belatedness makes it possible for him to run through the multiple opportunities offered by undoing for difference *within* repetition: "Sometimes an act is 'undone' by an opposite one. . . . At other times the same act is repeated but the meaning attached to it . . . is the opposite one. Or again, the act of undoing may be contaminated by the act it is supposed to annul" (Laplanche 1973, 477). The psychoanalyst, we note, permits, as a compulsive classifier like Klinkowitz does not, a wide spectrum of undoing's motives and effects that range from parody to travesty to imitation proper. All of these pertain in the relation Barth presents, for example, between his fictional poet laureate's first and second Maryland poems and the original 1708 poem written by E. B. Cooke (but there are several historical personages of that name); or between his *Privie Journall of Sir Henry Burlingame* and Captain John Smith's Pocahontas story in his own *Generall Historie* (of which there are four versions).

Barth's fictive undoings of history are generally being justified in *The Sot-Weed Factor* by a lot of evidence (gathered by Barth in the Maryland Archives of History) that history has always been fictionalized through and through. Clio, history's Muse—as the Author remarks in his Apology—"was already a scarred and crafty trollop when I found her" (743); and as an event under very subjective description, the historian's "fact" exhibits motives and consequences just as promiscuous as the authorial intentions behind the magical undoing of it. In the love/hate ambivalence behind any literary imitation and every obsessional undoing, the clinicians suggest, the analyst is seeing a contamination of the defense by instinct and would be well advised not to seek a single label for the symptomatic whole. *The Sot-Weed Factor* is a coat of many colors in its dealings with history and literature; and as Burlingame, "Suitor of Totality" and "Embracer of Contraries," is fond of repeating (with wide-ranging reference to sex, politics, language, and thought): "There are more ways into the woods than one."

Barth's three defenses are the means by which he distances himself from the realistic novels of the nineteenth century, by which he calls into question the preordered and fictive constructs that pervade their well-wrought mirrors trained on reality. Barth's materials, on the contrary, reflect a prodigious amplitude that is not simply his way with belatedness, but more pertinently the way of life when unrepressed appetite ranged the pre-industrialized earth, creating a fullness and disorder which novelists of that century did *not* prearrange, disarrange, or rearrange. What belonged to life then, and what belonged to the eighteenth-century novel's way of imitating it, Barth wants his book to leave comically undecidable. There is such an appetite for aggression, for role-playing and scheming, among the *Sot-Weed*'s malcontented tobacco planters, political conspirators, redemptioneers, disaffected Indians, runaway slaves, litigious barristers, and inglorious money-grubbers; yet can this fictional population of hundreds be so very different from colonial Maryland's ragamuffin demographics of Europe's castaways and castoffs? Sexual appetite ranges freely across the many options to sex served straight up, but in this fictional universe it is eternally uncertain whether Burlingame's disquisitions in praise of pederasty and bestiality are to be taken as summations or satires of colonial American sexual practices, or whether the gluttonous feasts and sexual rituals of the tribal Ahatchwhoops are imitations or parodies of their Native American originals.

Similarly, the huge appetite for language is well distributed between the author and his characters, between exposition and dialogue. Surely the paragraph-long sentence that opens the book belongs to Barth, as do the ongoing, scatological revelations of Sir Henry's journal, and the seven pages of bilingual insults traded off between a French and an English whore. But the omniscient narrator's voice gets lost in the crowd of seventeen storytellers narrating twenty-five stories (according to the tabulations of Charles Harris), who similarly pack their language with apostrophes and epithets, inventories and enumerations, similes and proverbs. Barth, depriving himself of his own language, picked the *OED* clean for the late seventeenth-century's English. Never since, except perhaps in the yarning of an old country cracker, has the language of everyday folk spewed forth such cadence and poetry (English seaman to principled virgin-poet Ebenezer Cooke: "'Sbody! ye mean to say a poet be like a popish priest, that uses his cod for naught but a bilge-pump? Ye mean to sit there and tell us ye never caulked a fantail in your life? Ye never turned the old fid to part some dock-whore's hemp?" [233]). *The Sot-Weed Factor* is always marvelously and sometimes conspicuously "written up," yet the reader believes in the transitive reality of those frankly appetitive drives that produced such astonishing language and such disreputable lives, that were expressed and acted on before everything natural and instinctual fell by the way with pasteurization and propriety.

The trope that will figure forth life as a banquet, and not as a closet drama, is *metonymy*, the trope of contextual amplification. When Barth puts synecdoche on the road, trundles that spatial form of part/whole out into the temporal world as metonymy, its infinite displacements appear as the ordinary and naturally imperfect noncompletion of any life or plot that just keeps on trucking until it stops. If metaphor, as Aristotle defined it, is an insight into likeness, a work of resemblance that implies a single iconic moment, then metonymy is that work of likeness which, subjected to the vicissitudes of interval, extends into difference. As a chain of substitutions taking the place of something else, metonymy begins in repetition and ends in difference, a *meta-onoma*, or change of name. In formal rhetoric, metonymy is a substitution of the external aspect of a thing for the thing itself (container for contained, effect for cause), but the metonymical chain can extend into metalepsis or even catachresis (the Latin *abusio*), whereby the legitimate function of substitution reaches illicit connections that jar the sensibilities (Quinn 1982, 52–56).

The massing of misplacements, which permits metonymy belatedly to trope an initial metaphor, is not only the method but the matter of Barth's book. Burlingame is a name-changing, face-changing master of disguise, who constantly materializes his metaphors of self on the world's historical stage and thereby brings forth and sustains most of the book's British/colonial political intrigues. His invented identities assure that he will be living his life in episodes, a cosmophiliac of difference, and he has a jaded view of any static schoolboy metaphor that isn't tested in metonymical action: Forget the sky as the "dome of heaven," Burlingame advises his ex-tutee, and sure enough, Ebenezer sees the night sky for the first time in his life (346). Ebenezer thinks he can storm Mount Parnassus if only he has enough learned similes salted throughout his jangling couplets; but Burlingame knows bad Hudi-brastic when he hears it, and so does the reader, who flinches at Ebenezer's puerile, pedantic use of figures yet relishes the metonymical uses that figurative speech is put to by others. Ebenezer's heap of similes merely repeats, whereas the opening simile of Mary Mungum-mory's tale of her wooing by Charley Mattasin, Indian half-brother to Burlingame and thus heir to the "particular shortcoming" of that male line, undergoes an escalation in repetition that, by sentence end, lands it far from the conventional sentiment with which it began: "my heart was a castle, and of two hundred men not one had come in sight o' it. But my Charley, that had not even a lance to tilt with, in two minutes time had o'ertopped the breastworks, spanned the moat, hoist the portcullis, had his will of every crenel and machicoulis, and raised the flag o' passion from the merlons of my keep!" (414). In *The Sot-Weed Factor*, metaphor that does *not* serve the appetitive life as metonymical double entendre is seriocomically criticized as a very poor thing indeed, by not only Burlingame but the Author, whose eighteenth-century chapter titles tend to promote just such metonymical displacements (*e.g.*, "The Laureate Indites a Quatrain and Fouls His Breeches").

Like its syntax, the book's stories are chains of metonymical devia-tion, always surprising in their complications. The reader, momen-tarily surprised by the poetic comparison of the male genitals to a leech or an eggplant, is thoroughly rattled by a tour through the tales of the Great Tom Leech and the Holy Rite of the Magical Eggplant. Barth's book gives generous space to the massy, muddy middles of the eigh-teenth-century novel, whose plots move through rank coincidence to a termination only casually related to a convincing dénouement: "Tales are like tarts, that may be ugly on the face of 'em and yet have a worthwhile end." This is not the stance toward plot taken by nine-teenth-century realism but, like *Sot-Weed*'s colorful multiplicities of sexual desire, a deliberate regression from the proprieties of shapeli-ness and singularity. Barth's plots make the novel much more multiple and metonymical than either the Victorian offspring of social realism or the modernist descendants of psychological realism. George Eliot and Virginia Woolf, for example, limit themselves to one story per novel and they stop their story along its metonymical way to organize it through metaphors of meaning (the pier-glass image, the witness box, the network; the envelope, the halo).

The Sterne/Fielding/Barth strategy, to the contrary, is to change the context of metaphor through metonymical excess, and thus allow metaphor to thrive at the lowest levels of formal organization. Happily, like the Traveling Whore o' Dorset, Barth's storytellers have a way with story as they have a way with words, and their digressive dramaturgy manages to herd all the little dogies into the corral by sunset. Part of the reader's fun with the book's multiple plots and marathon stories comes from watching how the author keeps all his balls up in the air without sacrificing any to gravity. Barth confesses to being "in love with stories at least as much as language" (*FB*, 105), and his authorial desire, particularly irrepressible in this instance, makes *The Sot-Weed Factor* indeed a "fancier" act of juggling than even *Tom Jones*.

By multiplying metaphor, yet keeping it submerged in his racy metonymical stream as the colorful flotsam and jetsam of its storytelling currents, Barth in 1960 is already beyond the structuralist definition of metaphor and metonymy as formulated by Roman Jakobsen. Jakobsen's separate assignment—of metonymy to the contiguous relations and contextual combinations of time-indexed prose fiction, and of metaphor to the imaginative similarities and spatial substitutions of temporally unmarked poetry—is useful as a blunt cut, but it does not allow for the distinctions within prose fiction I am trying to make between the eighteenth-century novel and the "Novel's" "bastard" descendants. It cannot in itself support my argument that Barth purposefully chose this historical example of the genre and consciously deployed his three defenses in order to slice out of the "true" history of the genre those intervening sober realists and artful modernists.

Jacques Lacan's post-structuralist application of a psychoanalytic analogy to the two figures—metaphor is a symptom, and metonymy is desire—makes rather more plausible the suggestion that the book's metonymical amplitude might be at least partially due to Barth's imitation of a period in history when quotidian life was more candidly appetitive and the drive for libidinal satisfaction more unselfconsciously out in the open. However, Barth is constantly destroying the ground of such mimetic assumptions through his impish scorn for any stable model of truth or reality; there can be nothing reliable to copy when the historical past is suspected to be a fictive invention, and when the book's fictional present is infested with such unstoppable metaphor-makings and self-creations.

One would not want to mistake literary creation for literary criticism and theory, but in the case of John Barth, an author situated in the academy and acutely attuned to its concerns, one does not err in seeking out a theorist whose interest in the history of the genre is equal to Barth's own. That theorist is the Soviet linguist Mikhail Bakhtin, whose theoretical summation "Discourse in the Novel" has been translated in *The Dialogic Imagination* (1987, 259–422). Bakhtin's insistence on verbal discourse as a social phenomenon and on its integration into the question of genre, I would argue, parallels Barth's achievement in his third novel. Bakhtin was arguing in the 1920s for the diversity of speech as the ground of style, in the face of prevailing "stylistics of 'private craftsmanship' that ignores the social life of discourse outside the artist's study" (259)—a stylistics which, in the spirit of Saussure's *parole/langue* distinction, was convinced that one's language is predetermined and inviolable, and that the artist's individualization of the general language was single-languaged and single-styled.

Such critics of literature, Bakhtin argued, were seeing but one of the two tendencies in life and language, the expression of the centripetal forces aimed at unification and centralization, while blinding themselves to the centrifugal forces uninterruptedly at work decentralizing and disunifying the forceful overcomings of reality by language. The novel is defined by Bakhtin as that genre which artistically organizes this diversity of voices, social speech types, and languages that are the *heteroglossia* of the human world: "the internal stratification of any single national language into social dialects, characteristic group behavior, professional jargons, generic languages, languages of generations and age groups, tendentious languages, languages of the authorities, of various circles and of passing fashions, languages that serve the specific sociopolitical purposes of the day, even of the hour" (262–63). Within this metnonymical cacophony every sort of discourse is oriented toward an understanding that is "responsive" (280), every prose word is "double-voiced" (327), every author is "representing another's language" (361), and every story is "not from the author" (322). Therefore, Bakhtin urges the literary critic to imagine the novelist as one who "ventriloquates" (299), and to think of his work as a rejoinder in a given and ongoing dialogue, instead of as a self-sufficient and closed authorial monologue.

Bakhtin's recognition of the likely distance between the creators of novels and their critics anticipates the storm of critical protest that broke over Barth's *Sot-Weed Factor*, and the terms of the negative responses. Long before Jerome Klinkowitz charged Barth with regression and parody, Earl Rovit (1963) was fairly sputtering over the fact that Barth had abdicated his monologic function and authorial voice for the representation of another's language—"for a twentieth-century writer to present an eight hundred page novel while denying himself access to the speech of his own time . . . that the question of identity so common to the concerns of contemporary fiction should be smothered in the excessive paraphernalia of authentic antiquarianism" (117). Rovit's "excessive paraphernalia" strongly intimates a distaste for any microcosm of heteroglossia that isn't tamed by the authorial voice, just as his dismay at Barth's self-denial of access betrays the Saussurean assumption that authorial *parole* can merely individualize the current official language. But Rovit knows full well what altar fire he's keeping lit and what leopards he's keeping out of the temple. This is what one might expect, he ruefully intones, from "the choice of Pope over Poe. . . . a hollow vessel, a cosmetic rather than a cosmic design, decorative, playful . . . the Novel as Jig-Saw-Puzzle" (121). Rovit wants the novel's First Stylistic Line, which triumphed only in the nineteenth century, and which displayed the Romantics' originary imagination as morally regnant in prose fiction, impregnable to fancy's liaisons with the outside. It would have had to be some prejudice of this sort against the Second Stylistic Line that motivated the moralized trope of Rovit's argument; namely, that Barth's dialogic imagination—his choosing of imitation, pastiche, and yes, parody—led him "inevitably to surrender his moral opportunity to create values" (119). For a critic such as Rovit, committed to an authoritative discourse, any reinvention that stops short of either redemption or revulsion is morally culpable, and therefore he was quite possibly immune to Barth's seriocomic dialogizings on the plain and significant virtues (171), on the linkage of mortality with morality (293, 579), on cynicism and basic trust (520–25), and on the distinction between a morality of motive and a morality of deed (628–29).

The traditional scholar, who seeks in the novel a symphonic, orchestrated theme rather than the entire piano keyboard, has always been able to find a fiction to his taste, as also has the lover of the double-voiced word. Bakhtin's uniqueness as a genre historian is to have traced prose fiction back through the prehistory of the novel, and found there a double origin, which became his First and Second lines. Aimed against the official language of its time, which always included a purified or "poetic" prose genre, heteroglossia at its inception was emphatically parodic; only over time, and especially in the merging of the two lines in the nineteenth century, did the parodic novel lose its distinction and come positively to inform the genre as a whole.

Staking out a finer line of classification than either Klinkowitz or Rovit, Bakhtin would not have characterized Barth's book as *parodic stylization*, in which "the intentions of the representing discourses are at odds with the intentions of the represented discourse; they fight against them, they depict a real world of objects not by using the represented language as a productive point of view, but rather by using it as an exposé to destroy the represented language" (364). Although Barth does re-create the language of the eighteenth century as an authentic whole, his overall conscious intention in re-presenting this "image of a language" is not parody, but *hybridization*—bringing into collision differing points of view embedded in a semantics that is concrete, social, and personal, multiplying encounters that either display the dialogized interrelation of languages or are apt to erupt into pure dialogues (358–63). Nowhere does Barth avail himself of the second language, his own century's, that is required for parodic stylization, although there is everywhere the contact of diverse speech that makes parody possible.

Bakhtin's careful distinctions, furthermore, let us discern the profit in Barth's deliberate regression to this particular century and in the hybridization that occurs between his double protagonists. Henry Burlingame III and Ebenezer Cooke are reinventions of the two marvelous types that carried the Second Stylistic Line through its most triumphant English century: the rogue and the fool (Bakhtin, 401–10). With the rogue we see the ground being prepared for a radical skepticism toward any unmediated discourse and any straightforward seriousness. Burlingame introduces, in Bakhtin's apt phrase, the "category of gay deception" (401), which opposes itself to the lies accumulated in structured and recognized professions, social groups, and classes. The rogue mocks the falsity of official languages, robs them of their power to harm, yet at the same time justifies the merry and intelligent deception precisely because it is directed against such liars. Burlingame's proliferating masks, which do so much to enhance the novel's Rabelaisian and carnivalesque flavor, have the additional and important function of forestalling the authoritative, lying impositions of political hegemony. When at book's end, he leaves his unborn son to be reared by his mistress Anna Cooke and her twin brother while he disappears into the Bloodsworth Island of his Indian heritage, the reader knows that this very useful rogue has what it takes to foment enough dissension among his chieftain half-brothers to prevent the Ahatchwhoops from going on the warpath until such time as "poor shitten Maryland" can get together its authoritative act as a properly constituted colony.

That he believes in and promotes reality as a fiction does not mean, however, that Burlingame takes its fictiveness less than seriously. As boyhood tutor and lifelong friend to Eben, Burlingame spends hours and years trying to wise Eben up to his own fiction-makings and those of the world. It is not for nothing that Barth's idealist poet of the mythopoeic Imagination and the virgin Soul must learn what's what from a Fancy-man tutor, or that the appalling sincerity and abstraction of Eben's bad art is submitted to abject comparison with Burlingame's own robust fullness in history. However, as wrongfully prideful as Ebenezer is of his "innocence," his story is not purely or mainly the authorial parody of the *Bildungsroman* that Heide Ziegler claims it to be (1987, 31–39); Ebenezer is quite another kind of fool. "Stupidity," says Bakhtin, "in the novel is always polemical" (403), itself a dialogic category like gay deception that can tear away masks. Eben's naiveté about the conventions of society as well as about the sexual desires of individuals exposes the conventionality of society and the tenacity of the instinctual. Like Voltaire's Candide, Barth's fool fails to understand even as he aspires to conceptualize the world, and this coupling of incomprehension with comprehension becomes a basic style-shaping factor of not only this novel but the Novel. As a fool with a rogue for a tutor, Barth's hero in this belated novel of education achieves a kind of prose wisdom, which retrospectively tempers the authoritative idealisms of nineteenth-century *Bildungsromane* with the conjectural possibility and speculative probability of amplitudinous double-voicing.

By taking this detour through Bakhtin, we should now be prepared to understand Bloom's assignment of *kenosis* as the revisionary ratio that coordinates the poet's psychic and artistic strategies at this third phase of his career. "Kenosis" is the term Saint Paul used to describe Christ's humbling of himself, the emptying out of his divinity, in order that he might live among humankind. Untypically, it is a ratio that seems directed at poets rather than poems:

every *kenosis* voids a precursor's powers, as though a magical undoing-isolating sought to save the Egotistical Sublime at a father's expense. *Kenosis*, in this poetic and revisionary sense, appears to be an act of self-abnegation, yet tends to make the fathers pay for their own sins, and perhaps those of the sons also. I arrive therefore at the pragmatic formula: "Where the precursor was, there shall the ephebe be, but by the discontinuous mode of emptying the precursor of *his* divinity, while appearing to empty himself of his own." (*AI*, 90–91)

By whatever criteria one may construe the "divinity" of the novel's First Stylistic Line of development—its fruitful adherence to the mimetic contract, its high moral seriousness, its deliberative objectivity, its rational arrangements of plot and characterization—Barth has comically done his best to compromise that divinity. His act of "self-abnegation," as regards his own language and contemporary times, is scarcely a "humbling," however, as regards the flamboyant life and language of colonial America, and the glorious abundance of the eighteenth-century novel. Nonetheless, Barth's regressive anachronism, performed at the expense of the nineteenth century, is not so far in motive from that which Saint Paul attributed to Christ: Barth, too, wanted his fiction to "live among humankind," and it was this fictional house with these fictional inhabitants which could encompass the astonishing vigor and scandal that is the human condition. Ultimately, Barth's kenosis gets him a direct route back to his own sublime, to the historical origins of his geographical home as a man, and to his roots as a writer in the English novel. As the contemporary direct descendant of the bawdy and enlightened Second Stylistic Line, Barth announces with his *Sot-Weed Factor* that comedy is primary, a mode that, like it or not, is eminently well suited to this American country of ours and to its great American novel. "It is hard work and great art," says Garp, John Irving's writerly protagonist, "to make life not so serious."

Chapter 5
Giles Goat-Boy (1966):
The Heroic Career, Beyond Oedipus

Image	*Trope*	*Defense*	*Ratio*
High and Low	Hyperbole	Repression	Daemonization

The crucial career question for Barth, after *The Sot-Weed Factor* was, "Where do you go from *up*?" Barth's private sense of his graduation into mature accomplishment was reinforced by the book's wide public review and successive paperback printings, which would keep his third novel in circulation among the college-educated counterculture, who were about to adopt his fourth as their campus classic. Looking back on these times in his foreword to the 1987 Doubleday Anchor edition, Barth thinks of *Sot-Weed* as "the novel that gives me the most satisfaction to remember having conceived, planned, and written" (vii). And he reserves special and uncommon praise for Ebenezer Cooke, not as a naive Candide, but as "a *writer*, sure in his calling though not in his gift," who throughout his book was "learning the hard way some facts of literary life, finding a real voice under all his rhetorical posturing and attitudinizing, discovering his true subject matter and most congenial form—in short, becoming the writer he had innocently presumed himself to be." Adds Barth: "So was I" (vi–vii). In 1960 Barth knew that he had made his "Crossing of Election" (Bloom's term [*PI*, 171] for the poet's triumph in the crisis of vocation), and soon the world would know that he belonged to the heroic fraternity of those who truly have the gift.

But if, newly elected, at age thirty you have already written your great American novel, what do you do for an encore at thirty-six? Riding high after Novel #3 and thoroughly daemonized in the strong *ethos* of a greatness of soul that puts him close to the gods, Barth reaches even higher in Novel #4 for the highest poetic genres of

Western culture, for its epic, tragic, and mystical sublimes—the Ur-Myth of the Hero, the *Oedipus Rex* of Sophocles, the biblical life of Christ. His answer to the career question is *Giles Goat-Boy*, the book whose plot is closest to Barth's definition of the heroic life as an obstacle course and scavenger hunt, whose heroic quest is closest to Barth's ideal of the literary career, and whose extravagant hero is closest to Barth's identification of himself as a poet. It is a hazardous book for the poet-as-hero who, in renewing his sense of personal power and announcing the advent of an agonistic Counter-Sublime, must make his transgressive Crossing of Solipsism over a purposeful and intense forgetting. *Giles Goat-Boy* is the glorious achievement of massive authorial repression.

These unfamiliar terms must give us pause. They testify to some rich elaborations that Bloom has worked upon his basic map of misprision, elaborations that tie the deviant and unnatural tropes ever more firmly to the poet's psychology and the poetic will toward persuasion. The six tropes should now be thought of as three pairs (irony/synecdoche, metonymy/hyperbole, metaphor/metalepsis), the first member of each conforming to the limitation, and the second, to the representation that is achieved in accordance with the dialectic of revision. Between these two opposed figurations of contraction and expansion, there occurs a moment of doubt, a question of uncertainty that is an *aporia* of the *logos*, a figure of shock or catastrophe, which Bloom's map designates merely as an unadorned "substitution." However, for the poet it is a crisis, crux, chiasmus that must be overcome, a crossing that must be made if he is to continue on his path to imaginative freedom, by making the lies he needs to believe in order to survive.

It is also useful to think of the six tropes as existing in two separate lines of descent, as tropes of limitation (irony, metonymy, metaphor) and tropes of representation (synecdoche, hyperbole, metalepsis), because this schema demonstrates that poetic meaning can be generated not only, as Freud thought, by means of the limitation that is sublimation, but also through the poetic representation of the repressed material heaped in the unconscious. Unlike the normal neurotic, who defensively turns away from instinctual representations and creates the unconscious by repressing them, the poet drives down to the unconscious, excavates the repressions, and represents them: "What the Romantics called creative Imagination is akin, not to sublimation and metaphor, but to repression and hyperbole, which represent rather than limit" (*MM*, 99). Bloom's third elaboration of his tropological schema involves his reappropriation of the original meanings of two Greek words, *ethos* and *pathos*, and his translation of them into the psychoanalytic recognition of the defect or excess within all human response, whether it is the failure to realize desire in an act that is *pathos*, or the successful but lying realization in an act that is *ethos*.

Because these completions by Bloom of his cartography are extremely pertinent to Barth's various mappings in *Giles Goat-Boy*, it behooves us to follow Bloom directly and at some length in his own summation, which occurs in his essay on "Poetic Crossing: Rhetoric and Psychology" (*PI*, 143–74):

> *Ethos*, the Greek word for "custom," "image," "trait," goes back to the root meaning of "self." We use it now to mean the character of an individual, as opposed to his emotions, or perhaps he meant what was permanent or ideal in anyone's character. *Pathos*, the Greek for "passion," goes back to a root meaning to "suffer." We use it now to mean a quality in someone that arouses feelings of pity or sympathy in anyone else, but Aristotle meant by it something like any person's transient and emotional frame of mind. . . . Quintillian's most useful insight is to associate *ethos* with irony and comedy, and *pathos* with tragedy; and so, by implication, with irony's rival as a master trope, synecdoche.
>
> In more Freudian terms, *ethos* results from the successful translation of the will into an act, verbal or physical, whereas *pathos* ensues when there is a failure to translate will into act. In the terms I employed in *Poetry and Repression*, *ethos* is a reseeing and *pathos* a reaiming, with the middle position between them in the dialectic of revision being taken by *logos* as a re-esteeming or re-estimating. (*PI*,150)
>
> I return to my map of misprision, with its three pairs of dialectical ratios, for I am going to complete it now by saying that a crossing is what intervenes at the crisis-point in each of the three pairs, that is, the point where a figuration of *ethos* or Limitation yields to a figuration of *pathos* or Representation. I think there are only two fundamental tropes, tropes of action and tropes of desire. Tropes of *ethos* are the language of what Emerson and Stevens call "poverty" of imaginative need, of powerlessness and necessity, *but also* of action, incident, character. Tropes of *pathos* are the language of desire, possession, and power. In poetry, a trope of action is always an irony, until it is further reduced to metonymy and metaphor; whereas a trope of imaginative desire always begins as a synecdoche, until it is further expanded to hyperbole and metalepsis, the trope that reverses temporality. (*PI*, 169)

Bloom's clarifying commentary permits us to review Barth's career up to this point and to stipulate the nature of his present task. Barth's single deployment of a trope of representation, the initial synecdoche of *The End of the Road*, confined its pathetic effects to the characters: The rational *ethos* of both Todd Andrews and Joe Morgan was troped by the *pathos* of Jake Horner's inability to act and of Rennie Morgan's acute suffering and grotesque death; thus, between the first two books, the *pathos* of a tragedy of adultery troped the *ethos* of a comedy of nihilistic thought. Barth's twofold deployment of the tropes of limitation, however, has been much more psychologically and rhetorically severe upon himself than upon his characters: The deathly *ethos* of Todd's verbal action was considerably ameliorated by Barth's humanistic perspective on him, and the life-affirming *ethos* of both Ebenezer's quest and Burlingame's intrigues was given hospitable range in the amplitudinous universe Barth created for them; the author, however, spared himself not at all in the sadomasochism with which he limited himself to the depiction of his opposite and curtailed the automimetic impulse in his first novel, and then emptied himself of everything close at hand for his third novel. In these extreme instances of self-abnega-tion and self-contraction, Barth has proven himself the poetic hero of *ethos*. Can he now succeed as well with the *pathos* of repressed desire and its expansive representation?

In his presentation of this fourth stage as "*Daemonization* or The Counter-Sublime" (*AI*, 98–112), Bloom prepares us for the ultimate deflation of the excessively inflated ephebe. As the strenuously sup-pressed representing force breaks forth into its fullest expansion, it expresses itself through hyperbole, "the trope of excess or the over-throw, that like repression finds its images in height and depth, in the Sublime and the Grotesque," and what it represents is the glory of repressive meaning heretofore buried in the unconscious; for "mem-ory and desire, driven down, have no place to go *in language* except up onto the heights of sublimity, the ego's exultation in its own operations" (*MM*, 100). But this "falling upwards" into extravagance of the ephebe leaves him susceptible to the vertigo of Binswanger's *Verstiegenheit*, and this "wandering beyond limits," which brings him close to the gods, also estranges him from human existence. The poet's daemonization as a challenger of the great, which thrusts toward a Counter-Sublime, is thus liable to a return of the repressed and its *pathos*, which will deflate the disproportionate distance the ephebe has put between himself and others (*AI*, 104–6). Bloom has many fertile insights about this phase of his map—grounded as it is in the Sublime of his favored Romantics and the Counter-Sublime of his greatest Covering Cherubs, Milton and Emerson—which shall receive a full airing as we proceed. First, however, we must hear how Barth, a theorist himself at this stage of his career, disposes of these same matters.

Barth does not present himself as a poet who has risen above human-ity to become a god himself, but as a humble ephebe who has been stunned by a shock of recognition. After reveling in *Sot-Weed*'s carnival of formlessness, Barth relates, he picked up by chance Lord Raglan's *The Hero*, and throughout the writing of *Giles Goat-Boy*, continued his investigations into the myth found in virtually all cultures, reading Otto Rank's *Myth of the Birth of the Hero* and Joseph Campbell's *The Hero with a Thousand Faces* (1949). Barth was captivated on two counts: (1) the regularity of the pattern that prevails, whether it is plotted in a linear trajectory by Raglan as the twenty-two steps that get the hero from home to Heaven, or is curved round upon itself in a circle by Campbell as the cycle where the hero's end meets his beginning; and (2) the integration, as successive stages in the journey of the hero, of "those two profoundest motions of the human spirit," Eastern mysticism and Western "tragicism." Ephebic astonishment and excitement are yet palpable in the 1965 public lecture that Barth delivered on "Mystery and Tragedy: The Twin Motions of Ritual Heroism" (*FB*, 41–59). I reprint below Campbell's diagram from his book (Princeton: Princeton University Press, Bollingen Series XVII, 1949) as amplified by Barth in *The Friday Book* (44):

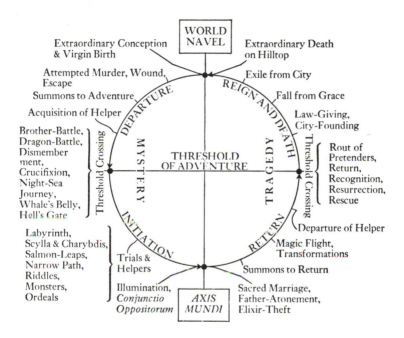

The first half of the hero's quest, the two quadrants of initiation and departure which Sophocles does not represent, belongs to myth and mystery—the hero's extraordinary birth, the attempt on his infant life, the spiriting away to foster parents, his unknown childhood, the journey to his future kingdom, his defeat of a creature from the daemonized sublime. The last two quadrants, return and reign and death of the hero, belong to tragedy proper—becoming king through marriage to a princess, reigning and prescribing laws, losing favor with the gods, being driven from the throne, meeting a mysterious death, having a sepulchre in which no body is buried, leaving no successors. The limit-experiences of the hero, his threshold points of illumination, are directly at the bottom and top of the circle. The mystical hero enters the *Axis Mundi* and, gloriously estranged from his illumination, disappears from the world; the tragic hero exits from the same place, goes out into the world, and has a public career before his tragic end. At the World Navel, both heroes meet their end in death, after which the mystery recommences.

Barth's daemonization—from the Greek root meaning "distribute" and "divide"—ensures that as soon as he finds Eastern mysticism and Western tragedy in collaboration, he will be putting them asunder. He begins by contrasting the path taken to knowledge by the Buddhist and by Plato's philosopher-king. The latter leaves the material reality of the cave because it is shadowy and inexact in its differentiations, and then pursues the sunlit dualisms of logical thought up the ladder of generalization and abstraction until he can gaze unblinkingly with his mind's eye "on Beauty Bare and the other Platonic Ideas" (*FB*, 49). Barth's hero ends neither in the illumination of Plato's philosopher-king nor in the insight-through-blindness of Sophocles' Oedipus Rex, although his way has passed through both these Western mistakings. Instead, like the mystic, he ends in the beyond of the East, in an "enlightenment in darkness" that is loyal to the *ethos* of the knowing self and far from the *pathos* of the madding crowd. Here is Barth's very Eastern interpretation of the quest of the mystical/mythical hero who completes the whole cycle:

> The mystic then is like the hero: Summoned by whatever voice, he comes to grips with the contradictions and self-defeating nature of differentiated reality (in the case of the Buddhists) or material reality (in the case of the Platonists); he leaves analytical consciousness behind him like Bre'r Rabbit's clothes on the Tarbaby, and after the very trying—and in the case of young Zen novices, often humiliating—ordeals of logical binds, despair, riddling *koans*, insults to "common sense," perhaps even physical mortifications, he is if he is fortunate vouchsafed a *satori*—an enlightenment as to the "true" (which is to say, undifferentiated) nature of reality: *prajna*. He sees that seamless nature knows nothing of the concepts and distinctions by which the "waking" consciousness apprehends her; that, in the paradoxical language of the mystics, I and thou, male and female, subject and object, good and evil, self and Buddha-self, are all aspects of the same thing, the One. Thus the paradoxical metaphors of rebirth in death, enlightenment in darkness, associated with the hero's arrival at the *Axis Mundi*: They become symbols of the mystical transcension of category. (*FB*, 49)

Ultimately then, the quest of George Giles, Goat-Boy is aimed not at the mastery of material reality and the self *through* thought, but at their recovery *from* thought. Which makes it all the more puzzling that the critics have persisted for so long (Scholes 1967; Tharpe 1974; Harris 1983) in interpreting the "mystical transcension of category" as the successful achievement of the Hegelian dialectic! As Barth the theorist is quick to point out, via William James, the four hallmarks of the mystic experience—passivity, noumenality, transience, and ineffability (*FB*, 50)—can have nothing to do with the logical contradiction and polemical disputation that operate the dialectic; a synthesis gained through the long labor of the negative is half the globe away from the oneness conferred as a gift upon the receptive, fusing, and non-negating mystic. George Giles may himself pass *through* his share of Hegelian positings, opposings, lifting ups, and surpassings, but the *Aufgehoben* doesn't get *him* through, and his final repudiation of that universe of thought proceeds very distinctly from outside it. To the Hegelian promptings of an interviewer, the creator of Giles responded with the snappish rejoinder that "I'm not sure synthesis is possible, and I'm not terribly interested in it anyhow" (Prince 1968, 47). Barth, in fact, has not been "terribly interested" in dialectic ever since he dragged rationality, its futility and its ill consequences, through the mud in his first two books, and then washed his hands of them. Life is too excessive to be depicted as or governed by a science of thought, and the abject gravity of the synthesists has caused them completely to miss, or misinterpret as a mockery of its hero, the mockery of Hegelianism that informs Barth's book.

Rather than referring the incredible botches of this Grand Tutor back to Giles's status as a parody or antitype of the true hero, they should carry their complaints to the author, who has hilariously rigged the Hegelian deck he gives his hero to play with. The dialectic might conceivably have functioned as a correspondence of thought with the quest of a hero who has been gradually prepared for it through a consecutive, graded sequence of initiation rituals, and then properly takes to the road—like Spenser's knight, or Christ, or any hero of a *Prüfungsroman*—for the successful completion of those tests, tasks, and ordeals through which he will prove his glorious *ethos*. However, much of the book's wild humor, and most of its catastrophes, come about because Barth has collapsed this rational step-by-step into a simultaneity, and Georgieboy—who is truly the good goat-boy his foster father Max keeps trying to believe he is—must practice his Grand Tutoring, under the sign of Hegel, before he has got the hang of it. His three descents into the belly of his father-computer WESCAC for enlightenment fixes do not issue in any dialectical progress; to the contrary, George's Hegelian three-step consistently confuses the minds and disarrays the lives of his eleven loyal disciples, who are waiting outside and hanging on his every Word from on-High. Wrenching their personalities and relationships to match the contraries of their Grand Tutor's yo-yoing thoughts, and faring no better when the yo-yo stalls and stutters in its overpassing, George's limp and battered eleven are the author's comic cautionary warnings against allowing this kind of thinking to lead you anywhere. The rampant inefficacy of Hegelian thought as a guide for living disqualifies it; it is at once a *pathos* of thought that does not translate well into act and a parody of any life lived under the gun of mentation.

Neither will the *pathos* of tragedy get you anywhere, enjoins our theorist of mystery and tragedy. The lecturer Barth in no way rejects the truth of Sophoclean tragedy, which he presents as four existentialist postulates: (1) that the world is morally ambiguous and brutally compensatory; (2) consequently, there are only different ways to lose; (3) the self is not transcendable; and (4) therefore, the human condition is essentially ironic and technically absurd (*FB*, 51–52). Indeed, Barth thinks that the tragic response is much more alert than the Platonic proposition that Truth is "a very fine thing to have." His quarrel, rather, is with those who drench themselves in the *pathos* of the tragic recognition. Any hero of Barth's is going to have to drive himself beyond the pathetic Oedipus, the blinded Oedipus dark with the revelation of tragic recognition, the human Oedipus whose affirmation of these tragic truths would terminate the hero's quest:

> Those who say of Oedipus, after the catastrophe, "But at least he *knows* himself now, and is ready for the condition of prophethood"—as if to say Truth is expensive, sure, but so are Rolls-Royces; you gotta pay for class—are being sentimental: Oedipus certainly doesn't feel that way; neither does the chorus, and neither does Sophocles. . . . "Affirmation of the human spirit . . ." all very well, as long as it's clearly understood that the affirmation doesn't *get* you anywhere: It is meaningless beyond itself, and people outside the drama too readily get sentimental about its terminal value. Be it repeated: On the tragic view there is not any way to win; there are only more or less noble and spectacular ways to go down. (*FB*, 52–53)

Almost at the center of *Giles Goat-Boy*, as if at its *Axis Mundi* of illumination, Barth has placed his scene-by-scene parody of *Oedipus Rex*. A performance of daemonized *ethos*, *Taliped Decanus* is Barth's coda to the impoverishment of tragedy through the humanization of comedy that prevails throughout the novel. "When the ephebe is daemonized, his precursor is necessarily humanized," says Harold Bloom. The daemonic ratio functions to humanize the sacred texts so thoroughly that they will seem to have been written by mere men, vaguely approximating in their *pathos* the gift of knowing that has been bestowed only upon the latecomer poet: "In *daemonization*, the augmented poetic consciousness sees clear outline, and yields back to description what it has overyielded to sympathy" (*AI*, 100–101). In his parodic centerpiece, Barth emphasizes all the instinctual lust and aggression that Sophocles' drama evades on its way to Aristotelian catharsis and tragic pleasure; and by retrieving the human middle ground, where desire overwhelms the moral imperatives of sublimated rationality, Barth subjects tragedy to the return of its repressed, representing all that heaps up its unconscious. Parody always says, "I know better, I see more clearly"—and it yields nothing to sympathy.

In Barth's parody, the very soul of tragedy, its *mythos*, is exposed as a trap for the readily gulled: How could King Taliped be expected to solve a murder that is nine years cold? How come over all that time Queen Agenora never noticed the scars on her husband's ankles? The psychoanalytical *pathos* of the Oedipus complex is rendered inane: An incestuous patricide should at least *know* the father he's killing and *desire* the mother he's sleeping with, but this oedipal kid's lust is all but henpecked out of existence by Agenora, who has cornered for herself all the randy sexual desire of this parodic present. Indeed, so dilapidated is the *ethos* of this latter-day Oedipus that Barth's *Taliped Decanus* is a tragedy without a hero. As a sporting lady of long reputation, whose hormones have been driving her for years to her present disreputability as a menopausal nymphomaniac, Agenora upstages Taliped every time she appears—joshing the male chorus about their dismal past records in bed, flagrantly vamping the handsome mailman, taking pokes at that swishy prophet-prof Gynander. Like Mae West oozing out of her corset, Agenora reminds us of how the putting on of comic flesh will obscure the skeletal form of the tragic figure; indeed, she reminds us of how any character who is living a myth instead of believing it will acquire the humps and bumps of instinctual nature that do not lend themselves readily to a scaling down or straightening out by the *mythos*.

When Taliped does manage to wrench center stage from Agenora— as "Master Sleuth, The Dean Who'll Dare Anything for the Truth!"— tragedy's high *dianoia* (Aristotelian rationality and moral excellence) is dragged low. In fact, it's a regular catfight of name-calling and insults between Taliped, his brother-in-law, and Gynander, who come from their corners with their claws out, spitting and hissing. (I take this as Barth's comic version of the mimetic conflict that René Girard [1978, 121–35] finds to be a staple of tragedy as well as comedy.) And, of course, Barth comically mucks up the *melos*, in order to limn with the pointed rhyme of his anti-heroic couplets the return of the comic repressed—aggression and sexuality—to the royal house of Thebes: sake! It/mother-naked; young/well hung; derrière/fairy; my past, sir/ bastard; riddler/diddler.

Like classical tragedy, which cuts itself a portion of familiar myth, both allegory and myth depend for their effects upon a skeletalization of form: The scenarios of which Oedipus, Christ, and Everyman are the heroes must be impoverished of all detail that is not obedient to the determinate schema of the received or second stor(e)y. Yet if tragedy sacrifices content to form, even more so do myth and allegory. In tragedy at least, the hero can give a personal answer ("I am the lover of my mother and the murderer of my father") to the question that is the occasion of all its *pathos*, "Who am I?" However, myth and allegory, those genres of *ethos*, assume that a generic answer will suffice, as if all that Oedipus ever needed to know was the "Man," with which he solved the riddle of the Sphinx. What is myth, after all, but the phylogenic experience of the species abstracted into a pattern? And what individuated human being, especially one holding to the ideal of professional herohood, could precisely duplicate that pattern, without falling short of it (the defective response of *pathos*) or going beyond it (the excessive responses of *ethos*)? Only an impossibly generic Man or mythic Woman could be bound to the stimulus/response form of behavior demanded of a character trapped in myth and allegory. That ontogeny cannot *just* recapitulate phylogeny is the bad news that *Giles Goat-Boy* sends back to the Monomyth and the Gospels.

Barth's comic strategy in the book, hyperbolic in each instance, is a double whammy, insisting at once on the generic allegorical form while making sure that his hero can only abort it. Any summary of Barth's allegory must manifest a manic proliferation of upper-case names and acronyms which would elicit the admiration of such champions of allegory as Edmund Spenser and John Bunyan. For instance: Ever since the end of Campus Riot II, the University has become increasingly nervous as New Tammany College of West Campus and Nikolai College of East Campus engage in a Quiet Riot. Both colleges are run by powerful computers, WESCAC and EASCAC respectively, which threaten all Studentdom with the hideous prospect of being *EAT*en through *E*lectroencephalic *A*mplification and *T*ransmission. The mission of George the Goat-Boy, son of WESCAC itself, is to prove that he is the *GILES* (Grand Tutorial Ideal, Laboratory Eugenical Specimen), relieve the pressure on the populace of WESCAC, and as Grand Tutor show all studentdom the way to Graduation. It is doomed to be a mission impossible.

Thus, *Giles Goat-Boy* is very much an allegorical guided tour for its hero, who traces the footsteps of Christ and Oedipus through the mire and fury of the Cold War politics of the 1950s and the uneasy détente of the pre-Viet Nam 1960s. George has all his mythic credentials in order according to Lord Raglan, but in every situation the content exceeds its container, synecdoche bursts into hyperbole, and both the transcendence and transparency of conventional allegory are con-

stantly at threat. High and low do not remain separated for very long
when a goat-god walks the earth, or when a comic *ethos* invades that
middle ground of the wholly human where instincts and morals clash
on the darkling plain. Barth's goat-god may be to either side of twentieth-century oedipal culture, but he is assuredly not above it.

The myth starts off well enough: Born of a royal virgin and a godlike
king in an unusual conception and then whisked off to the foreign land
of a foster parent—but then comic complications set in almost immediately to bring myth low. George's natural mother has become perma-
nently addled by her conception through computer console; his puta-
tive father has diverted all his programming into sexual and power
lust; the misanthropic foster father has reared our hero as a goat; and
"Billy Bockfuss" (our soon-to-be-rechristened George), suckled by a
she-goat and growing up on all fours, is a bundle of unrepressed
instinct about to be set loose in a culture of repression. In almost no
time, he whips himself through the Oedipus complex: strikes his dear
Max, tries to mount his mom, and for extra bad measure, kills his goat-
brother in what should have been safe and sane animal rivalry. During
the next seven years of his prepping, George remains the caprine and
capricious human animal, taking Max's historical facts, natural laws,
and philosophical concepts as if they were all prefaced with "Once
upon a time." Long past the day when he gets painfully up on his hind
legs and gets himself onto the great campus, the kid persists in thinking
of life as impromptu theater, self-knowledge as improvisation, and the
hero's cycle as an utterly free script. Not for the GILES are the guilt and
self-punishment of the pathetic Oedipus; his, rather, is the tremendous *ethos* that says, If I am the Grand Tutor, and I say this or do that,
then it must be right.

"*Ethos* is the *daimon*," intones Bloom, "and all things were made
through him, and without him was not anything made that was made"
(*AI*, 99). *Ethos* was made for the poet as maker; *pathos* won't get you
anywhere. The theorists Bloom and Barth agree: One reaches *ethos* by
shedding civilization, by "*backtracking* through the history of creation"
past the *pathos* of the human to the primal void (Barth, *FB*, 48); "to
daemonize is to reach the antecedent stage where everything passional is
ambivalent. . . . In the imagination, the Oedipal phase *develops backwards*" (Bloom, *AI*, 110). It is also agreed that this is a task suitable only
for an elite. The hero, says Barth with his eyes on himself, is "of the
intellectual, spiritual, and artistic elite; the masters in any field who
drive to the origin and first principles of their discipline in order to
turn round a corner" (*FB*, 48). The hero, says Bloom, is Emerson; and
to prove it, he quotes for his epigraph the famous passage from "Self-
Reliance" by the architect of the mystical, American Counter-Sublime:

And now at last the highest truth on this subject remains unsaid; probably cannot be said; for all that we say is the far-off remembering of the intuition. The thought by what I can now nearest approach to say it, is this. When good is near you, when you have life in yourself, it is not by any known or accustomed way; you shall not discern the footprints of any other; you shall not see the face of man; you shall not hear any name;—the way, the thought, the good, shall be wholly strange and new. It shall exclude example and experience. You take the way from man, not to man. All persons that ever existed are its forgotten ministers. Fear and hope are alike beneath it. There is somewhat low even in hope. In the hour of vision there is nothing that can be called gratitude, nor properly joy. The soul raised over passion beholds identity and eternal causation, perceives the self-existence of Truth and Right, and calms itself with knowing that all things go well. (*AI*, 98)

Analogous to the recognition scene of the tragic Oedipus, this is the "hour of vision" of the mystic. The gift of divination, where the *logos* ends and the mystery commences, has descended upon him, and the bestowal is met by a serenity that subsumes pain and joy. The poet of daemonized *ethos* no longer merely believes in a vague eternity, but knows it in its clearest and broadest outlines. Lamentably, the mystical experience lasts but an ecstatic moment, its unhappiest quality being that the "highest truth" will not lend itself to verbal or logical expression; the "soul raised above passion" has wandered beyond the limits even of speech, and, one assumes, that which cannot be said must go without saying.

Unless, of course, one is the daemonized poet John Barth, who is very much inclined to say what goes without saying. Although he bears all the proper marks of the mystic, how alien Emerson seems to Barth the poet! What appeal could ineffability have for this man of many words, or transience for this author for the long run, or passivity for a poet-as-hero? Surely, this cannot be the Counter-Sublime that Barth means to stand against the West's tragic Sublime. And yet his Goat-Boy ends exactly like Emerson at the height of his extravagance. In the beyond of the book, in the twelve pages of its "Posttape," a dozen years have passed since Max's voluntary Shafting, the ascension of Harold Bray the False Tutor from his stake, and George Giles' retirement from the Campus and humanity. George now sees all time as "cycles on cycles. . . . Unwind, rewind, replay," everything is a matter of "no matter," he neither agrees nor disagrees. He is beyond the *pathos* of "mortal studenthood," of those who still come to him with questions: "These things they ask in faith, despair, or hecklish taunt; I make no reply" (760). His once beloved Stacey has become the bullying organizer of his immortality—of Gilesianism, the New Curriculum, and the Revised New Syllabus we are reading—and the keeper of "His" son, whom George quite literally does not recognize as his own. Of the visiting Stacey, George says, "Let her wait." His single tenuous link with humanity is Tombo, the black boy with red hair, fatherless and abandoned by his mother, whom George plucked from the Unwed Coed's Nursery to be his errand-boy, and in whose eyes George sees "termless Truth" and "the reflection of myself, my hard history and my fate."

Like Emerson, Giles Goat-Boy has made his Crossing of Solipsism. The first Crossing of Election, between irony and synecdoche, answered the question, Am I truly a poet? and began the dialectic of the poet's freedom. This second crossing "struggles with the death of love, and tries to answer the fearful query Am I capable of loving another besides myself? This is the crossing between metonymy and hyperbole, or defensively between regressive and isolating movements of one's own psyche, and the massive repression of instinct that sublimely augments one's unconscious or inwardness at the expense of all the gregarious affects" (*PI*, 171). What Bloom is describing is the *pathos* of the man of *ethos*, of the mystic and the hero; the estrangement is glorious, but it is estrangement. Like Plato's philosophical ephebe who leaves behind the cave and its fettered men, and like the blind Oedipus who turns his back on kingdom and family, in the two great precursor poems of the Western Sublime, so also Barth's Goat-Boy has attained his noumenality through an intensely purposeful repression of everything human. The voiding in George of his sense of others, which Barth managed to exclude throughout the hectic Hegelianism of his Grand Tutoring, now reveals its repression at the book's closure as the death of the love of others, when the hero enters the inhuman and solitary transport where no Eros is possible except that of self-love. As Bloom says, in the falling cadence at his closure of "The Sublime Crossing and the Death of Love" (*AG*, 224–45), "knowing is itself a voicing of *pathos*," and that is where Barth's hero all but ends; yet "the marking, the will-to-inscribe, the *ethos* of writing" of the hero-as-poet drives Barth through George's crossing to the beyond of another scene, the scene of the Other.

At age thirty-three and a third, George knows that he has but a short time before they come to crucify him. But wait! The vision he leaves us with—of the "Commencement" that is at the end—is not of his Shafting on Founder's Hill, but of a mystical assumption into the lightning-struck oak and rock of "a riven grove beyond the Shaft." The fate that George will meet is the fate not of the voluntary scapegoat Christ or of the self-maimed Oedipus at the end of *Oedipus Rex*, but of the self-exiled Oedipus in *Oedipus at Colonus*. The questions implied by the exit of Barth's hero into a beyond of the tragic Oedipus are precisely those raised explicitly by Lacanian analysts and addressed to the conventional Freudians: Just how much recognition are we to give to Oedipus' recognition scene? Are we forever to be returning to the *pathos* of its cognition of incestuous and patricidal desire, or should we rather follow the wandering, performative Oedipus beyond his tragic recognition into the *ethos* of a mystical practice? With Barth, the Lacanians agree: Tragedy doesn't get you anywhere.

Shoshana Felman brilliantly schematizes the distinctive differences between Freudian and Lacanian practices in her "Beyond Oedipus: The Specimen Story of Psychoanalysis" (Felman 1983, 1021–51). For Freud, Sophocles' *Oedipus Rex* was the specimen story to which he could point for confirmation of his theoretical discoveries, and with this strategy he promoted the notion of psychoanalysis as a science founded upon a narrative. Lacan's return to Freud, however, is a return to *Oedipus at Colonus*—a retrieval that intends to take back for psychoanalytic *practice* a mythic Oedipus as the proper beyond of the tragic Oedipus which Freud translated into psychoanalytic *theory*; the Lacanians would then define their practice as a mystical bestowal beyond an act of narration. The Lacanians take Freud's "talking cure" very literally: it is through the "gift of speech" that one is mythically, mystically brought to health.

Wandering in the wilderness of his misrecognitions, the analysand, absent from the life of his history, tells his story; and the analyst— knowing his own exile from any "self-possessed kingdom of a theory," from any "non-mythical access to the truth"—listens for the "fictitious truthful structure" within the narrative symbolic logic. It is only through this speech-act space of narrative delay—which Felman terms "Lacan's uncertainty principle"—that the blessing of full, true speech descends upon the self radically expropriated in its own discourse, beyond ego and self-image and self-consciousness. Lacanian analysis answers affirmatively the question, with all of its *pathos*, asked by Oedipus at Colonus: "Is it now that I am nothing that I am made to be a man?" The insistent riddle of "Who am I?" whose answer was attempted by both Oedipus and Freud as riddle-solvers of great *ethos*, is ultimately answered by Oedipus and Lacan in the *pathos* of their exile: "I am a self expropriated in the discourse of the Other."

Through the Lacanian translation of theory back into narrative, we can better understand how the drama of the mystical Oedipus might inform the drama of a heroic career. With the making of literature, one exiles oneself from any non-narrative, non-tropological approach to truth; literature is no more a science of thought than psychoanalysis is a science of desire. Both the analyst and the author, radically self-critical and self-transgressive, commit themselves to a "destiny of erring," to performative acts through which the decentered self in its uncertainties assumes its history in the discourse of the Other, recognizes the symbol as the murder of the thing, and forgives itself. A career, like the work of a psychoanalysis, is destined to progress through the *pathos* of its recognitions to the *ethos* of its misrecognitions. The tale has no end or resting place; language always falsifies and the ideal of authentic speech is always ahead of one, but the hero-errant, in the exile of his *ethos*, is guaranteed continuance in an eternal relation to a future. Incorporating death into language in order to survive, the heroic maker is continually being reborn into his history through his stories and their truthfully lying symbolizations. Tropes of action and tropes of desire are his tenacities of error; one does not write to know, but rather to forget again and again. With Lacan, Bloom agrees: "that we do not father our own text, but that necessarily *our own text fathers us*" (*AG*, 245).

The poet-as-hero is what is permanent and ideal in John Barth's character. Although there is no way to win, on the tragic view of things, there are noble and spectacular ways to go down. Planning to major in professional heroism, George Goat-Boy asks the question that is his creator's: "How can anyone bear not to be . . . marvelous?" For the hero, greatness of character has only one opposition, petty-spiritedness; his only indignity, to be counted among the members of the chorus:

> Oedipus's choice, if he had any, was to take it on the chin in Thebes or in the back at Corinth, where presumably his fate would have sought him out: in other words, to be a tragic hero or a member of the chorus. Endowed with his temperament, he hadn't really any option. The pity and terror in our response to the tragic hero's fall, then, comes not from our feeling "There but for the grace of Zeus go I," but, more grimly, "There but for my petty-spiritedness go I." (*FB*, 52)

Just as tragic *pathos* chose Oedipus, so has comic *ethos* chosen John Barth and hauled him into the beyond of a heroic literary career. We recall Bloom's statement that gives everything to the performance of the poet exiled in his daemonization: "*Ethos* results from the successful translation of will into act." And when the daemonized Barth prefaces his conclusions about *pathos* above with a choice that for him has never been a choice—"You can 'not go gently to that last goodnight,' or you can go gently"—we recall also the last words of Jacques Lacan in 1981 when, gloriously estranged in the comic *ethos*, he went into the mystery: "I am obstinate . . . I am disappearing." It is here, perhaps, that one might begin to recognize the comic Counter-Sublime.

Chapter 6
Lost in the Funhouse (1968) and *Chimera* (1972): The Hero Minors in Metaphor

Image	*Trope*	*Defense*	*Ratio*
Outside and Inside	Metaphor	Sublimation	Askesis

John Barth prepublished the title story of *Lost in the Funhouse* in the *Atlantic* just three months after he had sounded his clarion call for a literary revival from those very same pages. Thereafter, critical response to Barth's "Fiction for print, tape, and live voice" would be forever attached, as proof to the pudding, to one's aesthetic response to "The Literature of Exhaustion." Was fiction-about-fiction just a stall and a sputter of exhausted artists before the whole enterprise went defunct, a drear foregrounding of form as a desperate alternative to representing a world gone to wrack and ruin? Could such a manifestation of artistic anxiety have any appeal for the larger public? Or was metafiction's "Principle of Metaphoric Means" the necessary and admirable Borgesian way of moving literature forward, as Barth had claimed? Does theoretical fiction truly bring the artist's "felt intimacies" to literary life with a "passionate virtuosity" that readers can respond to? Was Barth's *Lost in the Funhouse* the breakthrough he was prophesying as a theorist, or was it the breakdown that so many had read between Barth's optimistic lines?

One will think of Barth's fifth book as the peak or nadir of his career depending upon one's aesthetic: If the reader is generally inclined to welcome literary experimentation as having sufficient interest in its own right, and is willing to sublimate humanistic response in accord with the sublimated distance of self-reflexive fiction, then, like Max Schulz (1990), he or she will celebrate the volume as the "beginning of

Barth's career as a mature fabulist," as the "metafictional watershed" from which all later blessings flow (xiv). On the other hand, should readers distrust the usefulness of literary avant-gardism for the future of literature, and want to warm their hands at the fire of a fiction that brings them a world, then, with Jan Gorak (1987), they will find a theme of worldly loss and a scene of literary bankruptcy in *Lost in the Funhouse*—a withered world and sterile story presented by a writer similarly exhausted and infertile. There have been supporters even more effusive than Schulz and detractors more depressed than Gorak, but what there hasn't been is any mediation of a middle: The fate of *Lost in the Funhouse* was to be "praised or damned as conspicuously postmodernist" (Barth 1980, 66). Critical response to Barth's *Funhouse*, it would seem, has been heir to the same "fallout into hopelessly dualistic images" that is the destiny of metaphor and sublimation within Barth's book.

Thus alerted to the problem, the critic might look into the history of our current taste for innovation. It was not always so, René Girard reminds us in "Innovation and Repetition" (1990), an essay that ana-lyzes artistic production in the best and worst of times and concludes that the clamor of the new drowns out the continuity that actually pertains between innovation and mimesis. Girard takes "innovation" in the meaning closest to its original Latin form, as a renewal and re-juvenation from the inside, within the tradition and within mimesis (7–8). This was its historical meaning in the centuries when "external mediation" reigned, when literary works external to the contemporary culture were established as stable models for emulation, and artists were judged as good or bad imitators, strong or weak repeaters. But with the shift from theology and philosophy as modes of authority to science and technology as cultural models, especially in the social and political spheres, there quickly emerged a systematically positive view of innovation that overwhelmed any defense of traditional emulation.

In our contemporary times, Girard continues, "internal mediation" prevails, and the "terrorism" of innovation plunges artists into a "con-tinuous and monstrous rupture, not primarily with others, but with their own past" (12). No longer innovating by repeating established models, artists take as their models and rivals their own up-close and unproven contemporaries, engaging madly in a "reluctant mimesis" between look-alike equals that makes productive competition impossi-ble; and while the pressures of internal mediation assure the eternal presence of an avant-garde, they also force the consciousness of the individual artist to retreat within itself in solipsistic separation from the hue and cry (17).

Girard's description is relevant to both the general case of metafiction in the 1960s and the specific case of Barth and *Lost in the Funhouse*. Barth was certainly responding to the challenge of the "media street-smarts" that were being heard for the first time then, and in a reluctant mimesis of his contemporary times, he built a McLuhanesque fun-house of the electronic voice. However, Barth was a funhouse operator with an additional private program of his own, a program typical of one who is "of the temper that chooses to rebel along traditional lines" (*FB*, 65). Barth remembered what the noisier innovators forgot: that the spoken word had been at the origin of the printed tradition, and that their newest new was his oldest old.

Pursuing his own project from within the internal mediation of rampant experimentation, Barth saw how he could get himself to the stabilized, external mediation of ancient myth, where he might once again (as with *The Sot-Weed Factor* and *Giles Goat-Boy*) innovate through repetition. But before there could be *Chimera*, there had to be *Lost in the Funhouse*. That it would require a two-step process seems the Barthian presentiment of another Girardian insight: "Innovation is so contin-uous with imitation that its presence can be discovered *only after the fact through a process of abstraction*" (Girard 1990, 14; emphasis mine). Barth wanted not only to play ball with his contemporaries but to score off them, and he did so by holding up his funhouse mirror to their mutual "innovation" and revealing it as a literary debt to the recent past: The project of metafiction, Barth was announcing, is a foregrounding of modernist ways and means, the severely belated task of abstraction left to a "late modernism" in the aftermath of "high modernism." Only after the most unequivocal exposure after the fact of what has gone before is the literary slate cleansed of the portrayal of ultimacies, and literature itself enabled to move into its own unique future. Contempo-rary innovation, no matter how it may present itself otherwise, always has this prior task of clarifying the previous literary project through an emblematics of form, and thus functions not as a rupture into disconti-nuity, but rather as an interregnum within the continuity of literature.

Barth's news, in short, was that we are not yet postmodernists. *Lost in the Funhouse* was never meant to be that "literature of replenishment" which Barth in 1980 was still hoping postmodernism might become. He needed those two terms which he multiplied everywhere in his second theoretical essay—high modernism and late modernism—to drive a terminological wedge between the "*best next* thing" after mod-ernism, which was to be a replenishing postmodernism, and the "next-best thing" after high modernism, which was the late modernism of metafiction, his own and others (*FB*, 206). Through the writing of *Lost in the Funhouse*, Barth had to undergo a necessary disenchantment through a concerted sublimation before he could be re-enchanted and re-engaged once again in *Chimera*. As the critics have surmised, Barth's fifth book is indeed inextricably entwined with his two appearances as a theorist of narrative; *Funhouse*, however, is a matter of task, not taste.

Over an extended period of years, Barth has referred to his fifth book so elusively and contradictorily, in hindsight and in foresight, that only an unwary critic would cite Barth's wavering self-judgments as support for her own readerly taste or distaste for metafiction. As late as 1984, in a lecture to freshmen on "Getting Oriented," Barth was proclaiming his "pair of short ones," *Lost in the Funhouse* and *Chimera*, as "my favorites" (*FB*, 135); however, his judgment seems more likely a nostalgia for the brevity of *Funhouse*, since with *Sabbatical*, published in 1982, Barth had once again failed on his promise to himself to become "simpler." To take another sounding: As early as 1966, in the preface to *Giles Goat-Boy*, Barth was giving the critics everything they needed to develop the myth of writer's block. There, "J. B." is not an author at all but a middleman who hands over to his publisher these tapes of "The Revised New Syllabus of George Giles, Grand Tutor," which have been delivered to J. B.'s Penn State office by George's son, Stoker. J. B. is "disengaged" and "fretfully idling," a writer "whose Fancy is missing in action," and who is so intimidated by Stoker Giles's electronic tape that he has abandoned his current work-in-progress, *The Seeker*, to become "a humble Finder":

I knew what novels were: *The Seeker* wasn't one. To move folks about, to give them locales and positions, past histories and crossed paths—it bored me. I hadn't taste or gumption for it. Especially was I surfeited with *movement*, the without-which-not of story. One novel ago I'd hatched a plot as mattersome as any in the books, and drove a hundred characters through eight times that many pages of it; now the merest sophomore apprentice, how callow soever his art, outdid me in that particular. (*GGB*, xxiv)

Is Barth's characterization of himself to be received as a candid admission of well-deserved exhaustion, or as a sly reminder that authors who are not offering their wares for publication may yet still be writing? Is this Barth's preliminary announcement of sliding off the literary map, or of taking the electronic global village by storm? Barth's critics, I believe, have too precipitately seized upon such signposts as bane or boon—Barth is triumphantly acceding to the kingdom of contemporary experimentation, Barth is suffering writerly deplenishment. What they should have noticed was the authorial anxiety accompanying an atypically alien project that would demand of Barth a severe *askesis* of his powers: "How can a poet-as-Hero major in the minor?"

Where Barth does not waffle, where I think he can be trusted, is in the immediate vicinity of *Lost in the Funhouse*, in his explicit testimony during the time of writing it and within the space of performing it. It's a threaded commentary testifying to an anxiety about the project that precisely matches his unease concerning the theoretical closure in "The Literature of Exhaustion." In *The Friday Book*, Barth has included only one piece that is directly and entirely about his fifth book: the introduction he was accustomed to deliver to his audiences before he gave them the tape-and-live-voice performance of his book during the short season of 1967–68. In his introduction to that introduction, the 1984 Barth confesses that throughout the performing of *Lost in the Funhouse*, Socrates' demon—the little superego voice that was always telling Socrates, "for pity's sake, don't do that"—was perched on Barth's shoulder, telling him to cut short his tour of public readings that began on "Mayday, 1967," telling him that "for the writer as writer, show business is no business," telling him by no means to include an audio tape with his book (*FB*, 77). Barth may also have been recalling the Socrates of Nietzsche's *The Birth of Tragedy* (as Harold Bloom does in his chapter on this phase), whose perfect sublimation as "theoretical man" was the death of tragedy, and whose "ascetic ideal" was the triumphant blocking agent to Nietzsche's antithetical ideals, which would have allowed creativity to flourish freely throughout culture (*AI*, 115).

Moreover, the typically nonascetic Barth may well have been having second thoughts and first fears that his theorizing was trammeling up his creativity, for an acute uneasiness on this count surfaces in two of Barth's introductory statements to his audiences. In the first, contrary to the literary practice they are about to witness, Barth tells them that he doesn't "think it's a good idea, as a rule, for artists to explain their art, even if they can. Jorge Luis Borges puts it arrogantly: God shouldn't stoop to theology" (*FB*, 78). This sounds like consciously self-critical speech, coming as it does from a *deus artifex* who has been lately theologizing at a great rate and who has foresworn making stories for making metaphors that explain story. Second, as if already seeking forgiveness for the ascetic art he is about to lay on them, Barth begs his audience to understand that a professional literary career is not all smooth sailing, and that the author hopes "—since some of the legs of the journey are liable to be rougher than others—that his audience will stay with him across the troll-bridges and that they'll reach the sweet cabbage fields together. It may be that there is more troll than cabbage in these pieces. I hope not" (*FB*, 78). Yet the title that Barth gave to this Friday piece, "More Troll than Cabbage," seems to cut off that hope in a final judgment on *Funhouse* by the mature Barth, who is perhaps remembering what a fine fix he got himself into with metafictional nonfabulation.

Whatever other functions Barth's 1980 "Literature of Replenishment" was meant to serve as "companion and corrective" to his earlier
theoretical essay, it was also written, one suspects, to make sure that the
critics did not lose sight of the author's very qualified perspective on the
book that was contemporaneous with "The Literature of Exhaustion."
The metaphor of a necessary troll-bridge serves to justify Barth's new
division within modernism, and *Lost in the Funhouse* is offered to the
reader as the sole book within Barth's oeuvre that is "mainly late
modernist" (1980, 66). The metafictions of late modernism perform
valuable troll tasks in relation to the previous high modernism, but
they lack the "democratic access" and reader "delight and ravishment,"
which are Barth's two essential criteria for a positive postmodernist
fiction. In "Replenishment" Barth redefines the subject of "Exhaustion" as the completion in late modernism of the "aesthetic of high
modernism," of James Joyce and the other great modernists whose
works were marked by "their antilinearity, their aversion to conventional characterization and cause-and-effect dramaturgy, their celebration of private, subjective experience over public experience, their
general inclination to 'metaphoric' as against 'metonymic' means" (*FB*,
201). The true exhaustion of this modernist program—that is, its
thoroughly sublimated and ascetic completion—is the task of a next
best metafiction, which will foreground the aforementioned qualities
so that they might be apprehended in their starkest outlines. Only
through this abstraction by which the multiple is reduced to its essential is old literary business finished off, and the best next can begin to fill
the empty square again with content in the rhythmic continuity that
sustains literary production. One must bury one's recent dead before
literature can rise again.

Theoretically, this radical stance on innovation as a conservation
requires that Barth reshuffle his deck of authors and works in 1980 so
that they can be dealt out again as next best late modernists and best
next postmodernists. Nabokov's *Pale Fire*, Beckett's *Texts for Nothing*,
and all of his friend John Hawkes's works have become late modernist
(*FB*, 203); the divine Borges is now an emeritus "exemplar of *dernier cri*
modernism" (205); Italo Calvino's *Invisible Cities* is late modernist, while
his *Cosmicomics* and *The Castle of Crossed Destinies* are postmodernist, as is
all of the work of Gabriel García Márquez (196). Late modernism is
clearly no category of disapprobation; but at all costs, including the
sacrifice of his own *Funhouse*, Barth would save a truly innovative
postmodernist writing for the future of literature. In my schematiza-
tion of this crucial two-step in Barth's career, *Lost in the Funhouse* is his
troll-bridge and *Chimera* is his first glimpse of the cabbage fields.

Having taken this long detour through critical responses and theoretical essays, we are better prepared to hear from Harold Bloom about why and how the poet settles for such a desperate maneuver that can only produce a poem that evades itself in "a misinterpretation of what it might have been" (*AI*, 120). Much like the hysteric who, all emotions and theatricality spent, falls into anaesthesia and paralysis, so also the poet finds himself in a state of shock after his daemonic expansiveness. He then turns aggressively upon himself in a sacrificial process that purges the poetic self of its strength and internalizes the laws of culture in order to force the growth of a strong, even harsh, poetic will. Like the hysteric famous among psychoanalysts for *la belle indifférence*, the poet develops a counter-will of disinterestedness and through his internalization separates himself from culture, driving himself ever further with intense purgations into a state of contrary solipsism—a Narcissus who would also be the Prometheus of his culture (*AI*, 115–19).

This is the poetic strategy that the poet hopes will make his drastic surrender to the contemporary literary norm result in his superior individuation as a poet. His poetic weapons testify to the necessary gain and loss that mark every road to freedom, and to the terrible cost that must be paid for victory along its way: the ratio of *askesis*, the defense of sublimation, the trope of metaphor. What they all have in common is a tremendous curtailment of the poet-as-hero in forcing him toward normality, which "however desirable in persons, does not work in and for poems" (*MM*, 100). In the *askesis* that truncates his human and imaginative endowment, the poet "seeks transformation at the expense of narrowing the creative circumference of precursor and ephebe alike": contraction instead of expansion, concentration instead of prodigality, simplicity instead of complexity (*AI*, 118). Looking at the poems of Wallace Stevens, Bloom affirms that the strongest modern poetry is made through askesis; but a postmodern fictionist would have to disagree, recalling from Nietzsche that the triumph of the ascetic spirit would be the defeat of poetry itself.

For Freud, *sublimation* was the normal defense of acculturated man, who transfers his sexual energy, more or less successfully and without repression, to socially useful activities; by attaining a rational substitute for unattainable gratifications, we manage to modify ourselves without destroying ourselves. But for Bloom, contrary to Freud, an ego defense that works is "the one most impairing to the poetic self," creating a veritable halt in purgatory for poets, who need frustration and failure to accomplish the highest art. Furthermore, although Bloom recognizes the sublimation of the aggressive instincts as "almost identical with the process of misprision" (*AI*, 115), he cannot countenance Freud's incoherent and unconvincing argument for the sublimation of sexuality: Sublimation is "a too happily dualistic defense," which must fail in carrying such an "inside" as sexual desire to such an inapplicable "outside" as art (*MM*, 100).

Like sublimation, which is supposed to transfer energy to unlikely places, so metaphor carries its name to foreign objects; and like the defense of normality, the "trope of normality"—that "most-praised and most-failing of Western tropes"—promotes certain "perspectiviz-ing confusions" which tend to drive the poem into "hopelessly dualistic images of inside and outside" (*MM*, 100). These fracturings of a decep-tive unity thus reveal the limitations of metaphor, the unsuccess of sublimation, and the narcissism of the self in their failure to sustain a oneness. Nauseated by the taint of culture that contaminates his au-tonomy, the poet nevertheless pushes his poem toward even greater heights of sublimation, resulting in a forced development of the poetic will. It now becomes the imaginative equivalent of the superego; and harsher than conscience, the poetic will wields the forms, laws, rules, and norms of the culture that formed it (*AI*, 115–19).

Bloom's full description of this phase should alert us not only to how alien its weapons are to our postmodernist author, but also to how appropriate they are to his immediate predecessors. If we try to imag-ine a typicality to which Bloom's various attributes might apply—the nausea of the poet and his desexualization, his hatred of culture and his transcendent isolation from it, the reliance upon metaphor and myth in their normative and reinforcing aspects, the poetic will as a punitive and judgmental superego—we conclude unhesitantly that *askesis* is the ratio most compatible with high modernism.

Consider, for example, T. S. Eliot. What superego was ever harsher in its discipline of the self and its judgments of others? In his 1923 essay, "Ulysses, Order, and Myth," Eliot looks down with an Olympian eye upon the "immense panorama of futility and anarchy which is contemporary history," and applauds Joyce's sublimated use of Ho-mer's form as "a way of controlling, ordering, or giving shape and significance" to the catastrophic messes of Bloomsday. Temperamen-tally a royalist, Eliot welcomed the purgation of the self as a heroic means to royal art, and promoted art as a science of askesis, anti-affective and anti-intentionalist. We recall the dictum of "Tradition and the Individual Talent" (1919): "The progress of an artist is a continual self-sacrifice, a continual extinction of personality: It is in this deper-sonalization that art may be said to approach the condition of science" (Lodge 1972, 71–77). Virginia Woolf was no less ascetic. In her 1919 essay, "Modern Fiction," written while she was seeing Joyce's chapters from *Ulysses* appearing in serial form in the *Little Review*, Woolf takes Wells, Bennett, and Galsworthy to task as "materialists," while "Mr. Joyce is spiritual; he is concerned at all costs to reveal the flickerings of that innermost flame which flashes its messages through the brain." We don't have to disagree with Woolf's assessments to see, nevertheless, where they were to take her—to a consciousness purged of impurities of the outside, to a solipsistic room of her own, and within the envelope and under the halo, to a "hopeless interrogation that fills us with a deep, and finally it may be with a resentful, despair" (Lodge 1972, 85–91).

Between Brahmin and Bloomsbury, there is nothing to choose for a postmodern novelist with a comic vision. Whereas the refinements out of existence might have been suitable, even desirable, to Eliot and Woolf, to a self-affirming, world-inventing fabulator like Barth they must have felt like the literary hairshirt to end all such. Granted that Barth's literary progress of two phases demanded this imitating backwards so that he could innovate forward, canceling out the debit column in order to bring on the credits; nevertheless, this is an extreme purgation for a poetic self whose creative health, unlike Eliot's or Woolf's, depends precisely upon its avoidance of the askesis, sublimation, and metaphor that worked for them. The essentially antithetical Barth doesn't like having a demon always at his shoulder, any more than the postmodernist Barth likes the metafictional negatives that come from listening to the poetic superego. Readers of *Lost in the Funhouse* have tended to focus on the pain of its poor lost souls, or on Barth's admirable essentializations of high modernism's literary means, without noticing the good-natured mockery that Barth makes of his own harshly willed, weakened position within his metafiction. Can there be more hilarious rue than that found in this authorial statement: "God comma I abhore self hyphen consciousness" (113)? Askesis does not become Barth, and he knows it.

However, by willing this askesis—willing, this one time, not to be the poet-as-hero—Barth does indeed achieve an astounding economy of formal effects, and it was the book's intricate unity that was immediately discerned by his critics. Barth himself points us toward that structure of control in his initial instructions for reading his fourteen pieces in sequence as a series, and in his initial "Frame Tale," which is a first page of cut-and-paste, a do-it-yourself circle with a twist, a Möbius strip. Taking the author at his word, Heide Ziegler (1987) privileged the three stories featuring the artistic coming of age of young Ambrose, Barth's alter-ego, and pronounced the book a "*Künstlerroman* with a twist" that takes the writer's art back to the anonymous bards of the oral tradition and myth (49–55). Charles Harris (1983) emphasized the paralysis that comes from Ambrose's artistic self-consciousness, and read the book's return to ancient myth as Barth's preservation of the "ontological conversation that is man" (106–26). Jan Gorak (1987) interpreted the Möbius strip as a depressing circularity, parodying the artist as godly maker who gives up, goes anonymous, and finally disappears into the text (157–66). Max Schulz (1990) focused on the chiasmus of the twist itself, arguing that there is "a dual story line continuously 'progressing' in reverse directions and alluding to origins and closures, progenitors and their progeny" (5–6).

These analyses are generally unexceptionable, persuasive in their own way, every one of them. Yet all betray the assumption that metaphor can effectively circumscribe metonymical realities and that one should congratulate the poetic superego on the success of its sublimations, whereas Barth's content everywhere suggests that neither trope nor defense can contain human and literary dualisms and that sublimation is not good for human and literary health. The "perspectivizing confusions" of the narrators in *Lost in the Funhouse*, contrary to its Möbius strip, reflect irrevocable artistic and psychic polarities, implying that this figural form, with its inside/outside integration, cannot be realized within human experience. Barth's book, despite and because of its impeccable networking, is ultimately a dis-couraging of poetic askesis.

The story that is Barth's coda for the critique of sublimation is "Petition," narrated by the sublimated half of a Siamese twin, who knows a "figurative Bangkok," as opposed to his brother who, he tells us, is forever literalizing, lying, and mistaking his outside/inside connections to the king of Siam, whom his ascetic brother is petitioning for the gift of surgery. Unlike the legendary twins Chang and Eng, joined at the navel in an "emblem of fraternity," who were "paragons of cooperation," these twins are joined front and rear, and our piggyback narrator is the monkey on the back of his Siamese twin, always carrying his *NO*-sign with him (60, 68). "I neither perspire nor defecate, but merely emit a discreet vapor, of neutral scent, and tiny puffs of what would pass for talc," sniffs the sublimated narrator—and the reader begins to sympathize with his belching, farting, "rutting stallion" of a brother (63). The alienating perspective of sublimation becomes even more pointed when the brother up front takes Thalia the contortionist as his lover, and the superego brother—having experienced coition once with Thalia ("I did not enjoy it"), after which she steadily ignores him—decides that he loves a second Thalia, the sublime, inner "prisoner" of this one.

Max Schulz wants this imagined Thalia to stand as the muse of metafiction and be united through the Möbius strip with the actual Thalia as the muse of comic realism. Yet his elegant and ingenious meta-argument for the "Thalian design" of *Lost in the Funhouse*, it seems to me, is controverted by the hopeless dualism that Barth assigns to our Siamese psyches in this story and others. Between the id and the superego, there is no direct communication; the unself-conscious brother is "incoherent but vocal, the self-reflective one is "articulate and mute" (62), and self-consciousness is responsible, of course, for that separation. Prepubertal Ambrose likewise learns about the absence within presence when he thinks during his first sexual experience, *"This is what they call passion. I am experiencing it"* (84); and thereafter as an adolescent in "Water-Message," his idealizing imagination is besotted with young nurse Peggy Rollins, who is lying down with her soldier boy, completely unaware of Ambrose's infatuation. Also undone by sublimation is the "first person tiresome," brother to Beckett's Unnameable, who produces the "halt narrative" of "Autobiography" out of his "pure and sour" self-consciousness: "Being an ideal's warped image, my fancy's own twist figure, is what undoes me" (38). The hopelessly divided self, endemic to Barth's book, is constantly undoing the hope held out by its formal twist figure.

Ambrose, on his way to becoming both a modernist artist and a metafictionist, suspects that much of life is secret and hidden from him ("All that normally showed was preparation and intermission"). Wanting to get at "the truth of the matter," he makes his way through the most worn and tired of metaphors, translating in ascetic fashion away from experience toward its veiling within expression—so this is what they mean by "a lump in the throat," by "breaking into a cold sweat" (42, 52). Even for an older, more literary Ambrose, metaphor's normalizing and reinforcing aspects overwhelm its potential for creativity, and metaphor is decisively desublimated as the sly and low pun that plays to the existential real. When Ambrose's father remarkably manages to light his Lucky Strikes with a single hand while driving the family car, or when Ambrose, under the pilings at Ocean City, hears the family laughing at sexual secrets which are "over his head," metaphor is deprived of any higher mission (74, 86).

In *Lost in the Funhouse* humankind is discovered most often as a victim of metaphor, not a victor through it. There is ever a great metaphor being dangled before us, but always it is an untrustworthy one that is no real matchmaker, the sublimated opposite of what experience tells us is real, a hollow form that is but an ironic negative of the present. This is the discovery of the smartened-up sperm who narrates "Night-Sea Journey," a swimmer who all his life has known only the water and drowning, in contrast to the wishful idealization of "reaching the Shore":

Supposing even that there *were* a Shore—that, as a cynical companion of mine once imagined, we rise from the drowned to discover all those vulgar superstitions and exalted metaphors to be literal truth: the giant Maker of us all, the Shores of Light beyond our night-sea journey!—whatever would a swimmer do there? The fact is, when we imagine the shore, what comes to mind is just the opposite of our condition: no more night, no more sea, no more journeying. In short, the blissful state of the drowned. (5)

For Barth's microscopic narrator, the self-consciousness that makes metaphor leaves one with little "except dull dread and a kind of melancholy, stunned persistence" in the face of the ascetic ideal; and the ego, poetic and human, would be happy to settle for a Her (9). Even a proper name is a separation from the self, as the divided title of "Ambrose and His Mark" antithetically indicates. Ambrose received his given name only belatedly, his German-American family having waited upon a sign sufficiently sublime to render the much-awaited heir at one with his name. All along, the family has been calling him by the homely German *Honig* (Honey), but it is not until the bees swarm and leave the infant unharmed that they find their metaphorical sublime in the legend of Saint Ambrose among the bees. Nevertheless, man and metaphor remain split into an inside and an outside: "Vanity frets about his name, Pride vaunts it, Knowledge retches at its sound, Understanding sighs; all live outside, knowing well that I and my sign are neither one nor quite two" (34).

Metaphor, especially when it is employed in the modernist funhouse to "make a figure out of a fact," is not going to get one through the maze of life. One might be hoping to be carried through by a valiant metaphor, but Barth's several pieces that anatomize writer's block indicate otherwise: Metaphor is simply an enervated writer's means of "filling in the blanks," a phrase that recurs in double digits throughout the nine-page story, "Title." This story and others mock their own writing processes, make a travesty of literary experimentation, and demonstrate the sterility of the modernist askesis. Stories—whether realistic, electronic, or mythic—that come down to the metafictional convention of a story about a writer writing a story are simply "fashionably solipsistic" (117), the result of a misbegotten urge toward transcendence that can produce only negative resolves and no heroes, fictive voices reflecting upon writerly incapability. The modernist troll-bridge in its entirety betrays the three characteristics that Bloom has discerned in every Crossing—a dialectical movement between sight and hearing, an oscillation between mimetic and expressive theories of poetic representation, and a movement toward an ever greater degree of internalization of the self (*PI*, 171–72). The metafictional "tale of shortcomings, lengthened to advantage" (100) exposes modernist sublimation as the "guileful art" of metaphor inspired by despair (115), and as the literary equivalent of the chemists' typical meaning for "to sublime"—to pass from a solid state (mimesis of the outside) to a gaseous state (expression of an inside) without an intervening phase of liquidity. The potential for multiple being and malleable truth cannot be realized when a voice-without-content is simply cannibalizing itself, or when the solipsistic self fastens only upon its own image. Between Narcissus and Echo there is only self-absorption and petty-spiritedness—"he perishes by denying all but himself; she persists by effacing herself absolutely" (102).

This is the tale of inside/outside imbalance told by the final two stories that constitute the last third of Barth's book. The narrators of the "Menelaid" and the "Anonymiad" have indeed become the "printed voice," a metafictional resolution of old myth and new media that Barth points us to in his 1968 authorial preface; but neither narrator appears very gratified by it all, and seems rather, in fact, to serve as a cautionary bad example of the loss of self that follows inevitably upon a hoodwinked faith in sublimation and metaphor. For Menelaus, the splendid metaphor that was Helen has been shattered into the literal reality of two Helens, one in Egypt and another in Troy, and with the fracturing of his beloved, his own self has split and lost its materiality. An artist who loses his body image loses the world, but to retrieve the material would be to lose the metaphorical sublime. Had Menelaus managed to wrestle Proteus successfully and wrest from him his innumerable, inexhaustible shapes (in the scene from the *Odyssey* that so charmed Borges), then Menelaus might not now "exist" merely as a confusing record of past dialogues, so trapped within stories-within-stories that quotation marks to the eighth power are required to indicate his encrypting within inscription. Barth pronounces his epitaph: "Menelaus cannot lie, worse luck; Menelaus' carcass is long wormed, yet his voice yarns on through everything, to itself" (167).

Barth's last narrator, however, fares rather better in getting the teller, tale, and told together, although he is still to this side of accomplishment in Barth's parable of the artist. A simple, rustic minstrel who wandered into the court of Agammemnon and Clytemnestra, he "was put down by the sheer energy of them. . . . No, no I was not up to life—but it was myself I despised therefore, not the world" (186). Nonetheless, the anonymous narrator has taken the modernist path of askesis, abandoned world and wife, and ended up in solitude on a desert island. So intoxicated is he with his new invention of writing—goat's blood and squid-ink on tanned goat hides—that he's prepared for the sacrificial process all over again: "Had Merope—aye, Trojan Helen herself—trespassed on my island in those days. I'd have flayed her as soon as I'd laid her" (194). A Barthian postmodernist word sounds here, but our minstrel is still an all-tech, no-vision solitary, "a survival expert with no will to live," when a bottle with an indecipherable message floats ashore; and knowing now that there is an audience out there, he can recommence telling his stories, "written from my only valid point of view, first person anonymous" (199).

There are enough ironies besetting the situations of Barth's last writer-narrators for his readers to drop the notion of a happy ending, despite the author's cunning circle-with-a-twist that loops back to his first story of the "Night-Sea Journey," connecting the first and last as the biological and mythic origins of the artist, or as the reunion of voice and writing, or as the integration of realism and metafiction (in Schulz's argument). Neither Barth nor his various narrators have yet made it through Bloom's Crossing of Identification, which is the facing down of death, for all are still yearning and yarning for a written immortality that would sublimate the fear of death. Nor does Barth deceive himself by thinking that with *Lost in the Funhouse* he has reached the shores of replenishment. Many critics would not follow Edward Said in characterizing modern writing as a dire sublimation of "what is natural and human"; however, in his meditation upon the sterile writing that can afflict an author at the midpoint of a thriving career, Said comes close to what I take to be Barth's conviction of the ultimately defeatist divide between life and mind of the modernist askesis that is magnified in late modernist writing: The author, Said says,

> may endlessly bewail his inability to appear, and even do his complaining in writing. Writing about writing can then be not writing at all, from his point of view, just as appearing . . . is entirely sterile, without issue, almost as bad as not appearing at all. . . . Modern literature converts a dependence on writing into a method for isolating writing and the writer from what is natural and human. Writing is an acquired mannerism, a performance, a characteristic gesture of inscription that separates the spaces of the page from the spaces of "life." (1975, 236–37)

At the 1978 University of Cincinnati symposium on fiction, six years after the publication of *Chimera*, Barth spoke with John Hawkes about his intentions for that book and also gave voice to a rather unqualified rejection of the volume preceding it:

> I have at times gone farther than I want to in the direction of a fiction that foregrounds language and form, displacing the ordinary notion of content, of "aboutness." But beginning with the "Chimera" novellas—written after the "Lost in the Funhouse" series, where that foregrounding reaches its peak or its nadir, depending on your esthetic—I have wanted my stories to be *about* things: about the passions, which Aristotle tells us are the true subject of literature. (Hawkes and Barth 1979, 32)

The formal spatial problem of foreground and background translates as the human problem of inside and outside, self and world. In his sixth volume of fiction, Barth sets about correcting both problems, passing beyond *Lost in the Funhouse* through technical revisions on all four fronts of the modernist ratio, trope, image, and defense. In *Chimera* we encounter (1) an egalitarian participation in myth from the inside by present reality; (2) the making of a spatial metaphor of form that evades the separating out into dualisms; (3) a desublimation and resexualization of writing that equates it with sexual potency; (4) a facing down of death and a facing up to love through a heroic philosophy of "as if."

The modernist use of myth reflected, perhaps first of all, a grand case of separation anxiety. After the Great War, the next news after God was dead was that mass man was on the horizon, and classical myth was to provide a pattern for comparison and emulation for a formless society. The seasonal myth of vegetation for *The Wasteland*, the *Odyssey* for an anarchic Bloomsday—these were the distanced shadows of *in illo tempore* that might serve as archetypal model or ironic commentary for a degraded contemporary culture. In the three novellas of *Chimera*, Barth collapses that distance into collaboration and collective effort between the author and his mythic characters. Barth now is Muhammad gone to the mountain, a postmodernist who knows that myth needs the present to preserve its vitality. As the genie out of his bottle in the *Dunyazadiad*, he tells back to Scheherazade her stories, read by him in the twentieth century from *The Thousand and One Nights*; in the *Perseid* he commiserates with his middle-aged Perseus as an author who is himself looking at the second half of his life; and in the *Bellerophoniad* the author becomes a guest lecturer on the pitfalls of pattern-following, which beset the novella's false hero. "What Barth has done by grabbing the 'other end' of the mythopoeic stick," said one prescient critic, "is to treat myth realistically, instead of treating 'reality' in accord with archetypal patterns" (Powell 1976, 60). Says another, characterizing the effect on the reader of this reversal: "We're surprised, charmed, pleased to laughter, and enormously impressed. We're looking at things as if from the bottom of a swimming pool, from inside the mind of a character we have known only from the outside" (Bryant 1980, 214). *Chimera*, and not *Lost in the Funhouse*, is the Barth book in which outside and inside come together.

In this decriminalization of the Möbius strip's precarious and prevaricating unity, neither space nor time relates to each other as an inside to an outside. Barth's new metaphor of spatial form is the spiral, a metaphor whose realization prevents polarities from crystallizing out of the narrative solution by keeping them in constant motion toward an open-ended future—no opposite without its sameness, and no closure in view. Perseus, down and out in Calyxa's temple and reading his past but not his future in the spiraling mural the priestess has painted, knows the spiral as the form of his life in time. Bellerophon, his failed cousin, discovers that his own slavish imitation of a real hero has made of his second cycle a vicious circle rather than a liberating spiral. The genie and his "publish-or-perish darling" Scheherazade, more daringly, are figuring out how the spiral might serve as the shape of a narrative in progress. Sherry's younger sister Doony eavesdrops on their high-tech talk:

They speculated endlessly on such questions as whether a story might imaginably be framed from inside, as it were, so that the usual relation between container and contained would be reversed and paradoxically reversible—and (for my benefit, I suppose) what human state of affairs such an odd construction might usefully figure. Or whether one might go beyond the usual tale-within-a-tale, beyond even tales-within-tales-within-tales which our Genie had found a few instances of in that literary treasure-house he hoped one day to add to, and conceive a series of, say *seven* concentric stories-within-stories, so arranged that the climax of the innermost would precipitate that of the next tale out, and that of the next, et cetera, like a string of firecrackers or the chains of orgasms that Shahyrar could sometimes set my sister catenating. (*C*, 32)

In each of Barth's three realistic reinventions of myth, the spiral functions also to ensure—contrary to the inverse ratio demanded by Freud's theory of sublimation—that writing and sex will go together in a relation of reciprocity, with potency or impotency in the one area reflecting or conferring the same quality in the other. More of one is more for the other; one pot does not have to be emptied out for the other to become full. Unlike the ascetic modernists willing to pay the sexual cost for writerly potency, Barth and his mythic cohorts are stubbornly disinclined to sacrifice or purge one for the other, since both activities are life-affirming. In the case of Scheherazade, the metaphor is literalized: Her narratives do not serve to substitute for sex with her sheik, but storytelling and sex in tandem do defer, for every one of her 1,001 nights with him, her murder, which is supposed to happen every one of those mornings. In *Chimera* the spiral form permits a doing that exceeds mere reflexiveness and its potential for paralysis that was so evident in *Lost in the Funhouse*. One rids oneself of writer's block by writing, and of sexual impotency by multiple, vigorous, imaginative copulations; "the key to the treasure *is* the treasure" means that metonymical action legitimizes metaphor in a risk-taking that proceeds beyond analogical naming. The resexualizations of Barth's spiral form—a form that, for instance, will not permit the fallout polarities of "active" and "passive" as regards the typically patriarchal definition of gender—extends outward to the erotic collaboration between the author and his audience:

> The very relation between teller and told was by nature erotic. The teller's role . . . regardless of his actual gender, was essentially masculine, the listener's or reader's feminine, and the tale was the medium of their intercourse. . . . He had not meant to suggest that the "femininity" of readership was a docile or inferior position: a lighthouse, for example, passively sent out signals that mariners labored actively to receive and interpret; an ardent woman like his mistress was at least as energetic in his embrace as he in embracing her; a good reader of cunning tales worked in her way as busily as their author; et cetera. Narrative, in short—and here again they were in full agreement—was a love-relation, not a rape: its success depended upon the reader's consent and cooperation, which she could withhold or at any moment withdraw; also upon her own combination of expertise and talent for enterprise, and the author's ability to arouse, sustain, and satisfy her interest—an ability on which his figurative life hung as surely as Scheherazade's literal. (C, 34)

One of the beauties of the spiral as metaphoric emblem of life and career is that one always has an unforeseeable future in the immediate and mediate distance, which in itself tends to mute loud judgment calls of success or failure along the way, while the call to explore potential tends to silence the sublime clamor for poetic immortality and permit the unsentimental recognition that literal death, somewhere up ahead, will mark the closure of a generous continuum. Barth's *Perseid* can begin with the reality-tested, desublimated statement—"Stories last longer than men, stones than stories, stars than stones" (67)—because there is no pecking order of mortality or immortality; whether the writer will be petrified in stone (just dead) or constellated as a star in the heavens (just immortalized) ultimately comes down to the same state of "suspended animation" in which one's identity and narcissism are relinquished to cosmic incorporation.

Perseus, the golden hero who tamed Pegasus and beheaded the Medusa, discovers the second time around that Medusa was truly the love of his life. Their "immortal parts" are now joined as constellations in the night sky, and although the lovers' "mortal parts will never touch"—holding Medusa's head by the hair, Perseus can't even see his beloved—Barth writes them a lovely, if falling, finale: "I'm content, So with this issue, our net estate: to have become, like the noted music of our tongue, these silent, visible signs; to *be* the tale I tell to those with eyes to see and understanding to interpret; to raise you up forever and know that our story will never be cut off, but highly rehearsed as long as men and women read the stars. . . . I'm content. Till tomorrow evening, love" (41–42). Yet even Belleropheron, that rank imitator and therefore false hero—whose greatest exploit, the slaying of the Chimera, may have been but a non-episode consequent upon a meta-phoric slip in translation for *kamara*, or chamber—has an even cozier, in-the-flesh immortality with his Amazon Melanippe; having gotten himself a life, they live happily ever after, transported by Pegasus from their "little rented cottage out in the marsh" to "restaurants and the-aters and museums and such" (299).

Not everyone can follow the high road to the stars. Most of us, the genie tells Scheherazade, find our "civilized delights" in living out a metaphor, in the philosophy of "as if," a brave self-mystification that at once lets man and woman love each other and poets believe in their own immortality. Scheherazade and her little sister stay their hands against the royal brothers who hold them captive, once they learn that both brothers are eager to trade away the hate between men and women for an as-if philosophy of gender equality and fidelity. At the end of his *Dunyazadiad* Barth himself speaks out for death—and not immortality—as the edge that makes life sweet. In doing so, he retires the ancient metaphorical cover-up of "happily ever after" for a much more severely metonymical personification of death, a figure that evades neither death's power nor our pain. Having just passed the halfway mark of his own life, Barth refuses to falsify what remains with any foolishness about a beautiful ending—yet one can have a way with words:

Dunyazade's story begins in the middle; in the middle of my own, I can't conclude it—but it must end in the night that all good mornings come to. The Arab storytellers understood this; they ended their stories not "happily ever after," but specifically "until there took them the Destroyer of Delights and Desolator of Dwelling-Places, and they were translated to the ruth of Almighty Allah, and their houses fell waste and their palaces lay in ruins, and the Kings inherited their riches." And no man knows it better than Shah Zaman, to whom therefore the second half of his life will be sweeter than the first. (*C*, 64)

By Barth's standards, *Chimera* is a small book of three hundred pages, and although less is never again going to be more for this author of the long ones, it is easy to understand Barth's affection for it, and perhaps also why this work won Barth the National Book Award. Its gaiety is mature, as is its comic wisdom, and one can *hear* the unclut-tered, joyful conviction (that love and language are quite simply mar-velous human inventions) because the self-reflexive authorial voice and the godly maker of forms are so naturally accommodated into story itself. But *Chimera* means most to Barth, I suspect, because it is his coming through the bad times onto the cabbage fields, not here through any ascetic path of sublimation, but rather like Shah Zaman, who has also made his Crossing of Identification and knows death's

knife at his balls as never the modernist kings of literature did—as the
edge that sweetens the hero's Second Revolution.

But I would like to close this chapter, which for the sake of argument
has had to be less than friendly to modernism, with what I take as a
recapitulation of this rough bridge-crossing in Barth's career. The
passage comes from Barth's commended work of late modernism, Italo
Calvino's *Invisible Cities*. The cities all belong to Kublai Khan, who has
never seen them, and who therefore has hired Marco Polo to report
back to him with descriptions of his "invisible" cities. Marco Polo's cities
remain invisible to the great khan because they are metaphors of cities,
places of possibility rather than actualities of designation and specifica-
tion, and because the explorer delivers his reports in the mute commentary or mime of silent mental communication. Occasionally in the
book's frame interludes, the emperor of the Tartars and the young
Venetian meet in the great gardens. In this instance, as they are playing
chess, Marco Polo breaks into language, and takes the conqueror from
the metafictional exhaustion of his cities to their postmodernist replenishment:

> The Great Khan tried to concentrate on the game: but now it was the game's reason
> that eluded him. The end of every game is a gain or a loss: but of what? What were the
> real stakes? At checkmate, beneath the foot of the king, knocked aside by the winner's
> hand, nothingness remains: a black square, or a white one. By disembodying his con-
> quests to reduce them to the essential, Kublai had arrived at the extreme operation: the
> definitive conquest, of which the empire's multiform treasures were only illusory enve-
> lopes; it was reduced to a square of planed wood.
> Then Marco Polo spoke: "Your chessboard, sire, is inlaid with two woods: ebony and
> maple. The square on which your enlightened gaze is fixed was cut from the ring of a
> trunk that grew in a year of drought: you see how its fibers are arranged? Here a barely
> hinted knot can be made out: a bud tried to burgeon on a premature spring day, but the
> night's frost forced it to desist."
> Until then the Great Khan had not realized that the foreigner knew how to express
> himself fluently in his language, but it was not this fluency that amazed him.
> "Here is a thicker pore: perhaps it was a larvum's nest; not a woodworm, because, once
> born, it would have begun to dig, but a caterpillar that gnawed the leaves and was the
> cause of the tree's being chosen for chopping down. . . . This edge was scored by the wood
> carver with his gouge so that it would adhere to the next square, more protruding. . . ."
> The quantity of things that could be read in a little piece of smooth and empty wood
> overwhelmed Kublai; Polo was already talking about ebony forests, about rafts laden with
> logs that come down the rivers, of docks, of women at the windows. (Calvino 1972, 131–
> 32)

Chapter 7
LETTERS (1979):
Funerary Fare-Thee-Wells

Image	*Trope*	*Defense*	*Ratio*
Early and Late	Metalepsis	Introjection, Projection	Apophrades

In the seven years between *Chimera* and *LETTERS*, Barth aged forty. With comic ebullience and aforethought, and for the good of his career, Barth advanced himself in his imagination to a serene eighty years. The three fictional male heroes of *Chimera*—Perseus, Bellerophon, the Author-as-Genie—are all anxious forty-year-olds caught in mid-life and mid-career crises, "sea-leveled, forty, parched, and plucked" (*C*, 60). However, in his interview with *Publishers Weekly* on *LETTERS*, published the year before his fiftieth birthday, Barth is sounding off on his "octogenarian theme": "As you approach fifty, you feel that even if you're going to lead a writerly life as long as Thomas Mann's or Nabokov's—and I think I will—it still adds up to about eighty years. That only leaves three decades, and there's so much one wants to do. . . . I intend to reach my peak only as an octogenarian, and then go into a *very* slow decline" (*PW*, 1979, 6).

This is Barth's imaginative copping of a future, his anterior appropriation of what he can come to only very late, a reveling in the perfect future of the future perfect: By eighty, I *will have* had/done/written/been. It's a sleight-of-the-calendar trick triggered by Barth's exaltation at discovering that what looked like death at forty had been realized as rebirth and renewal by fifty, and hereafter in his writing, as the strong poet of the future anterior, he will be found affirming the fundamental virtue of death as the precious edge that lends latter-day life its unique savor. But first, there are murders to commit. With *LETTERS*, the aging-quick Barth, as indisposed to nostalgia as to despair, throws up a solid barrier between past and future, splits himself into a precursor Early Barth and an ephebe Late Barth, and cleans house on the first half of his career—six volumes of fiction to be shifted to the attic for storage or, better yet, flushed down the waste disposal. This, for the author, was what *LETTERS* was for: To get an unencumbered and indeterminate "second revolution" for Late Barth (who will be seabound and traveling fast and light) by killing off the progeny of Early Barth.

"What it's for?" is not considered in formalist circles the proper question to ask of the literary text, since it adulterates critical response with readerly reactions and/or authorial motives. Early Barth himself cautions against its use as regards himself, since an author's intentions in writing any book are sure to be "multifarious"; it is better, says Barth in 1960, that we critics stick to the formalist question of "what the book is" (*FB*, 28, 29). The steadiest focus of this study has all along, to the contrary, been fixed on the career-advancing strategies of an author whose poetic anxiety is invested in continuance rather than influence. If with *LETTERS* we fasten even more doggedly on the career question, to the relative subordination of a book that is a monument of marvelous structuration, we do so because only at this stage of his career does Barth duplicate in his *content* the *forms* of the sixth and final phase of Bloom's map of misprision—a sure sign, on the scale of logical typing, that the past-forty Barth is kicking things up to a higher level: Finality must be made to foster commencement. For those with Bloomian eyes to see, it will appear as if a grinning and cocksure Barth were writing *LETTERS* with his spatializing left hand/right brain while holding Harold Bloom's *The Anxiety of Influence* in his temporalizing right hand/left brain, and performing a wholesale comic revision in Barth's seventh upon the ratio, defenses, trope, and images of Bloom's sixth.

Nowhere is Bloom more in sympathy with the dark task the strong poet must undertake than in his chapter on "Apophrades, or The Return of the Dead" (*AI*, 139–55). The terror experienced by the ordinary Athenians during those "unlucky days" of *apophrades* when their dead ancestors returned to reoccupy the dwelling-places in which they had passed their lives is shared by the uncommon poet who, having made his distinguished career by troping against his precursor in one strong misreading after another, now discerns to his horror in his late work the return of the precursor, intact and strong, an uncanny déjà vu and hallucinatory double thought to have been banished long ago. "Our own rejected thoughts, returning to us with an alienated luster," says Bloom in *The Breaking of the Vessels* (1982), "are what account for the uncanniness of the strong reading experience" (*BV*,

28). The dead must return only "in one's own colors" (*BV*, 88), if they are not to impoverish the late poet, whose "later visions must cleanse themselves at the expense of earlier ones," if the poet is to capture and retain priority over his precursors (*AI*, 139). The strong poet will have to utilize to the maximum the trope that tropes directly against the tyranny of anteriority, *metalepsis*—the far-fetching trope of transumptive allusion that now bears the current name of "intertextuality"—in order to achieve the "ultimate placing and reduction of ancestors" to the past and to claim his definitive gift as his own. Only the strongest poets—Browning, Yeats, and Stevens in their late phases, and Late Barth in his—acquire that invulnerability to the past which is necessary for this conversion of death into rebirth. They are aided in the feat by an extraordinary narcissism beyond the instinct for mere self-preservation, an excess of self-love that from the beginning of the poetic career has included the poetic self and now surges forward as itself a return of the early in the late. Bloom recapitulates the role of narcissism in the antithetical creative process:

The mystery of poetic style, the exuberance that is beauty in every strong poet, is akin to the mature ego's delight in its own individuality, which reduces to the mystery of narcissism. . . . Any departure from initial narcissism, according to Freud, leads to development of the ego, or in our terms, every exercise of a revisionary ratio, away from identification, *is* the process generally called poetic development. If all object-libido has its origin in ego-libido, then we can surmise also that each ephebe's initial experience of being found by a precursor is made possible only through an excess of self-love. *Apophrades*, when managed by the capable imagination, by the strong poet who has persisted in his strength, becomes not so much a return of the dead as a celebration of the return of the early self-exaltation that first made poetry possible. (*AI*, 146–47)

Unlike Bloom's strong poets seeking terminal clarity of self-definition at their Romantic or modernist sixth phase of finality, the postmodernist Barth already has a future anteriorly in mind, and all he wants is some elbow space to get on with it. Because Barth in his exultation over his continuance sees no near end to it, he comically and capably "manages" the return of his own dead beyond Bloom's wildest imagination: He fetches his dead from afar and invites them to return, welcomes the characters and their offspring from his first six fictions to his seventh—but he is a devious host who, unlike his flattered guests, knows what will happen after the feast is over. This is an authorial father who, in his eagerness to self-destruct his precursor, Early Barth, will not stop short of other-destructing the offspring of Early Barth, for if Late Barth is to be the wandering Aeneas of contemporary fiction and make the triumphant trip into advanced age with neither poetic progenitor nor poetic progeny aboard, he of course must murder the old to ring in the new. "What the strong poet truly knows," affirms Bloom, "is only that *he* is going to happen next" (*AI*, 152). Playing the dozens on Bloom's apophrades, *LETTERS* may thus be functionally described as a cast party after the curtain calls and before the ax falls, a Halloween Eve for his characters before their All Souls Day, a hello-again that is a goodbye-forever, and—beyond all this gleefully murderous intention of the kiss of death—a *bon voyage* party thrown by Barth for Late Barth alone.

Perhaps my reader demurs. This may seem to be a rather tall tale to spin out of a bit of authorial whimsy about an octogenarian future. Yet when the best critics of Late Barth ask the formalist question of *LETTERS*, "what is it?"—even when they update it to the structuralist idiom of "how is it made?"—their answers, as complimentary as they are to Barth's superbly formalist imagination, nevertheless seem like old wine in new bottles, a re-vintaging of the "mostly late modernist" Early Barth of *Lost in the Funhouse*. Barth has lured them into this trap of critical recycling on his very title page. Despite the fact that this hefty fiction, unlike the slim *Funhouse*, is packed full of the "aboutness" of early American history and the contemporary American sixties, Barth's canniest critics, encouraged as structuralist sleuths by their author, have fastened on the book's structuration as it is displayed in its title. Of the seven capitalized letters of *LETTERS*, each represents a month of epistolary letters on a seven-month calendar (March through September 1969) laid on its side, with an alphabetical letter assigned to each epistle according to its date and day of composition—eighty-eight letters in all which, when read in sequence left to right, reveal the subtitle, "An Old Time Epistolary Novel by Seven Fictitious Drolls and Dreamers Each of Which Imagines Himself Actual." Ignoring the uncanny revision of "Fictitious" into "Actual" in this last flip (upon which I will fix), Barth's respectable interrogators then proceed to the body count of Barth's returned dead. The eighty-eight letters that constitute the book's 772 thick pages are written by seven correspondents, six of whom are either characters from his former fictions (Todd Andrews, Jake Horner, Ambrose Mensch, the Author) or their heirs (the great-grandson of Ebenezer Cooke, the son of Harold Bray the False Tutor). Among the critics, moreover, there is no inordinate pause over the single exception and only new character (about which more later), Lady Germaine Pitt Amherst, who at book's end is over fifty and pregnant.

Instead, Barth's late modernist critics respond to his fiction as more of a system than a novel, each developing an intricate dominant paradigm that attempts to accommodate *LETTERS*' ingenious patterns. Reaching back to the Möbius strip that framed *Funhouse*, Patrick

O'Donnell (1986, 41–72) projects it upon the waterway geography of Barth's Eastern Shore as an emblematic seascape that is his paradigm of the circulation that governs the everything-that-goes-around-comes-around of Cooke's exposures of diplomatic intrigues in American history, the madness and sanity bouts of Todd's friend Harrison Mack, the corporate enterprises of Jane Mack, and Ambrose Mensch's theories about the making of literature. Tom LeClair (1989, 175–203) brings O'Donnell's circulatory metaphor into his own central systems concept of recycling, connecting it to Barth's preferred metaphor of artistic creation—regression, reenactment, reorientation—and to a second concept of interfacing, which mingles dualisms in a common boundary and thus enhances circulation. Max Schulz (1990), whose structuralist bias leads him to propose a Late Barth beginning with *Funhouse*, suspects recycling as a metaphor of dead-end repetition, and offers in its place the double helix of the DNA, the genetic coding that divides and recombines organisms toward unpredictable biological growth rather than to predictable closures of reenactment; for Schulz, *LETTERS* is "The Great Recombinant Postmodernist Novel."

One is tempted to nod one's head yes to all these bright and comprehensive paradigms (as Barth somewhere comments in another context), but then one reconsiders. Haven't we heard this before? Not only the inside/outside Möbius strip in O'Donnell's new application of it, not only Charles Harris's homely "synthesis" behind LeClair's "interfacing" (of realism and irrealisms, time and space, metaphor and metonymy, old and new), but also behind the quarrel between LeClair's systems metaphor and Schulz's biological one, Barth's own dialectic between the circle and the spiral in *Chimera*, where Bellerophon, the dull repeater and thus false hero, traces a closed circle that fails to get him to heaven, while Perseus, a prescient renewer and thus true hero, spirals his way up to the stars. Since *Chimera* is also the volume where Barth introduced the notion of the Second Revolution as the recycling of the first half of one's life, and since *Chimera* is not really a precursor of Barth's seventh but rather a piece of it that was published in advance under separate cover, it would seem wise to return there, rather than to *Lost in the Funhouse*, for heraldings of *LETTERS*. We will not return, however, to Heide Ziegler's *Chimera*, from which Barth has exhaustedly refined himself out of existence so that he can replenish himself with "a foothold in reality" in the "Supra-Realistic" *LETTERS*, with his Literature now battling Jerome Bray's Numerature (1987, 64, 78); Ziegler's seesaw of exhaustion-and-replenishment, always more creaky than well oiled, does not function at all in this instance.

Our Early Barth, rather, is the drop-in artist of *Chimera*, the Author-as-Genie, who has taken his own "dead reckoning" of life and career

(Barth's navigational metaphor for going forward by going back, which is the recycling principle in any self-regulating system); who has lost the spiraling growth of the Maryland snail that "carries his history on this back, living in it, adding new and larger spirals to it from the present as he grows"; and who now spills his bankrupt beans to Scheherazade on his initial visit to her, as first reported by her little sister Dunyazade and then confirmed by the Genie himself:

> His own pen (that magic wand, in fact a magic quill with a fountain of ink inside) had just about run dry. . . . he was distractedly in love with a brace of new mistresses, and only recently had been able to choose between them. His career, too, had reached a hiatus which he would have been pleased to call a turning-point if he could have espied any way to turn: he wished neither to repudiate nor to repeat his past performances; *he aspired to go beyond them to a future they were not attuned to* and, by some magic, at the same time go back to the original springs of narrative. (*C*, 9–10; emphasis mine)

> That snail's pace has become my pace—but I'm going in circles, following my own trail! I've quit reading and writing; I've lost track of who I am; *my name's just a jumble of letters; so's the whole body of literature*: strings of letters and empty spaces like a code that I've lost the key to. (*C*, 10–11; emphasis mine)

If this is indeed an authorial quandary, it is mighty prophetic. Barth seems to have pre-knowledge of not only the material ("the original springs of narrative") that will appear in the first three books of his first dozen years in the future anterior, but of what has to be done to get there: Make all letters—alphabetical, documentary, and literary—make sense, and make sure all your dead are good and buried. Although Barth's wake, like *Finnegans*, will last long into the night despite whatever palimpsests of pattern the critics lay over it, its pragmatic importance for the author's career, I believe, far exceeds the high-tech lusters of its complex design. As Barth's comedy of exultant narcissism, as his replenishing version of Bloom's and Beckett's endgames, and as his triumphant thumbing of his nose at a predatory past that threatens to "manure" his future, *LETTERS* puts Barth back at the helm of his ship, and the captain's first message to his crew is: *You* end, *I* (re)commence.

The strategies by which Barth executes their death sentences are every bit as intricate, and more humanly ingenious, as those of open systems and the DNA helix. Many of Barth's readers were stunned by the unseemly good cheer with which *LETTERS* produced its immoderate destructions, which in themselves can be justified as imitations of the paranoid conspiracies of a violent American history or of the velocities of unruly change in the sixties. But critics know the difference between actual homocide and literary murder, and they were especially appalled at the exuberant carnage of the book's violent finale, in which Barth not only explodes the boatful of passengers left unexploded in his first novel, but leaves a bomb ticking in Marshyhope College's Tower of Truth that could cause even greater devastation. To an interviewer sincerely puzzled at what seems to be excessive authorial aggression, Barth responded with his most insouciant remark on record: "It's odd, but there is an awful impulse one has at the end of a long project to sort of blow away a healthy portion of the cast of characters" (Reilly 1981, 17). Whether the "long project" Barth refers to is the seven years it took to design and write *LETTERS*, or the quarter-century of his career, Barth is remarkably at ease about the decimation of his significant others: as if he were saying, It's the kind of thing that happens at the end of a decade spent at the barricades, a revolutionary history will always pile up the bodies (19). That his authorial replenishment depends upon the murderous exhaustion of Early Barth goes without saying.

But if Barth's is the killing hand of the plotter, the "Capital-A Author's" is the glad-hand of the host: Come back home and help me out on my work-in-progress; update your life histories for me, discuss narrative strategies, give me your theories of everything. This is not a confidently invulnerable Barth speaking, but instead his henchman the strengthless Author who, under the ruse of an SOS sent out to the family, poses before his grown-up children as a fledgling author and floundering father. However, there is little familial collaboration here. The author may be among his dead, but he is not of them; they tell and tell, while he remains silent, passing himself off as relayer, compiler, clearinghouse—in Max Schulz's witty metaphor, "a dead letter box" (89).

The frenetic epistolary activity is almost all one-way correspondence, the Author breaking his silence mostly initially, with his invitations to return, and at the end of each month of letters, in comparatively brief and even cursory responses. If the Author is not yet expiring, he most certainly is unavailable. Strange action for a father who invites his prodigal sons home again and then resolutely holds them at a distance! Because Jacques Lacan is going to pick up as Late Barth's psychoanalytic navigator where Bloom and Freud left off, and because we eventually must deal with Lacan's concept of *forclusion* (of the Phallic Signifier, the paternal metaphor), I introduce the concept now in its several, generalized meanings as the English "foreclosure," all of which apply to Barth's coordinated actions with his Author vis-à-vis his characters: (1) to deprive a mortgagor or pledgor of the right to redeem his property; (2) to shut out, bar, hinder, prevent; (3) to establish an exclusive claim to; (4) to close, settle, or answer beforehand. Surely the letter-writing progeny of Early Barth must be feeling slightly dis-owned, a little orphaned, foreclosed on when they appeal to the Name-of-the-Father; so rarely do they get an answer.

It is as if their authorial father had said, "Come under the shadow of my roof," and then slammed the door in their faces. The invitation is a near paraphrase of Arthur Quinn's biblical example of a *metalepsis*, "a metonomy apparently involving a double substitution," with "roof" a synecdoche of "house," and "house" as a metaphor for security and protection (19). The concealed two-step of metalepsis, Quinn avers, comes close to abusing the legitimate function of substitution—that is, there may be no room under its roof, metalepsis has no space of its own on which to stand as substitute figure. Nor, Bloom suggests, has it a time of its own, for metalepsis "lies about and against origins" in its revenge against time, from a crippling sense of belatedness (*BV*, 89). Flinging itself between early and late, metalepsis creates (in John Hol-lander's phrase) "an ellipsis of further figuration," with only the most extreme images of apocalypse or farce left available for its representa-tions (*BV*, 13).

Picking up on the farcical alternative, Quintilian (Bloom reports) declared metalepsis to be good only for comedy, not at all the major mode of poetic allusion and transumptive intertextuality that metal-epsis has become since Milton. As a transitional, change-of-meaning trope, with no meaning or space-time presence of its own, metalepsis betrays a "tone of conscious rhetoricity," according to Quintilian," that "can seem comic in its surrender of the living present" (*MM*, 102). Moreover, the absurdly self-affirming rigidities of metaleptic repeti-tion remind us that Freud's compulsion-to-repeat, adduced as the man-ifestation in human lives of the antilife death-drive quietly and always at work, can also appear as the French farce of Bergson's definition of comedy, "the mechanical encrusted over the human," as well as the terrifying and uncanny question—is it alive or dead?—that emerges at the apocalyptic edge of psychosis. All of these interpretations of meta-lepsis, I propose, come together in a comic mirage of psychosis with which *LETTERS* frames—confines and sets up—its characters, for the rescue of John Barth from his writerly past.

This may appear to be a wild interpretation, but it has two virtues not easily found elsewhere in the critical bibliography: It accommodates Barth's seriocomic view on a broad range of apocalyptic yet farcical realities, psychic and historical, and it retrieves the comic edge missed by those reviewers who admired the book but also disliked it. As example, we might consider Barth's recurring engagements through-out *LETTERS* with the altogether serious Karl Marx. Marx's theory of a revolutionary history that depends upon a resolute junking of the past certainly cannot have much appeal for a novelist seriously attempting a literary conservation of the past in his works, nor from the perspective of Barth's anxiety of continuance can Marx's determinism be anything but anathema to his indeterminate future. Barth's doubled vision—that we must preserve the past while liberating ourselves from it—accounts for the comic variations he works on the motto, *praeteritas futuras stercorant*, which take it from "the past fertilizes the future" to "the past craps up the future" (*L*, 12).

On the eve of his own Recommencement, Barth is interested above all else in deciding between good and bad repetitions, and is thus much more fascinated with Marx's renowned pronouncement in the *Eighteenth Brumaire* that "tragic history repeats itself as farce." After Napoleon comes his feeble nephew, and in Barth's hands Napoleon's godlike sense of self becomes Harrison Mack's farcial imitation of it in his madness. In *LETTERS*, the fate of Marx's historical repetition is echoed in the self-repetitions of the characters, who are seriocomic analogs to Marx's first-time tragedy and second-time farce. Jan Gorak's excellently balanced discussion of the Marx-Barth connection approximates this seriocomic ideal: Gorak gives serious attention to the commodifications of postindustrial capitalism as they are amply represented in *LETTERS*, and then he moves Marx's theater from the political-economic infrastructure to its impact on individual lives, crediting Barth with a Balzacian "creation of a *comédie humaine*," of characters who likewise exhibit the solipsistic self-enclosure and narcissistic self-centeredness that proceed from the commodification or "fetishization" of the self (1987, 173–91). Just as the War of 1812, the "Second Revolution" in A. B. Cooke's historiography, is a farcial repetition of the Revolutionary War, also farcial are those Bellerophonic characters in *LETTERS* who dwell in/on their past and repeat the first half of their lives in the second half, a fate that separates them from a career-oriented Barth and "a future they are not attuned to."

The argument, ultimately, sinks or swims with the reader's experiencing of *LETTERS*. For me, Barth's progeny kept popping up like puppets, fidgeting through their obsessive repetitions and narcissistic fetishizations with a preposterousness just barely saved, on this side of neurosis, from the mechanism and madness of true psychosis. What could be more farcial than Todd Andrews, at sixty-nine, still writing to dear dead Dad, still making money for the Macks, still lusting after Grandma Jane, still trying for suicide, and still being a connoisseur of ironies? Although Jacob Horner is now among a new generation of the sixties who are stumped at the Remobilization Farm, his personal weather hasn't changed since 1954; he's still an immobilized person-in-pieces, with his current therapy at the low level of his "Anniversary

View," which sorts persons and history according to mere dates. The Cooke/Burlingame generational doing and undoings of history continue to repeat themselves through an extended family line of incestuous loves and nefarious political intriguing for the game of it all. While Todd might just get himself dead in his own fashion this time (although the ending suggests he may well not), while Jake will finally escape Joe Morgan and get himself eloped with an allegorical Marsha Blank, and while some of the Cook heirs will become seriously committed in the sixties—the sense of change is largely conveyed not through character growth but through the normal differences promoted by historical rather than personal development. If we laugh at these characters rather than view them as failed, it's because we are prompted by Barth's humane forgiveness of their botched lives and his admiration for their tenacity of survival.

The two characters who are closest and farthest from Barth—one of whom he has identified with in the past, the other whom he projects outward as his own worst future—relate to the Author in the same capacity. Ambrose Mensch, Barth's "old altered ego" and an artist-in-the-making when last seen in *Funhouse*, is the Author's confidante in all matters of literary practice and theory, and as close as Barth has come, thus far in his career, to an identification with one of his characters. Mensch, nonetheless, is a formidable formalist and rabid repeater, who often appears like a failed hero imitating the pattern (decidedly preposterous, for instance, in his manipulation of his love affair with Germaine to correspond to his past affairs with other women). The Author's enemy is "the other J. B.," Jerome Bray, Barth's projection of a failed Late Barth as a perfect RESET computer novelist, a mad Rex Numerator who would end all literature with his numbers, and halt the Author's career with Bray's maniacal repeat of it in LILYVAC's *Numbers*. It is significant that of the two characters who can be related to Barth's own introjections and projections, the swallowed-up Ambrose woos and wins the new woman for their indeterminate future together, while the spit-out Bray reels on to ever greater heights of apocalyptic farce.

In addition to the serious social satire that informs the content of *LETTERS*, I am arguing that there is also a comic "Great Divide" that Barth builds between himself and his characters, a barrier of spatial and temporal alienations that can be comprehended through the psychoanalytic revisions worked on the antithetical defenses of introjection and projection by Lacan, a revisionary task that extends their relevance across the spectrum of normality, neurosis, and psychosis. The widespread, psychological meaning of projection that connects subjectivity to the world is generally useless to us. As the externalization of the self through an attribution of one's feelings, thoughts, and attitudes to other people or objects, projection can refer equally to the savage mind that naively "projects" a universe, and to the civilized novelist who consciously "projects" a fictional world. In neither case is the creative, living self expelling something distasteful to himself.

But we cannot get very far with projection before encountering this very definition of it by Freud, who situated projection, along with the twin defense of introjection, as the earliest defenses of the human infant already individualizing himself through a definition of the me and the not-me. As Freud schematizes these double defenses, they proceed from a more primary history of the forces of attraction and repulsion, whereby what is foreign or alien to the initial body ego is "bad" and projected outward, and what is considered "good" is intro-jected inward. What I like forms my inside and what I don't like forms my outside. Freud's biological model for these psychic defenses is the suckling and vomiting infant, with his "I should like to eat this"/"I should like to spit this out." Bodily incorporation, as the first introjec-tion, then leads directly into the later process of identification, whereby the subject assimilates an aspect, property, or attribute of the other and is transformed, wholly or partially, after the model that the other provides. It is through a series of such identifications, Freud argues, that the normal, mature personality is specified (Laplanche 1973, 229–30).

Freud's analysis, however, focuses on the inside/outside and there-fore can offer no insight on the seriocomic early/late division that Barth puts between himself and his characters. Harold Bloom, con-trary to Freud, emphasizes the differential *temporal* results of introjec-tion and projection, as they produce either an "idealized past" or a "hoped-for future," a revision toward metalepsis that corresponds to Barth's most basic career-intention with the writing of *LETTERS*. Says Bloom: "Either there is a spitting-out and so a distancing of the future and so a swallowing-up, an identifying with the past, by substituting late words for earlier words in an anterior trope, or else there is a distancing, a projecting of the past, and an identifying with the future, by making a substitution of early for late words" (*MM*, 103). Although Lacan's revision of Freud's psychic defenses leaves much more to be said, Bloom's revision of Freud points well to the temporal reversal between Barth and his characters: Because Barth is confident about his career future since he knows how to cut off the past, he can let his correspondents do the telling in their early words as a substitution for his late Author's present silence; because his returnees identify strongly with their pasts to the relative exclusion of their future, their late words are destined to be mostly repetitions of their early ones.

Consequently, they will not have a future, whereas Barth will, and his replenishment will be predicated on their exhaustion.

Yet it is Lacan, and not Bloom, who in his return to Freud aids our comic appreciation of the book's representations, aside from Barth's authorial motive. Lacan does not like the "totally uncritical use" that psychoanalysts have made of Freud's introjection and projection, as if they were a simple scheme of infusion or expulsion. Thus, he sets about making the crucial distinctions that will distribute these defenses across the three Lacanian orders of reality—the Symbolic, Imaginary, and Real—and will resuscitate the half-life that projection lives on its own in relation to psychosis. In Book I of the English translation of the ongoing *Seminar of Jacques Lacan* (1988), Lacan breaks the direct line from physical incorporation to psychic identification that traditionally defines introjection. The oedipal child does not literally devour the father, but rather internalizes (introjects) the Name-of-the-Father as his own superego, in a self-mastery that does not proceed through the stomach; introjection is always an internalization of the *speech* of the other and thus belongs to the Symbolic order (83). This first cut into Lacan, however, permits us only a weak misreading of Barth's letter-writing progeny as perfectly normal neurotics, good citizens of moral conscience, and docile oedipal kids all, who have introjected the Name-of-the-Father as culture's Law, and who, as fictional characters whose only origin is their creator's ventriloquated voice, repeat his prime writerly attribute with their interminable epistles in their own en-feebled, Symbolic realm. This is to say little more than that all fictional characters are sometimes more, sometimes less sons of the father.

A stronger misreading emerges when we follow Lacan on the traditional party line in its relevance to a definition of psychosis, a trajectory traced in the English translation of his *Ecrits* (1980), through Lacan's essay "On a Question Preliminary to any Possible Treatment of Psychosis" (179–221). When Freudian analysts interpret introjection and projection as "a sort of pumping in and out of the libido by the *percepiens*," they give too much responsibility for reality to the ego (which Lacan's lifework has shown to be significantly unreliable), and too much leeway to themselves for defining psychosis along a vague continuum as the point when an excess of deflation is supposed to have occurred and the psychotic has suffered a "loss of reality." Psychotics, Lacan argues, do not suffer a subtraction from any bogus totality that normal people are supposed to have a hold on, for the norms have their home in the Symbolic, not the Real. The cut between neurosis and psychosis depends, not on the absence of a *whole*, but rather on the presence of a *hole* in the Symbolic for the psychotic (188). What is lacking to the psychotic is the Name-of-the-Father: Where the Law outside should respond as the Name-of-the-Father, there is only this gap in the Other. It is this "foreclosure of the signifier," and not some unspecifiable loss of reality, that defines psychosis; the "inadequacy of the paternal metaphor," and not the absence of the real father, accounts for the psychotic's nonrelation to the Symbolic and his consequent captation in the Imaginary order of his hallucinations and delusions.

Even an eighteen-month-old infant, Lacan argues, knows better than the psychotic. At six months the jubilant infant, seeing his mother's unified image in the mirror, stole for himself an Imaginary mastery that he had not yet attained, a misrecognition (*méconnaisance*) that followed upon the attributive judgment of introjection, "I should like this." However, as a year's graduate of the mirror stage, the older and wiser infant knows that his mirror image is "nothing more than an appearance," a truthful judgment of existence that follows from his new power of negation, "This is not real" (*Book I* 1988, 168–69). With the resolution of the oedipal conflict, the normal child has learned negation on both counts of the not-me and not-real, repressing the not-me into his unconscious and carrying his not-real/not-true judgments into the realm of symbolicity. The psychotic, on the other hand, does not take to oedipalization and therefore does not repress meaning, but treats it as if it doesn't exist, having never introjected the Name-of-the-Father and thus having forfeited the power of negation of an internalized superego. When the repressed returns for the psychotic, in Anthony Wilden's words, "There is nowhere for the 'return of the repressed' (the psychic symptom) to return to (as it returns to the subject's history in neurosis)." Without a home of its own in the unconscious, shut out and excluded, the repressed then returns from the outside. This is what accounts for the Imaginary of the psychotic which he takes to be Real, and for the terror he experiences at the uncanny déjà vu that occurs when "what was abolished internally returns from without" (Wilden 1981, 168–69).

This more complex relation between representation and perception, which Lacan takes to be the issue in defining psychosis, leads directly to my alternative description of *LETTERS* as Barth's comic illusion of an "as if" psychosis. In inviting his dead to return, Barth has uprooted them from the homes in their Symbolic books and expelled them out into the erratic Real by functioning as the silent Other where the Name-of-the-Father should be. Far from knowing themselves as the offspring of Early Barth's Symbolic, they think that they are Real, "seven fictitious drolls and dreamers each of which imagines himself actual," unable themselves to judge between appearance and apparition. Resolutely expelled from the author's psychoanalytic history as

well, Barth's dead must return from the outside, like Imaginary hallucinations, insistent and self-repeating storytellers who, having gained
none of the neurotic's relief through repression, are condemned to
hauling their own stuff over and over again down the same towpath.
Foreclosed from the property proper to the fictional character—his
author and his book—these orphans of the Symbolic order babble on
and on, like former doubles of the author unable to get themselves a
time and space of their own, condemned on the rebound to regular
reappearances as the living dead, as repetition-compulsives farcical in
their mechanical reenactments. In Lacan's phrase concerning the psychotic's hallucinatory reality, Barth's characters are all "punctuation
without a text," whether they are apprehended from a frame outside
the fiction, from Barth's and his readers' perspectives, or at the textual
level of the viewpoints of the Author and his correspondents. Their
fruitlessness is the direct consequence of Barth's across-the-board divestment.

Such a mirage narrative of Barth's creative strategy, when baldly
foregrounded as above, may seem extravagant, yet Barth's other critics
have noted his tactical deviousness, while keeping any suspicions about
his motives to themselves. Charles Harris (1983) labels *LETTERS* "a
Derridean plexus of intertextual traces," and places those many characters who emulate their past selves "in the context of the Archetypes
of the Eternal Return" (165, 162). Heide Ziegler (1987) is closest to my
own perceptions when she characterizes the novel as a "gigantic exercise in the *exorcism* of every one of the author's possible limitations,"
and remarks on the comic effect of the "vicissitudes of rigidity" that
plague the characters, condemned to repeat the limiting former stages
of the author's development (78, 73). Schulz (1990) notes Barth's "bar-
ring" of the "Author" from the other drolls and dreamers, reaffirming
his own position as *deus artifex*, and with this inside/outside "strange
loop" promoting the persistence of "a knowing more" (74–76). Even
the more negative assessments can be recuperated as the underside of
my mythopsychotic scenario, as when Tom LeClair (1989) criticizes the
novel's "authorial imperialism," its "often inert formalism," and the
absence of characters in the literal sense, these serving only "to fill a
textual or dramaturgical niche" (187, 184); or when David Lodge
(1980) attacks the book as "an eccentric and extravagant production . . .
parasitic upon the past and sterile as regards the future" (607).

An author's intention remains an outside recourse for contemporary
literary critics, partly because they are exercising a polite tact regarding
authorial privacy, and partly because they are much more intrigued by
the public text. The analyst of a literary career, however, must per-
severe through the author's possible motives and their practical literary

consequences, until she reaches what appears to be something like an adequate resolution of process and product. In dealing with an author such as Barth, whose anxiety of continuance surfaces most readily between his books, the career-analyst is well advised to persist, particularly when the critical paradigms devised to explain the book when it appears fall far short of answering the question, "What is it for?" An extravagant project, like the *LETTERS* of Barth, demands an extravagant answer, not to be found in metaphors of form and systems of functioning. My answer, instead, is that through comedic caricature of his former characters, Barth aesthetically accomplished a creative subtraction from himself, the unburdening of an accumulated identity that would leave him free to assume an undetermined literary future. The complex structurations of the book, its attention to historical detail, and its concern for the continuity and coordination of its fictional biographies all testify to its author's painstaking labor; the fruit of that labor is authorial divestment.

The single character whom I have saved from psychosis and saved for consideration until now is Lady Amherst, who is not a returnee from the dead but the first offspring of Late Barth. Because she has not served in the first half of her life as a character in Early Barth's previous fictions, she does not dwell in the psychotic Imaginary in her second half, but is, instead, herself a presager of Barth's own Second Revolution. Here, in an interview with an ex-student of his, is Barth's sketch of her:

As for my Lady A: In better days she has been the Great Good Friend of a number of this century's celebrated novelists. She has even been impregnated by a few of them, though all the pregnancies have failed to reach term for one reason or another. In 1969, the present time of the novel, she's fifty and has a new American lover, who does not always manifest his love with the dignity and courtesy she deserves. He's a failed last-ditch provincial modernist; a sort of marsh-country mandarin. But he is possessed of an unreasoning obsession to impregnate my heroine one last time and bear a child with her, despite her age and their unimpressive track records. You get the idea. (*FB*, 174)

Barth's formalist critics, delighted by Lady Amherst's allegorical status as the Muse of Literature, the Great Tradition, and the Realistic Novel, and despite her protests to the contrary (*L*, 57), have interpreted her marriage to Barth's alter-ego Ambrose as the transcension of literary contraries that Barth took as the sign, in his *Atlantic* 1980 essay, of a future literature of replenishment. However, in his exhaustive interview on *LETTERS* with Charlie Reilly in 1979 (published in 1981 in *Contemporary Literature*) Barth speaks much more directly to this study's career view of literary production. After Barth had decided on the form and structure of the novel suitable to his "*Jaws II* theory of literature," he tells Reilly, Lady Amherst was the first character he invented, and "the other characters, to me at least, are clearly ancillary, complementary, supplementary; her voice is the sustaining one" (14–15). Indeed, Germaine's voice sustains about a quarter of the book, and it is the voice of a lively, intelligent, and terrifically attractive person, in contrast to the other characters whom Barth admits (with reference to the psychedelic sixties) "to some extent . . . are meant to be caricatures" (17). Furthermore, while Barth promises that he has "no intention of ever bringing any of those characters back again," Lady A. is very much going to accompany Late Barth into his unique future.

If Lady Amherst is exempted from Barth's funerary fare-thee-wells, it is because she is the only character who gets inside the author, the one whom Barth introjects and identifies with, the only writer who is with child. Pregnant now with books and a future of his own, Barth's cross-gender identification gets him a new metaphor for Late Barth's creativity. No more penile assaults by the male upon the exterior, but rather a fullness of interior female space will become in Barth's next two books the paradigm of creative replenishment: female pregnancy rather than male potency. By 1982 in *Sabbatical, A Romance*, Lady A. will reappear as the bawdy and wise mother of the wife who will jump into Late Barth's lifeboat with him; and it is this pregnant wife who will so agitate the one-in-two and the two-in-one that the psychosis of *LETTERS*' hallucinated characters will seem to be but the exemplarily sane schizophrenia of the happily coupled. The whale-road may get rough, but the ship is yare. Funerals are out; rebirth is in.

Chapter 8
Sabbatical, A Romance (1982): Literalizing the Lateral

Image	*Trope*	*Defense*	*Ratio*
The Incestuous Couple	Synergism	Schizophrenia	Chiasmus

Barth will now set sail for the beyond of Harold Bloom that is the postmodern literature of replenishment. Replenishment was never intended to be accommodated by Bloom's map of misprision. In his first seven fictions, our novelist-as-hero admirably dispatched the images, tropes, defenses, and ratios with which Bloom's map challenged and championed the strong poet. The broad historical relevance of the map extends from the post-Enlightenment through late modernism, a commodious stretch of time that saw the mature consolidations of Platonic philosophy in Kant, of an orthodox psychoanalysis in Freud, and of literary irony in the Anglo-American New Criticism. For the poets and poems within these historical limits, Bloom has meticulously fashioned a functional, diachronic and synchronic explanation of the creative process that ties the poetic psyche to poetic rhetoric in persuasive analogy. The creative process as described by Bloom, however, is a tragedy of self-wounding, the voluntary and heroic shouldering by the poet of culture's "narcissistic scar" as represented in the tragic Oedipus. Moreover, Bloom's map, haunted as it has always been by Bloom's theory of the anxiety of influence, not only begins in irony but ends in it: The ephebe who tropes and defends every which way against the presence of his precursor ironically suffers the precursor's triumphant return in the poet's late texts, and thus he never attains a land of his own.

The comic postmodernism of Barth's Recommencement is a robust and forthright rejection of the psychology of lack inherent in the father's return, of the belated tragic vision that modulates toward cynicism, and of a decadent irony that impels the comic into the depressive position of snide aggression. In his upcoming literary voyages out, Barth cannot make use of Bloom as his navigator, for Bloom's modernist map does not acknowledge the post-ironic heterodoxies visited on philosophy by Jacques Derrida, on psychoanalysis by Jacques Lacan, on post-structuralism by Gilles Deleuze and Félix Guattari, and on Newtonian science by post-Einsteinian physicists. These incursions upon the official disciplines are the postmodern supports for the tangential tactics of an ascendant post-ironic humor, which makes forward progress by moving sideways, ignores the perpendicular limits of both physical space and logical thought, and makes the whole cosmos its home.

Therefore, while Bloom's fourfold classificatory schema will be retained for its valuable psychotextual analogies, his ratio, image, trope, and defense will appear as familiar containers of unfamiliar cargo. Especially the rhetorical "trope" and the psychic "defense," which assumed a normal neurosis of text and psyche, should be understood as inscribed within quotation marks. Missing from the anti-gravity offensives of post-ironic humor are the notions of limit and lack that sustained both Freud's analysis of neurotic humankind and literary modernism's mimetic/ironic relation to reality. The unconscious, which for modernism was the ultimate limit, the world elsewhere of Freud's *eine anderer Schauplatz*, will now increasingly be explored as a world next door in a *para*-space beside quotidian reality, as a second reality that is lateral and alternative to that which culture has trained our perceptions and language to sanction. No longer submitted to the warring parts of the tripartite psyche, which reach their limits in the nightdream, the poet recommences in limitless daydreaming. No longer submitting his poetic task to the threefold dialectic of limitation/substitution/representation, the comic poet breaks out of the hostile interiors of the psychic and writing processes and activates a fourth possibility—of connecting to an amiable exterior, of hooking up to a collaborative outside, of mapping an adjacency. With Plato in pieces, not only does the limit recede but so also does the stolid illusion of mass and wholeness that sustains all paranoid and antagonistic confrontations at the boundaries.

Images now need not represent the either/or extremes of a homogeneous space and time (as in Bloom's presence and absence, part for whole and whole for part, fullness and emptiness, high and low, inside and outside, early and late). Beyond the tragic and ironic perceptions of the whole, imagery may now frolic in hybrid and mongrel couplings that are often the provisionary possibilities or illicit opportunities presented by a destabilized space-time of gaps and fissures, breaks and flows. The "tropes" are likewise partial, multiple, and mobile maneuvers of syntax, rather than substantive carriers of figural meaning, and they also tend toward the outside, drawing perhaps more on postmodern mathematics and science than on traditional rhetoric. The newly unemployed psychic "defenses" divorce themselves from the drive and point instead to discoveries that are more found than sought, and they manifest themselves as amateur and ad hoc psychic tactics of advantageously decentered characters who affirm individual mobility and multiplicity. The ratios of the second revolution, also undreamed of in Bloom's philosophy, appear as overall strategies for gaining a world without losing it, for multiplication without subtraction, and for a revisionary process without the demands of poetic self-sacrifice. On the sly and on the run, aside from culture and not up against it, Barth's post-ironic comedy affirms the availability of alternative universes on the most homey and homeliest levels of acquisition. The strangeness of this new map of re-reading is the result, not of an upsurgence of wild fantasy, but rather of our own unfamiliarity with being at home on the outside.

Official culture designates those of its citizens who are neither neurotics nor norms but who are outside of normal reality as psychotics, and diagnoses the alternative worlds of madmen as extreme defenses against the external frustrations and unbearable burdens of a reality that has been too much for them. Conversely, madness has also always been venerated as the source and homeground of poetry. In the sixties the ancient analogy between the madman and the poet came together with the more recent one between the poet and the child in the generalized amelioration of schizophrenia undertaken by British psychiatrist R. D. Laing, who glorified for a large readership the absence of normal neurosis and presence of poetry in these natural rebels without a cause. Through the seventies and eighties, in the original French and English translations of their two volumes on "Capitalism and Schizophrenia," Deleuze and Guattari have argued even more radically for a properly managed and exemplary schizophrenia as a breakthrough rather than a breakdown.

John Barth has also wondered, more moderately and hesitantly, whether, in the current state of global capitalism and imminent nuclear apocalypse, an emulation of schizophrenic disorientation might not be an eminently "sane response to a deranged but inescapable set of circumstances," whereas to orient oneself "sanely" to a world that is looking increasingly crazy would be wholly self-destructive. Schizophrenia as a leap into sanity rather than a lapse into psychosis? Citing Laing as his authority and in an explicit reference to his eighth novel, Barth teases his critical reader with the possibility: "My little novel

Sabbatical, A Romance (1982) carries this Laingian scenario farther" (*FB*, 140).

Barth's particular image of schizophrenia-as-cure, the incestuous couple, entails for its understanding an uncommon recourse by Barth to his own biography. Barth begins his *Friday Book* with a self-introduction that is a reprint of his contribution of May 9, 1982, to an ongoing series in the *New York Times Book Review* under the "general and hokey" title of "The Making of a Writer." His first answer to the question implied in his own "counter-hoke" title, "Some Reasons Why I Tell the Stories I Tell the Way I Tell Them Rather Than Some Other Sort of Stories Some Other Way," is that he was born an opposite-sex twin. Customarily, throughout a long history of snappy remarks to the critics, Barth has deployed this anonymous sister as a comic explanation for "Why I write my books in pairs" or "why I over-use the semicolon"—an absurd reduction of cause clearly intended to ward off through mockery any critical endeavors to trace Barth's bibliography back to his biography.

But in this instance of his return to the theme of twinship, there is additional development that strongly suggests that Barth is in earnest this time about the connection between his art and his life, and that we should take him semi-seriously. Beyond mere personal whimsy, Barth appeals to mythic authority in his citation from Plato's *Symposium* of Aristophanes, who declared in effect that "we are all of us twins, indeed a kind of Siamese twins, who have lost and who seek eternally our missing half." Barth then observes that "a writer who happens to be a twin might take this *shtik* by the other end and use schizophrenia, say, as an image for what he knows to be the literal case: that he was once more than one person and somehow now is less" (*FB*, 3). Barth also reveals the name of his twin sister, letting his readers know that Jack and Jill Barth went through their young lives as flesh-and-blood literalizations of the literature of the nursery, a "literal case" of materializing a metaphor that hints at Jack Barth's identity as being bounded not by his own body but by JacknJill's. Moreover, twins already lateralized in the womb, according to Barth, enjoy a relation to language different from that of us solitaires:

Much is known about identical (monozygotic) twins, less about fraternal (dizygotic) twins, less yet about us opposite-sexers (who, it goes without saying, are always dizygotic). But twins of any sort share the curious experiences of accommodating to a peer companion from the beginning, even in the womb; of entering the world with an established sidekick, rather than alone; of acquiring speech and the other basic skills *à deux*, in the meanwhile sharing a language before speech and beyond speech. Speech, baby twins may feel, is for the Others. As native speakers of a dialect regard the official language, we twins

may regard language itself: It is for dealing with the outsiders; between ourselves we have little need of it. One might reasonably therefore expect a twin
who becomes a storyteller never to take language for granted; to be ever at it,
tinkering, foregrounding it, perhaps unnaturally conscious of it. Language is
for relating to the Others. (*FB*, 1)

These authorial pronouncements linking schizophrenia to twinship
deserve our concerted attention for several good reasons: because they
appear in the year of publication of Barth's eighth work of fiction,
which is the first book of his Recommencement; because in this book
for the first time in Barth's literary career his fictional "hero" is a
happily married couple, each born a twin, who are hand-over-hand in
all they undertake—making love, making sail, making stories; and
because Susan Rachel Allan Steckler and Fenwick Scott Key Turner
look very much—much too much, their author is going to come to
believe—like Jack and Shelly Barth. Let me elaborate these considerations going from the last to the first, as befits the recommencement of
a Second Revolution.

It may seem passing strange that, in a study focused on the relation
between psychology and rhetoric, so much has gone without saying
concerning John Barth's life which, at this point in his career, has
reached its fifty-second year. If the critic now suddenly jumps with both
feet into his biography, it is because *Sabbatical, A Romance* demands
such a leap; this book is the closest that Barth has ever ventured to a
direct connection between his life and his literature. Heretofore, I have
respected his abhorrence of unimaginative and uninventive "confessional" fiction, which appears again and again in his announcements
for the public record, and the basic "shop rule" of his writing—that
there shall be "no autobiography, except in the Nabokovian way."
Barth tells us that this special aspect of his broad admiration for the
Russian-American writer hearkens back to a remark made by Nabokov
in interview, to the effect "that while he deplores autobiographical
fiction, he will on occasion bestow upon one of his invented characters
a detail from his own life, 'as one might award a medal'" (*FB*, 178).
There is a lot of medal-awarding and general bestowing in *Sabbatical*,
so much that perhaps one may respond to one's author with the
Zarathustran wisdom that, as one's life grows happier and healthier,
the bestowing virtue overflows and indeed is the very sign of the
overman who has come through.

Barth's biography, in fact, began to play patty-cake with Barth's
bibliography on the eve of the second half of his life, when both his life
and his writing appeared to be beckoning him to the "best, next thing."
Lost in the Funhouse (1969), Barth's goodbye to late modernism, coin-

cided (a term we shall not take lightly in *Sabbatical*) in Barth's life with the death throes of a long marriage beset with diminishing returns. Soon after *Chimera*, Barth would remarry, move to his beloved marshlands on Maryland's Eastern Shore, and, in violation of another of his shop rules, would dedicate his next five books to his second wife, Shelly. As his casual remarks will thereafter testify, it has been a happy marriage for Jack and Shelly (an ex-student of Barth's who is now a teacher of literature), and a coupling that is passionately collaborative. The right woman, the right place, the right job—who is to say that when a man's cup runneth over, some of it shouldn't spill out into autobiographical bestowal, or that the Barths shouldn't award themselves a medal whenever they are so inclined!

Until Novel #8, the well-conjugated couple has not been a hallmark of Barth's fiction. In the first pair of his books, the couple was split asunder into an adulterous triangle; in the next pair, the picaresque Ebenezer and the questing Giles were solitary rolling stones that gathered piquant but ultimately ancillary females; by fictions #5 and #6, the couple had become a fanciful vision, an unrealized ideal, a consummation devoutly to be wished. In the words of the desperately self-conscious and blocked narrator of *Funhouse*'s "Title."

> The times be damned, one still wants a man vigorous, confident, bold, resourceful, adjective, and adjective. One still wants a woman spirited, spacious of heart, loyal, gentle, adjective, adjective. That man and woman are as possible as the ones in this miserable story, and a good deal realer. It's as if they live in some room in our house that we can't find the door to. (*LF*, 10)

By 1972 and *Chimera*, there are women abounding and Barth jumps into his book with them, to face down the problematics of *equality* that are inevitably exacerbated in the "mixed" marriages between male and female. Bellerophon, who doesn't seem to get much else right, seems to have authorial approval for his love-and-writing affair with Melanippe, the sexually frisky and self-sufficient young Amazon whose "Lethelike" memory has failed to preserve the stale antagonisms of gender battles. About sexual equality *Chimera*'s true hero, Perseus, has learned the hard way, from his wife of long standing: "Andromeda, in my opinion, had near henpecked me out of cockhood; but I learned from her what few men know, fewer heroes, and no gods: that a woman's person is her independent right, to be respected therefore by the goldenest hero in heaven" (84). Even so, Perseus has to admit that too often in the past, in service to his insufferable male ego, he has tended to propose "three parts Perseus to one Andromeda."

But then the equalizing Perseus is brought up short by his darling priestess Calyxa, who is aghast at the idea of sexual parity and reciprocity. Having spent her young lifetime aiding and abetting, entertaining, and sexually servicing the mythical heroes dropping by her temple, Calyxa is all in favor of the *complementarity* of a coupling relationship in which the male pitches and the female catches. By 1979 and *LETTERS*, we find Lady Germaine Amherst Pitt still oscillating between reciprocity and completion on this matter of the couple. Germaine has as much of the temple priestess in her as the independent Amazon, and she concludes that although she sometimes regrets the former tendency toward "intense complementarity," it may well be ineradicable: "What rot, the old female itch to be . . . not *mastered*, God forfend, but ductile, polar to the male, intensely complemental" (247).

But it is with Scheherazade and her little sister Dunyazade that these pre-*Sabbatical* concerns with gender sameness and difference get provisionally settled. As collaborating storyteller (three parts of) Barth-as-Genie ends up agreeing with Scheherazade that "to say men and women are equal is to say nothing: Authors are essentially active and masculine, readers primarily complementary and feminine; however, this is also to say nothing, since all appreciators of narrative, like imaginative lovers, switch positions after Position One" (34). To her surprise Dunyazade learns, while holding a razor to his royal genitals, that the younger brother of Shahryar has had a way with women quite different from that of Sherry's lover. Instead of deflowering and then murdering *his* virgins, Shah Zaman has sent them secretly out of the country—intact or impregnated as they choose, but each with a vial of diamonds in her vagina—to found a gynocracy where more peaceful and freer relations between the sexes might prevail. Give up your sister's plan for a double regicide, Duny's shah cries out, let us marry and pledge ourselves to an "as if" equality:

"Let's end the dark night! All the passion and hate between men and women; all the confusion of inequality and difference. Let's take the truly tragic view of love. . . . Nothing *works*! But the enterprise is noble; it's full of joy and life, and the other ways are deathy. Let's make love as passionate equals!"
"You mean *as if* we were equals," Dunyazade said. "You know that we're not. What you want is impossible.
"Despite your heart's feelings?" pressed the King. "Let it be *as if*! Let's make a philosophy of that *as if*!" (61–62)

Literalizing the metaphor? Living a lie? The strategies that Shah Zaman is here suggesting are those proper to the schizophrenic. Whether or not they can work for this couple we never learn in *Chimera*; Barth does not give us the story of their life together because, as he more than candidly admits, "in the middle of my own, I can't conclude it" (64). Even for a genius of fictional invention, there are some things that can't get into the bibliography until they have enjoyed a run in the biography.

But by 1982 Jack and Shelly have themselves enjoyed that run, and Barth finds himself writing about a couple who in the seventh year of their marriage have taken sabbatical leave from the world, and after nine months of cruising the Caribbean are coming home to shore through Chesapeake Bay. These two very qualified partners in sailing and love are also the dual narrators of *Sabbatical*; Fenn and Susan, in fact, are about as *co-* as it gets. Theirs is a story of the his and her working beautifully in sync; their story and their life make headway through hisnher ordeals, hisnher dreams, hisnher flashbacks, hisnher stories-within-a-story, hisnher asides, hisnher footnotes. Their intra-marital dialogues ping and pong crisply with all the in-house compressions, ellipses, shortcuts, and alphabetic notations that supplement what goes without saying between well-conjugated, albeit "incestuous," twins. The rule of dual narration dictates that there shall be no I/thou, neither first-person nor second-person singular aboard the *Pokey II*; storytelling is in first-person plural or, when they hand the helm of story over to the author, third-person singular. Aimed for novelty as well as efficiency, these house rules produce a swinging narration of pronominal switcheroos, tense changeovers in midstream, buffered interruptions, and syntactical shortcuts—all of which the reader soon gets the hang and delight of. Between this couple of corroborating and collaborating co-sailors and co-narrators, reciprocity redounds, symmetry shimmers, synergy sings its songs.

Thus, *Sabbatical* does indeed read as a romance of "as if" equality between man and woman and as the literalization of that philosophy of metaphor discussed by Dunyazade and her shah ten years earlier. Barth probably knows that, in literalizing metaphor, he is turning to his active couple's advantage precisely the major problem of the true schizophrenic who is unable to distinguish the metaphorical from the literal and thus would understand a metaphorical expression like "jumping to a conclusion" only in the literal sense of a suicide leaping to his death from an open window. Indeed, the literalization of the fantastic and marvelous is responsible for much of the narrative action in Barth's book. But literalization, which is here the generalized transfer of trope to the subjective actions of life, is not thereby the troping of a trope *by* a trope; and for that reason, and because of Barth's special privileging of schizophrenia as twinship, *synergism* has been chosen over "literalization" as the trope of this phase. Permissibly, Barth has defined his schizophrenia through a mathematics of less-than-one and more-than-one, taking the divided or split self of the schizophrenic directly to the doubled or multiplied self, while evading the possibility of one. If JacknJill are indeed the whole body, then synergy, from the language of kinesiology, is an accurate trope for the cooperative and combined action of two muscles of that body working together. Synergism gets additional mileage as a postmodern trope from the language of pharmaceutics—"the joint action of agents which when taken together increase each other's effectiveness"—and from the language of theology—"the doctrine that the human will cooperates with the Holy Ghost in the work of regeneration."

If Barth's concerns had been merely autobiographical in *Sabbatical*, he could well have characterized the onebody of the couple as Mr. and Mrs.; but because his fix is in the foremost formalist, and because his formalism extends to the structuring of a career whereby each book hopefully is "pushing the same payload to Heaven," Barth needs at this phase the synergistic regeneration of the JacknJill for his structuration even more than he desires to celebrate the synergistic effectiveness of the MrandMrs. An author who is by nature a coupler and by literary preference a repeater, whose literal case is that of a doubled origin in the womb and at birth, will have to be reborn into his Second Revolution with a "sister" sidekick incestuously attached to himself through marriage, if he is to catch the *à deux* windfalls of language bestowed upon the schizophrenic more-than-one.

No other explanation, it seems to me, suffices so well as this structuralist one to justify the messy clutter of family with which Barth loads down his well-married couple. As dual narrators, Fenn and Susan are champs at the Aristotelian pacing of dramatic incident, "working in the exposition with our left hands as we go along" (*S*, 72) to insure that their hisnher story proceeds unimpeded. Yet even they are somewhat weighed down by their extensive, left-handed footnotes in the first chapter, through which the reader is introduced to the two colorful lines of descent that come together in this advantageously incestuous, marital alliance. The Turners are Fenn, an ex-CIA officer who has written an exposé of that agency and who is thinking of becoming a novelist once again; his old-time Marylander parents, Chief and Virgie; his ex-wife, Marilyn Marsh Turner; their son Orrin, a post-doc in molecular biology who, with his wife Julie, is about to make Fenn a grandfather; and above all, Fenwick's fraternal twin Manfred, a mysterious prince of darkness and the suave "Count" of high CIA intrigue, whereabouts presently unknown, his disappearance coinciding with that of his son Gus, last known to be engaged in an anti-CIA terrorist activity in Chile. Gus is likewise the son of the Gypsy-Jewish merry widow and crack businesswoman, Carmen B. Steckler: daughter of ancient Halvah, survivor of the pogroms and the camps; mother to Fenn's Susan, a bright young professor of American literature and creative writing, and to Susan's sororal twin Mimi, radicalized in the sixties and since freaked out in the aftermath of Iranian torture and multiple rapes. Carmen's Place, in the boozy Fells Point district of Baltimore, is a restaurant as accommodating as Alice's. It now houses Mimi's common-law lover, a refugee Vietnamese poet; and Carmen's new lover, the gypsy bartender, Dumitru (Do-Me-True).

No matter where one penetrates its tangled foliage, this is a family tree riddled with incest. But not to worry: This is not the tabooed relation universally suppressed by all cultures, not the serious incest between parent and child or siblings within a single line of biological descent. This is incest through marriage, culture itself having made the mess, a comic incest of inadvertent alliance, the very adventitiousness of which provokes all along the dynastic line only hokey and harmless variations on the theme, "I'm my own grandpa." Through his marriage to Susan, for instance, Fenn has become a brother-in-law to his mother-in-law, nephew to his twin brother, husband and "Virtual Uncle" to his wife and "Niece-in-Effect." Surely on this point Barth is using *Sabbatical* to pay merry homage to two of his most admired authors: Vladimir Nabokov of *Ada* and Gabriel García Márquez of *One Hundred Years of Solitude*. Nevertheless, Fenn and Susan are being played for higher stakes.

There is yet another way to characterize this alliance of twins, this incest through marriage. In Derridean terminology, it is the lateralization and literalization of the *doubled origin*. When Derrida, like Barth, reaches back to Aristophanes to correct the concept of a single origin or originary center, what he finds at that origin—in lieu of the "schizophrenia" Barth found through the mathematics of less-than-one and more-than-one—is *differance* (Derrida 1976). *Differance* is the wrecking ball that Derrida has deployed to bring down the house that Plato built, and from it depend other terms designed to scramble categorical thought—the *supplement*, the *copula*, the *hymen*—all of which terms are also implicated in conjugality (Derrida 1982). According to Derrida, there never has been the full presence of one, but always already a small, local difference that separated the one from itself, a spatial divergence within presence, a temporal delay and deferral within simultaneity—just as twins are never exact repetitions of each other, but are initially re-differentiated through the temporal interval of their delivery. *Differance* is minuscule, ephemeral like a gesture or glance, less solid than speech—something like what goes without saying between twins in the womb and afterward.

Moreover, Derrida rejects the motivation of absence that is supposed to drive Aristophanes' halved creatures into one another's arms. The supplement is not a reliable addition to a subtraction, but rather an exorbitant and excessive surplus that plays freely with the perspectives of every split and doubled self; what completes the copula of "to be" is always a *non*-essential predicate, the hot fudge sundae of metaphor and not the bread and butter of conceptual definition. Supplementarity never closes off or completes, but rather opens up to the more/less, neither/nor, both/and—to that in-betweenness figured forth, for instance, in the hymen. The hymen names neither virginity nor marriage. All it can "mean" in its alternative logic is the indeterminate play of syntax that invokes the interminable dialogue which repetition holds with difference. Barth's incestuous twins are not only bifid and (doubly) doubled, but they're asymmetrical too; thus the cozy *co-* of the copulating couple is going to have to be modulated throughout by the *con* inherent in any conjugality.

True to Derridean prediction, the not-so-happy Turners, each keeping silent about what should not go without saying, are already tipped toward difference. Fenn and Susan are at least one heartbeat away from each other. There is one hisnher secret unshared, a double omission on which the plot turns, a *differance* that makes all the difference. Barth offers these two heartbeats of *differance*, of the absence within presence, early in the book:

> You're my island, sleepy Susan murmurs, kissing her husband's chest. She lays her head briefly there in the salt-and-pepper fuzz, then sits up: to hear his heart beat breaks her heart.
> He kisses her lap. You're my cove. Puts an ear to her tidy belly as if to listen to a heartbeat there. (26)

For Fenn and Susan, the tragic view of love reduces to an irreversible inequality between their separate-but-equal parts, a temporal deferral and delay, a discrepancy in numbers: Fenn is fifty and Susan is thirty-five. The occasion of the voyage they have all but completed was Fenn's first heart attack, Susan's first ache over being childless, our indecision about what to do in the face of the above. So *co-* is fraternal twin Fenn that he even jots down his writer's notes in the form of dialogues with Susan, but about one ordeal he will remain wordless: He has had a second attack. So *co-* is sororal twin Susan that she survives a day out of Fenn's presence only shakily, yet her ordeal will likewise go without saying: She is pregnant. Reciprocally stalled between new life and near death, Fenn and Susan spend a week paddling around the Chesapeake, their sails luffing, reluctant to tie up to the mainslip and confront decisions that can no longer be postponed. Now, as at the beginning of their voyage, each has the same question, yet each has a private complication: Boyoboy, where do we go from here, and how the effing *how*?

Perhaps they might make headway by a lateralization toward the outside, by extending it out there to the world, to the unexpected lateral *co*llision between two discrete linear trajectories which in everyday life we call *co*incidence. Believing in "the voltage between two people, the pressure cooker of the single heart," Fenn also believes in the magic of coincidence for life and story, just as he has faith that, having lost his precious Basque beret for the third time in twenty years, his *boina* will return as it has twice before, at the efficacious moment when his trajectory and its coincide. Fenn also notes that when coincidence gets escalated into the uncanny, there is a literalization of the marvelous, and perhaps if their coincidental dream images were materialized on the outside, as phantasmatic images become concrete events, the literally marvelous might get our schizo-couple to dry land: "Realism is your keel and ballast of your effing Ship of Story, and a good plot is your mast and sails. But magic is your wind, Suse. Your literally marvelous is your mother-effing wind" (137).

It would seem that Fenn has a way with metaphor, and that, as above, metaphor can be easily and directly literalized for life and narrative. But in fact he has little interest and less talent for metaphor as decorative description, for the classical Aristotelian notion of metaphor as an ornament detachable from language. Fenn's failure with metaphor is demonstrated on his bus ride to Washington: "Indeed, when somewhere along Maryland 5 two Porsches pass the bus in quick succession, one the color of buttermilk and the other of tobacco, Fenn cannot summon up better adjectives for them than yellowish-white and brown, though the highway at the moment happens to divide a tobacco from a dairy farm" (138).

On the use of metaphor, Fenn and Susan are much closer to Vico's poetic primitives, to Claude Lévi-Strauss's "savage mind," to schizophrenics and children, for whom—in Terence Hawkes's words, well-chosen but out of context—"metaphor, in short, is not fanciful 'embroidery' of the facts. It is a way of *experiencing* the facts. It is a way of thinking and living; an imaginative projection of the truth. As such, it is at the heart of the 'made'" (Hawkes 1972, 39). Only the made-by-metaphor life makes life worth living; only an aesthetic existence, said Nietzsche, can justify life. The very distinction we make between the "literal" and the "metaphorical" is indeed available only in societies that have acquired the capacity for abstract thought; these oppositional categories are unavailable wherever thought is concrete. And what is more concrete than our couple's avocation of sailing, whose literalities can provide all kinds of metaphors for lovers and storytellers to re-literalize? "One is forever in fact making things shipshape from head to stern, getting under way, making headway, giving oneself leeway, taking a different tack, getting the wind knocked out of one's sails, battening down the hatches, making for any port in a storm, getting swamped or pooped, putting an anchor out to windward, enjoying a snug harbor" (162). For this couple, the lateralization of metaphor becomes a virtue only when it becomes invisible as rhetoric and is literalized in concrete action.

Like the doubled origin, like the married couple, metaphor is thus also a threshold site of *differance*, from which all our hard and fast categories of identities and oppositions will arise. Maybe Fenn and Susan are looking for too much perfection through their twinship advantage, two much sameness in their repetition-completion? Certainly Susan is making too much of the contraries they are, taunting Fenn with not only their divergent WASP and Jewish heritages, but with his Francis Scott Key (eighteenth century, Enlightenment, Apollonian, Mozart, tinkle-tinkle) versus her Edgar Allan Poe (nineteenth century, Romanticism, Dionysian, Beethoven, boom-boom). But comes now to the rescue that prize schizo and lightning rod of energized difference, that Apollonian Dionysiac, that moustached and cigar-smoking complement of a gypsy lover who wears the earrings in the house—Carmen B. Steckler. Perhaps the White Witch of Fells Point has some schizoid, differential counsel for our pooped lovers and their story?

She does. First there's an evening of *ca dao*, the oral folk poetry of the Vietnamese that puts special emphasis upon the form of its traditional rhyming couplet, the *luc bat*, in which "the 'male' and 'female' couplets are coupled like the couple: the poem is a loving, sportive sally between the 'truly wed' " (272). Carmen's kid and her husband should please notice that there never is exact rhyme and rhythm in repetition-completion, without the spacing and delay of *differance* making couplets and couples an affair of tangential, asymmetrical inclinations. Carmen's second narrative boost comes from her wholly "kerflooey" version of the facts of life: Our children are actually our grandchildren, our literal children being the sperm and eggs which each gender engenders asexually. Ergo, we are all merely "make-pretend" sexual, for only our sperm and egg "parents" achieved through sex the union of contraries that we humans can never achieve; and what Aristophanes should have said is that the search for our sundered half is motivated, not by lack and absence, but by our unconscious memory of being sexually conceived. Crazy like a fox, Carmen B. wants to console her daughter for not having had "grandchildren." She knows that her daughter never really wanted to have children—Susele's ideal of motherhood is so high as to be self-defeating—but *having* had them, she would be of the same grandparently age as Fenn, thus putting under erasure the temporal difference that presently plagues them.

Carmen's conceits get Fenn pondering the twin sets of dreams dreamt by these married partners of the dizygotic egg, all of which feature a geography of Y. In their coinciding dreams, Y is the literal site in the Chesapeake Bay where Fenn and Susan first became slightly incestuous lovers—at a Y where two channels converge into one or, alternatively, one channel diverges into two. But this dream site seems also to be a metaphor for the female anatomy: the twin fallopian tubes converging at the uterus for the Y at which sperm and egg meet. Susan's dream has her and her twin floating in water like two big, plastic eggs; Fenn's dream has him and the Turner man swimming madly upstream, as giant sperm resembling the paisley figures on his headscarf. Our unconscious discourses are apparently lateralizing and literalizing to make lots of headway; might not we in our married life seize upon an exorbitant supplement, an excess of metaphor, for this Y—and thus reliteralize what our dreams have metaphorized?

Fenn is so lost in his meditation upon its possibilities of play between life and dream that he hardly reacts to Susan's horrified confession: that on a past black Friday the thirteenth, she got herself not one abortion but two, that what the double schlup of the vacuum aspirator meant was that she had aborted *twins*! So, says the distracted Fenn, I had a second heart attack, we're even. But now nothing can save this doubled double-negative for reaffirmation except the literally marvelous, and thus our story "sails out of James Michener into Jules Verne": *Pokey*'s bow is crossed by the rolling hulk of "Chessie," Chesapeake Bay's own, often-sighted sea monster. In his scramble to get a photo, Fenn's *boina* replacement (the headscarf of paisley spermatozoa) goes overboard, their vessel reaches the go/no-go decision point at the Y of the channel marker, and Susan goes beserk: Everything is garbage—our story, kerflooeyhood, coupling—let's get a divorce. Leaping about in a frenzy (Omygod, thinks Susan, I've caused him his third), Fenn goes over the side and (the *co*-magic of Chessie getting up speed now) comes up like a "surfaced sea-god," topped with his "Sopping, Seaslimed *Boina*." The veils fallen from his eyes, Susan's twin of a husband orders the Dom Perignon from below, toasts Aristotle on coincidence, and heads the *Pokey* "for the crotch of the Y. The hub of the wheel. The place where three roads meet" (350).

And there the couple will dwell happily ever after. Fenn's Derridean illumination has been that at every Y with three legs there is a fourth possibility hidden from ordinary view. One need not go right, left, or backward; one may choose the intersection, the crossroads, the *chiasmus* itself, which "is not a matter of answers, or even a philosophical position: just a perspective. Our perspective" (360). Building their home at the site where all coincidences converge and thus literalizing the copula, the Turners will make their peace with the Nietzschean perspectivism that is the doubled origin of all metaphor—at the blank square, where "our house is our story is our child" can become the nonessential predicate, where "the thing that's both of us and neither of us" can celebrate the schizophrenia of the couple as the difference of numbers that are never prime, where life and script double themselves at the end just as they split themselves at the beginning: "The doing and the telling, our writing and loving—they're twins. That's our story" (365).

In order to get to the chiasmus where Fenn and Susan await him, Derrida likewise had to dispense with the *V* (the "crisis of Versus" endemic in Western conceptualization) and deconstruct the *Y* (the oedipal/Christian/Hegelian intersection where the three roads of the dialectic meet). The *X* of the chiasmus will then open the third side of the West's triangulated formulations to a fourth domain of possibility and indeterminacy where phenomena belong solely to perspective. Here is where the seed of the father is freed of the father, shattered and scattered in dissemination, in the prismatic, none-and-all perspectives of those who camp out at the chiasmus at the fruitful mercy of the wind and tides. Thus, *Sabbatical, A Romance* is like/as if *Of Grammatology, Writing and Difference*, *Positions*, and *Dissemination*.

This coincidence between our comic novelist and the father of deconstruction can be extended backward over all of Barth's literary production, demonstrating the interconnectedness in our contemporary times between creative making and nomad thinking. *The Floating Opera* is Barth's meditation on absence and presence, and his inquiry into the equivocal man of reason who seeks to master all equivocality. *The End of the Road* pits this integral man against a man of differance, whose multiplying perspectives seem adequate if disabling reflections of a cosmic ambivalence. *The Sot-Weed Factor* dilapidates the center and its continuities with the supplements from the circumference, placing *sous rature* both the history of the colonial seventeenth century and the literature of the English nineteenth century. *Giles Goat-Boy* features a hero of the in-between, a carrier of neither message nor code, who signifies nothing at all except the hymen/hinge upon which the various representations of his disciples and detractors will depend. *Lost in the Funhouse* is Barth's probing of several Derridean problematics—the presence-bearing illusion of the voice, the erring of the proper name, the origins of writing. *Chimera* introduces *differance* into the copula of metaphor, rendering myth and reality a Möbius strip and making the spiral a fourth option arising from the double session. With *LETTERS*, Barth fosters dissemination, disowning his textual progeny and turning them into Derridean traces of lost texts.

That Derrida's radical deconstruction can be mapped onto Barth's experimental fiction seems these days a coincidence more canny than un-. Even more than schizophrenia perhaps, lateralization opens to a problematics in these postmodern times that encompasses not only language (as metaphor), the psyche (as split and doubled), and gender relations (coupling), but also the cross-disciplinary study of all of these human areas. All knowledge is presently rearranging itself across the disciplines, and as each discipline tests the waters at its margins, it discovers that elsewhere an analogous domain is being traversed, in which discovery itself comes on the wings of analogy, homology, the isomorph.

The voyager without parallel among these spaces of knowledge is Michel Serres, whose *Hermes* (1982) is a sampling in English of the several numbered volumes under the same title in French. Serres might have disabused the Turners early on of the illusion of any easeful reciprocity between two distinct entities; the navigation is tricky enough to confound any optimism about direct lateralization. Heretofore, human thought has assumed that the space of knowledge was homogeneous, that the local was included in the global, that there was a clearly charted course from part to whole, that couplings could be essentially coupled. However, on Serres's map of knowledge there are only "heterogeneous spaces" and "regional epistemologies," which our professional discourses have isolated into little islands of local truths, each built from its own underlying presuppositions and none connected through an exact route of translation. On his voyage through the heterogeneous spaces of literature, science, and philosophy, Serres is guided by a single, fixed star of conviction: "The identity of a culture is to be read on a map, its identification card; this is the map of its homeomorphisms" (Serres 1982, 45).

Serres thus stands for the optimism of lateralization, but it is an optimism subdued and tempered by the warnings issued by deconstruction that insist on setting out from a doubled origin and not from a One. Over a lifetime of exploring these uncharted waters, and literalizing in brilliant applications across the disciplines the lateralizations of analogical thought, Serres has helped to draw that map, on which the following couplings, among many others, are seen to be homeomorphs: Turner's painting and Carnot's steam engine, Descartes' reason and La Fontaine's fables, Socratic dialogue and Pythagorean geometry, Michelet's historiography and the prebiotic soup. Serres's couplings run the range from mundane comparison through beautiful metaphor to shocking metalepsis, but any way he goes, it's analogy that gets him there. For the destination of knowledge, however, what counts—what ensures the time of arrival—is the threshold site itself.

Only by beginning from an entropic, heterogeneous totality—from a site like the hymen or the chiasmus, where in-betweenness is held in (irre)solution by maximum oscillations of repetition and difference—can thought sail on into the global. Otherwise, the inadequate premises/premisses at the origin of a homogeneous totality—a totality that permits no repetition without shame for its doubleness and no difference without hostility toward an alien singleness—will fling thought back to its impoverished localizations, where the likes of a Derrida will deconstruct it directly.

Furthermore, we should note that the homeomorphs of Michel Serres are not only reflections of each other's structure and function, but also refractions deflected back upon the one by the other, the message returning otherwise in the rhetorical inversion we call—after Lacan as well as Derrida—a chiasmus. Any coupling that occurs at this site, therefore, will be the lateralization between two familiars, each of whose discourse comes back to the other as a repetition with a difference, revealing the other as unfamiliar and unsettling. The fullness of knowledge that comes with this lateralization will always seem novel to most of us, for it is the gift of a totality that cannot be grasped by the normal search-and-seize procedures of Western reason; it happens out there at the limit where science ends and poetics begins, at the threshold site where Freud and Lacan have situated the relay station of psychoanalysis.

This "discourse of the Other" is the unconscious, and the unconscious is the one concept that Derrida has found to be inde(con)structible. He cannot deconstruct it because the unconscious marks an alterity, an alternating Otherness, that refuses to show itself under any process of representation. Its primary process thinking makes endless sport with substitution, doubling and coupling; it is all free play and indeterminacy—no stabilized identity, no contradiction, no cause and effect, no negation, and no revelation of presence. Therefore, whenever we try to represent the unconscious with the signifiers that honor these boundaries, it folds back on itself and escapes us. Derrida prefers the decentered and decentering unconscious of Lacan's description to Freud's unconscious, which over the years has acquired too firm a center in the Oedipus complex: not the unconscious at the Y, where the doubled parental heritage converges in the child, that single channel that will later bifurcate into normal or abnormal socialization; but the X of the unconscious, where the couplings of chains of oscillating difference and repetition merge the two-in-one and release an exorbitant surplus of human potential for both conflict and cooperation. Because this Lacanian unconscious is a site of irreducible *differance*, it is Derrida's unique untouchable.

Indeed, although it is lurking there in disguise all the while, the unconscious will receive but meager mention in the discourses of the three islands of knowledge we are about to sail to—the science of the split-brain, the technology of artificial intelligence machines, and the anthropology of handedness. Typically, our informants will speak of a much-to-be-desired coupling of the right and the left: but because they commence thinking with the assumption of a homogeneous totality in which each part is subservient to the whole, they end up with a concept of coupling as complementarity, whose single choice for active (male) dominance or passive (female) submission creates an impasse where a bridge should be. What occurs in gender relations then, rather than the schizophrenic two-in-one, is a splitting of the woman, despite the fact that she is always in the same place, into a moralized metaphor for what culture venerates on one hand and degrades on the other. It is no wonder that women want out of that angelic/demonic bind that becomes their reward or their punishment—having been denied equality, reciprocity, "twinshiphood"—for failing to fit complementarily into a totality defined as male. Within the homogeneous totality of the phallic signifier, there is only one gender (plus-or-minus male). Barth's answer to Lacan's charge of "hommosexuality" (after the French *homme*) is a coupling as reciprocity between a brother-husband and sister-wife, "peer companion(s) from the beginning." Fenn and Susan are Barth's post-structuralist experiment with the reciprocal sexual relation much rarer than the complimentary.

Voyaging now to heterogeneous spaces, we approach "the woman question" from the outside of its current confinement, and comprehend the schizophrenic totality of Barth's married and twinned couple through their negation in other, analogous domains where the homogeneous, organic ideal prevails. As we come to recognize everywhere the same dismal dénouement—the nonliteralization of the coupling ideal which follows upon the refusal of the less-than-one and the more-than-one—we will want to keep in mind that for Fenn and Susan, marriage is the hymen that hinges consciousness to the unconscious within the discourses—jokes, dreams, slips of the tongue—between significant others. When our informants speak of brain and hand, we are permitted to send back "psyche." As we thus tack against the wind, we will pick up some leeway, as the domains switch from head to hand, through an auspicious literalization in the human anatomy of the chiasmus, the X that marks the spot for both Derrida and Lacan. This is the "chiasma," the anatomical term for the site at the base of the brain where the optic nerves intersect and cross over each other, a crossing that ultimately connects the right hand to the "male" left brain and the left hand to the "female" right brain. In the subsequent assessments of "woman" by a culture that denies fortuitous reciprocity in gender relations, the woman will be at once denigrated as the left hand and sacralized as the right brain, showing herself to be the demon of disorder that we take the unconscious to be.

What scientists tell us is that there is a certain division of labor in the processing of information by the brain, a functional bifurcation in which the left hemisphere processes verbal input, and the right, non-verbal. Because hemisphere specialization is unique to human maturity, found in neither other primates nor the human infant, the researchers have concluded that hemispheric difference is attributable to the acquisition of language. Within this couple that is the mature human brain, there is maximum differentiation: The left brain, the locale of our speech centers, is verbal, analytic, rational, reductivist, sequential, time-oriented, and discontinuous; the speechless right brain is nonverbal, visual-spatial, holistic, synthetic, intuitive, timeless, and diffuse. There is, nevertheless, a maximum of communication and cooperation between the two less-than-ones, made possible by a bridge that connects them, the *corpus callosum*, a conductor route that looks even more like an *X* than like two *Y*'s connected at their stems. For full mentalization each hemisphere must complement the other, lift it up and out, save it from its own inadequacies: The right brain of itself would never solve a problem, resolve a conflict, or make a decision, were not the left brain to seize the function of making these rational closures; the Cartesian left brain would be at the mercy of its premises and programmed sequences, were not the right brain offering it alternative patterns and multiple perspectives in order to reorient it down a new path. No doubt about it: Two brains, all four halves working together, are better than one for synergistic effectiveness.

But such total collaboration is not easy to obtain, as no one knows better than Allan Newall, creator of a sophisticated thinking-machine called SOAR (Newall, 1985). The problem for Newall as an artificial-intelligence simulator is not how to get cooperation between two entities of such oppositional difference as the left and right brain; he can build into his computer simulation of human thought all kinds of *corpora collosa*. Newall's problem is with the right brain itself, which he redefines in a significant opposition to the left: Our brains are undifferentiated on the right, differentiated on the left. The left ("male") brain displays specific, complex structures and performs sequential, digitalized operations that can be easily duplicated by computer technology; not so the right ("female") brain, which is a vast area without structure and with functions that are elusively open and unbounded, an area devoid of the hardware and software components directly imitable by computer models of artificial intelligence.

In the mental environment of SOAR, the right brain brings "a knowledge of the whole" to the tunnel-visioned left—a knowledge, granted, that must be called the "universal weak method" when contrasted to the brute power of the left's problem solving and means/ends analysis. However, Carmen's kids should please notice that, although it must eventually turn over its possible other wholes to the "decision cycle" of the left, the right brain is a long-term memory bank of pattern recognition, and its "elaboration phase" of unfamiliar and heterogeneous totalities is crucial to thought that is not to be a stale repetition of old equations. It is only through the inclusion and cooperation of the right brain (unconscious, "woman") with the left brain (consciousness, "man") that "modulations of the total environment" can be effected. The more that the right brain sounds like the unknown but all-knowing subcontinent of the psyche we call the unconscious, the more that Newell's successful SOAR sounds like a successful psychoanalytic excavation of it, and the more it confirms Serres's threshold site and Derrida's doubled origin.

But once this success story tries to repeat itself outside in culture, it fails utterly, for culture refuses reciprocity and fosters hostility even between such exact repetitions as mirror images, the right and left hands. Before we ever got inside the brain, anthropologists knew that throughout primitive culture a similar disvaluation of the right brain occurs which, in the chiasmic crossover that connects the right brain to the left hand, lumps them both together in opprobrium. From the pioneering essay by Robert Hertz in 1909 (Needham 1973, 9–31) to the recent structuralist analyses of Claude Lévi-Strauss, anthropological research has confirmed split-brain research, while significantly failing to accord any *co-* status to the two hands or two brains. In pre-literate cultures—as interpreted by left-brain dominated researchers from a left-brain dominant culture—the mirror-image right and left hands are almost universally unequal; and grounded in this inequality are all our pervasively dual symbolic systems of classification and organization in which the right hand (left brain) is all that is good, high, and inside while the left hand (right brain) is bad, low, outside. Those long lists of the binary oppositions that stabilize primitive man's social organizations offer overwhelming evidence that for the savage mind the left is the side of the uninitiated, uncooked, polluted, junior, subordinate, weak, small, passive, difficult to control, wild, dark, deathlike—of the woman, the woe-man.

Nor can we congratulate ourselves that this prejudice marks a discontinuity between our culture and theirs. Geoffrey Lloyd reminds us in a stunning essay (Needham 1973, 167–86) that the primitive preference for the right-handed was carried over into Greek philosophy through the science of Aristotle, who inherited the bias from the Pythagorean Table of Opposites, where the male right and light is opposed to the female left and dark. More than any of his contemporaries, Aristotle made himself familiar with broad varieties of biological behavior, and experimented under laboratory conditions with the internal and external organs of animals. Nevertheless, when push came to shove, when dogmatic belief was discomfited by empirical results, Aristotle went to enormous lengths to make his laboratory results conform with his ideological bias for the right. Aristotle is probably best known in this area for his efforts to prove that gender is determined by the right (male) or left (female) testicle, or by the right or left side of the womb. For myself, I like to imagine his embarrassed distaste at discovering that the very pump of life, the heart, was located interspatially on the *left* side of the body. Lloyd offers an amusing account of the elaborate, irrational ruses by which Aristotle explained away this appallingly perverse placement on the left: First, he had to posit, outside of any investigative results for support, a bilateral heating system for the body, in which the left was lesser by the un-virtue of being colder; then, he had to attribute to an intentional left side the teleological need for a heart to warm it up!

Nor can we consign Aristotle's ruse to the rubbish bin of medical quackery, for some version of it is still with us, surfacing whenever any trained scientist or social scientist has failed to check for the subjective machinations that underpin his assumedly "objective" analyses. This can happen to an anthropologist as renowned as Rodney Needham, to whom we are already indebted as the editor of the seminal collection of essays referred to above, *Right and Left: Essays on Dual Symbolic Classification* (1973). Even Needham can be seen to stammer when he must account for the leftness of the Mugwe, who is the supreme religious dignitary among the Meru of Kenya. Elsewhere in their symbolic organizations the Meru are resolute observers of right/high and left/low distinctions, but here is their Mugwe: a holy man whose left hand is the source of all sacred power and tribal veneration, who is always robed in the black of the profaned left, who must passively wait to be asked in marriage by the subordinate, the polluted, the wild-card woman.

Concerned to rationalize the exception, Needham argues that this leftness effects a humbling of spiritual authority (the spiritually high Mugwe must bow down to the political headsman, after all, just like everybody else in the tribe)—an argument that ignores additional field data which would corroborate leftness as the source of a holy man's sacralization by the tribe. The Mugwe's leftness is, in fact, a manifestation of the sacred that is generalized throughout tribal cultures. Among the Ngaju of South Borneo the religious functionaries are often women, but when men assume that function, they also assume female status; among the Chukchi of Siberia, the holy man adopts a woman's hairstyle, wears woman's dress, undertakes woman's tasks, and may even "change sex" by taking a husband and claiming to give birth to children (Needham, 109–26).

Ultimately, Needham's blindness comes with his being a supreme product of left-brain culture, which activates only three possible models for dealing with two: The two are infused with sameness, as in copies and mirror images; or they are binary opponents, modulating from hostile reciprocity to dominant-submissive complementarity; or they can be uplifted, surpassed, transumed, *Aufhebung*ed into a third, synthetic unity. But the boundary-adoring left brain will not see the fourth possibility that the boundary-blind right brain adores: that the Mugwe is, in his himnher self, a couple at the crossroads, where the left-brain choices for both/and, either/or, or a synthesis of repetition and difference do not pertain. Only *neither/nor*, the repudiation of all boundaries, occurs at the chiasmus.

Preliterate man does indeed dump everything he doesn't understand and which therefore terrifies him on the unbounded right brain and the sinister left hand, but his thinking takes an additional right-brained turn that most Western researchers fail to recognize or participate in: Its common unboundedness and undifferentiation assures that what the savage mind relegates to the profane, it will simultaneously venerate as the sacred. That the violent and the sacred are tied to a single two-in-one entity is the post-structuralist discovery of René Girard, whose studies on the doubleness of the scapegoat and on the triangularity of desire are brilliant implementations of that initial insight. But what we want to retain just now is the place of the sacred for primitive man: Sacralization occurs only at the chiasmic conjunction of left and right. If we take our twinned, married couple as a manifestation of the single Mugwe, and venerate that coupling as a heterogeneous totality of repetition and difference held in irresolution, it is because thereby all that culture has symbolically designated as "lower" now enjoys "as if" equal status with the "higher." The right brain, the unconscious, and the female have been lifted up through the fourth possibility at the chiasmus.

One can comprehend why such a solution is alien to a feminist politics that distributes its resolutions across the first three possibilities. The hard-core lesbians, like their counterparts among gay males, advocate a relation of sameness, which excludes the *differance* of half the living human world and eschews opposite-sex lateralization. The unhappily sexed androgynists, holding to the Mugwe ideal of the two-in-one realized in a single self, cannot literalize their fantasy of difference in a nonhermaphroditic body. The mainline militants ascribe so much difference to the other gender that it hardly seems they could be in the same pot with men, even though it is the pot that culture stirs to the mutual disadvantage of both sexes. Thus feminist militancy blinds itself to the "love" part of the love/hate relation, inconvenient to gender politics, in all "marriages" that create a heterosexual, rather than a *hommesexual*, totality. And whenever they advocate role reversals between men and women, feminists reinscribe women into the patriarchal totality, thereby revictimizing themselves as mirror-image repetitions without ever disturbing, and possibly enhancing, the prevailing structures of duality.

Women themselves do not have the answer, any more than men themselves do, and neither is Woman the answer. Poetry and magic are always threshold phenomena that happen between two at the chiasmus, in metaphoric exchanges that supplement sexual difference with an exorbitant "as if" equality. If I have offered John Barth's homey celebration of the well-wed couple as *corpus callosum*, as the in-betweenness where the rare, ambidextrous couple can practice *ad hoc* subversions of the antagonistic limits set by a left-brained culture—I do not then expect an immediate and widespread cultural turnaround, thanks to a few scattered couples who, two by two, hop on the ark and sail off into the cultural unknown. This is not one of the short-term gains of a politics of women's liberation; indeed, coupling, as Barth has written it and I have interpreted it, suggests that "liberation" is the wrong word entirely. There may be more drastic and direct rebellions against cultural dominance, but what recommends the model of the couple-as-opposite-sex-twins is its availability and normalcy as a lifetime experiment in cultural evasion and—with the letting-out-of-the-closet of the right brain and the psychoanalytic unconscious—in self-awareness.

The right brain and the unconscious may not be empowered to say the "no" of socialized man, but they have a corner on the "why not?" of the gods of creation. Within their processes, where similarity encounters difference with neither vanquishing the other, lies a grand opportunity to counter the dogmatisms of the left brain and to make a lively totality of what has been kept hostilely separated. Lateralization is the strongest defense we have against the high tech of the left-brain; nevertheless, it is a troping, not by the right brain, but by synergistic collaboration. Right-brained, we all become analogical thinkers and poets of metaphoric relation, letting desire out of its cavern and releasing creativity from the nightmare hours of dream, content to let the antagonisms of gender politics proceed without us.

That the right brain, the unconscious, and woman can bring on the metaperspectives of a god—an artist obsessed with and smart about

patterns, plans, models, maps, grand designs, overarching purposes—
is attested to in the "birthing" of *Sabbatical, A Romance*. Before *Sabbatical*, Barth was at the chiasmus, in the same position as Fenn and Susan
at the end of their novel. At its inception, the new Perseus and his new
Medusa were snug in their new home on the Maryland shore, a home
perched on a point where a river forks Y-like into two branches. As he
describes it to his interviewer, pre-*Sabbatical* Barth had an exorbitant
surplus on his hands, two writing projects instead of one: this novel,
and a television play from the perspective of an egg in transit, occa-
sioned by the coincidence of his daughter's pregnancy with his own
public readings of "Night-Sea Journey."

What Barth did next represents the windfall of "us" and the first-
person plural. His act would certainly earn the applause of Michel
Serres, whose significant supplement to Western knowledge inheres in
the copula of his conviction that, sitting or sailing, "the wise man *is* the
basic world," a resolute materialist who avoids the violent idealisms of
politics and history by sticking with the world and its geography. What
does our armchair navigator do in his house at the chiasmus, upon
contemplating the gift of his cup-runneth-over? He picks up a map. It
is a map of Chesapeake Bay, and once Barth locates their own spot on
the map, the right brain, the unconscious, and woman take over the
helm and creatively negotiate the difficult passage between the heterogeneous islands of fertilization and geo-graphy, the birth at once of life
and writing: "I was struck by the fact that it (our spot) looks like
nothing so much as two fallopian tubes conjoining in a uterus. And
there I sit—serendipity!—working on a plot where I have two eggs
coming down, about to encounter a spermatozoa . . . and my next novel
is going to have to wait until the story is finished" (Reilly, 21–22).
Barth's sequentially ordered left brain was wrong about that; *co*incidence had its day and say, and the novel didn't wait to be born. But it
retained its birthmark in the local metaphor from which it grew into a
global construct of literalized and lateralized repetition and difference.

Somewhere, I would like us to imagine, a Mugwe is smiling in
approval—at seeing, finally, a coupling for the long run.

Chapter 9
The Tidewater Tales (1987):
Conjugality's Cartography

Image	*Trope*	*Defense*	*Ratio*
The Nomads	Anadiplosis	The Refrain	Chaosmos

Barth's ninth novel was warmly welcomed by the reviewers, who regarded it as a showcase exhibit of the "literature of replenishment" that Barth had foreseen on the postmodern horizon in 1980, a buoyant literature to be distinguished from modernist fiction by its accessibility and from contemporary metafictions of exhaustion by its thick content of "aboutness." "Without question the richest, most ebullient and technically daring of any novel he has hitherto written," said the *Washington Post Book World*; ". . . probably the only piece of experimental fiction that can double as summer reading," said the *Library Journal*; "Barth has never been more engaging, nor more engaged in his narrative complications," said the *New York Times Book Review*. So engaging was Barth, in fact, that his reviewers failed to remark that the more ravishing *Tidewater Tales* was a replay of *Sabbatical, A Romance*. Barth had said back in 1980 that, as it was with good jazz and classical music, so would it also be with a literature of replenishment: "One finds much on successive listenings or close examination of the score that one didn't catch the first time through; but the first time through should be so ravishing—and not just to specialists—that one delights in the replay" (*FB*, 203–4).

In this instance, it is Barth himself who has closely examined "the first time through" in *Sabbatical* and made an *end-run* (italicized to signal its schizo literality) around his eighth novel with his ninth. Yes indeed, there is once again a happily married couple who sail for two weeks, without itinerary or destination, around a Chesapeake Bay afloat with literary marvels and CIA intrigue, and return to shore more soundly wed than when they left. But this is a repetition with a replenishing difference, "the repetition of an end at the next beginning" which, despite the forbidding clutch of syllables in its Greek name, is a nomad trope that names nothing more foreboding than a sequel that is a non sequitur: *án-a-di-pló-sis*.

Before we consider Barth's replenishing tropological strategy, however, we must confront the subject of Barth's book, what its aboutness is about. With only one novel about wedded bliss, we could perhaps have evaded the issue, but with this couple of doubles of the couple, we are impelled to note that happy matrimony is just about the only theme prohibited to the novel—a threshold perhaps to be anticipated but never to be crossed, stigmatized in the aura of the dead-end, a tabooed representation that must not appear if the novel is to have any dramatic life at all. It is a truth universally recognized: "Happily ever after" may be the perfect ending for a fairy tale, but it must never begin a novel. If Kitty and Levin thrive in the married state, they do so as a sideshow luxury Tolstoy permitted himself after responsibly writing in the necessarily adulterous affair between Anna and Vronsky as his novel's main show; the well-wed have never managed to hold center stage on their own two pairs of feet. Even as Barth is an intrepid recycler, he is a plotter and pacer without peer, and he cannot be unaware of the sound dramaturgical reasons for excluding the happily married from novelistic fiction: Nothing happens, moves, changes, or makes a big bang in the future assured by matrimony. Most marriages are not becomings or discoveries for either partner, but rather steady states of conjugality—a territory of two that has been thickened, made sluggish, and locked into rigid segments by those various recodings and reterritorializations of the State which bind the couple to the hard rock of the strata.

These objections are advanced not by John Barth, however, but by Gilles Deleuze (well-wed philosopher) and Félix Guattari (militant antipsychiatrist) in their two volumes that treat capitalism as the disease, and schizoanalysis and nomadology respectively as the cure, *Anti-Oedipus* (1983 [1971]) and *A Thousand Plateaus* (1987 [1980]). Deleuze and Guattari come down hard on marriage because the nuclear family is the prime target and locus for capitalist recoding, the nefarious and ubiquitous capture of all codes by which capitalism sustains its global triumphs. Just at the paranoid logic of late capitalism created the form of bureaucratization to recode the sphere of production and the forms of advertising and mass-marketing to recode the sphere of consumption, so also did Freud, capitalism's henchman of the psyche, invent psychoanalysis to recode the sphere of human desire. Freud's Oedipus is a paranoid construct intended to confine desire to the meager and boring cartography of "I want to sleep with my mother, I want to kill my father." Many distant domains on culture's map have been colonized by capitalism according to this two-step logic of decoding and recoding: first, the rampant elimination of all preexisting multiple meanings and partial codes; second, the relentless round-up of everything into the large, paranoid masses of crowd control. Historically, conjugality has been a con of the State, which seeks to annex marriage as one of its official territories to the great molar aggregates of religion, economics, law, and social custom. It is because of capitalism's expertise at reterritorialization, Deleuze and Guattari argue, that marriage is so often a "bad line," conned into treading the molar line of well-defined segmentations within the striated space preferred by the State, which can then bind these well-articulated and firmed-up segments to the other paranoid aggregates of its strata.

Nevertheless, there is hope for even the most well-conjugated of couples. Schizoanalysis rejects the definition of desire as oedipal lack and limit promoted by psychoanalysis and engineered by social systems of representation, and retrieves a truly molecular unconscious where authentic, schizophrenic desire puts itself in immediate and unmediated connection with part-objects, tries them out and tries them on in a workshop of desire that bears no resemblance to the classical oedipal theater with its rigid stick-figures of Daddy, Mommy, and Me. Seeking a society that would least contradict this logic of the unconscious—in the diplomatic phrasing of Eugene Holland's very perceptive essay on the *Anti-Oedipus* (1986, 293)—schizoanalysis recommends a "better line," the molecular line of supple segmentarity, and a "best line," the unsegmented, nomadic line of creative flight, by which conjugality, hooking up with an outside, might enter into becomings of its own, and thus become a fit, even ravishing, object of novelistic representation.

Deleuze and Guattari in *A Thousand Plateaus* demonstrate the literary-critical use of schizoanalysis through the Henry James novella, "In the Cage," a title appropriate to their definition of State marriage, yet a story that also points out the line of escape from its confinements:

The heroine, a young telegrapher, leads a very clear-cut, calculated life proceeding by delimited segments: the telegrams she takes one after the other, day after day; the people to whom she sends the telegrams; their social class and the different ways they use telegraphy; the words to be counted. Moreover, her telegraphist's cage is like a contiguous segment to the grocery store next door, where her fiancé works. Contiguity of territories. And the fiancé is constantly plotting out their future, work, vacations, house. Hence, as for all of us, there is a line of rigid segmentarity on which everything seems calculable and foreseen, the beginning and end of a segment, the passage from one segment to another. Our lives are made like that: Not only are the great molar aggregates segmented (States, institutions, classes), but so are people as elements of an aggregate, as are feelings as relations between people; they are segmented, not in such a way as to disturb or disperse, but on the contrary to ensure and control the identity of each agency, including personal identity. The fiancé can say to the young woman, Even though there are differences between our segments, we have the same tastes and we are alike. I am a man, you are a woman; you are a telegraphist, I am a grocer; you count words, I weigh things; our segments fit together, conjugate. Conjugality. A whole interplay of well-determined, well-planned territories. They have a future, but no becoming. (1987 [1980], 195)

For our two anarchist thinkers, the significance of James's story is that the heroine effects a sort of escape from the molar through the molecular line, a line on which "a present is defined whose very form is the form of something that has already happened" (196), something that travels too fast for ordinary perception, but can be caught on the wing by switching one's attention from the macrolevel to the microlevel, where schizzes and their part-objects fly free of the large molar aggregates. One day a deterritorializing male customer enters her couple-domain from the outside, and the telegraphist begins "a nonlocalizable passional relation" with him, as with a hallucinated double or a schizophrenic peer. Although the micropolitics between them in James's story cannot rival the micropolitics of Barth's well-charted couple, it does allow for the materializing of a phantasy as an event, and it points us forward to the techniques of evasion that might yet make of marriage an adventure *à deux*.

Unlike Derrida, who dilapidates philosophical thought by placing its firmest concepts (such as inside and outside) *sous rature*, Deleuze and Guattari—with Nietzsche as their mentor in all these matters—hang thought on the outside, insisting that no theory has value unless it is also a practice that issues in politically effective interventions in the real world. Derrida's intensive, programmatically irregular thinking is essentially a task of destruction—little traps baited with D-Con set all around to catch the big rats—but Derrida is no pragmatist or materialist. Deconstruction may herald the end of Western metaphysics, but it remains a discourse of philosophy.

As an example of their difference, we might briefly consider the nomadic strategy of Deleuze's early book, *Différence et répétition* (1969). Deleuze's critique follows Derrida's in their mutual anti-Platonism: The West's concept of homogeneous unity consigns repetition to a weakness or deficiency within representation (the copy, simulacrum, replica) and deploys difference as the contradiction or opposition within this unity. But from the outside of representation, nomadic repetition and difference are positive concepts that signify the diversities excluded and the multiplicities unacknowledged by the inside system organized toward exact resemblance in the perfect adequacy of word and thing. Deleuze's discourse deals with the materiality of incorporeal things—with phantoms, idols, simulacra and their angles, flashes, membranes, and vapors—that Deleuze insists must participate in any "unity of the multiple," in any heterogeneous concept of the totality. By encouraging the "small talk" from either side that Plato excluded, Deleuze has articulated, in Michel Foucault's assessment,

a philosophy of the phantasm that cannot be reduced to a primordial fact through the intermediary of perception or an image, but that arises between surfaces, where it assumes meaning, and in the reversal that causes every interior to pass to the outside, and every exterior to the inside, in the temporal oscillation that always makes it precede and follow itself—in short, in what Deleuze would perhaps not allow us to call its "incorporeal materiality." (Foucault 1980, 169)

If Foucault anticipates Deleuze's distaste for the currently fashionable oxymoron, which is the fate of all binary oppositions when put under erasure by Derrida, it is because he knows that Deleuze, above all, wants his own diagrammatics to be "a decentering for the people." As the absolute pragmatists of theory, Deleuze and Guattari mean their proliferating metaphors to be functional; the nomad, the schizo, the rhizome, the refrain are all metaphors of what has not yet been thought by the Western mind, and they are made for the active use of the little guy in the post-ironic, intent upon making a life in the enclaves indiscernible to the paranoid vision of global capitalism. The "nihilism" attributed to these two French thinkers by their detractors is, in fact, a positive retrieval of the connective procedures of the small and multiple that never got on the maps of the West; their anarchy is an affirmation of the right of the people to trade in their cultural ready-mades for a home-made life.

Looking for the difference within the repetition of Barth's two-in-a-row (and thereby getting a preview of how *anadiplosis* works its magic), we find it in this divide between Derrida and Deleuze, between an antiphilosophy and a positive pragmatics: It is the difference between making an accurate map and fully occupying a domain. We recall that a map figured in the scene of *Sabbatical*'s origin: Barth sitting in his armchair in the house at the chiasmus, fingering a map and marveling at the analogy between the Chesapeake Bay's geography and the female's reproductive anatomy. Whereupon Barth's fertile right brain went mad for the map, overlaying his couple with pattern and symmetry, twinning and doubling, and over-relying upon the coincidences of metaphor to carry the multiple to this marriage. But sometime in the five years intervening, Barth must have translated the "as if" philosophy of metaphor into the "can-do" action of metonymical metalepsis, for *The Tidewater Tales* reads like the materialization in fiction of Deleuze and Guattari's palimpsest of motifs.

We might even imagine a scene of origin for the book, as Deleuze and Guattari storm the pre-*Tidewater* study of our armchair navigator: Drop that Rand-McNally, abandon all tracing and copying concepts, practice nomad geography. Map with your sails, not your mind; forget incorporeal premises and take heed of corporeal premises. Get off your butt, cautiously cast off your moorings one after another, and go sailing on the smooth space of the primal soup. Make marriage a vector of changing longitudes and latitudes, turn speech into speed, deterritorialize your home refrain, open it to change, form temporary assemblages with the outside. Heed chance and convergence, develop drift as well as speed, prolong and relay the supple and nonsegmented lines of flight. Enjoy weightlessness and transformation. In each instance subtract the value of a concept and disperse metaphor throughout the vibrating plane of consistency. Materialize the phantasm in the event—have an affair with one of your fictional characters, fix another up with some women of your party, invite a couple of others over for cocktails on shipboard. Eventually, when enough outside passes to your inside and vice-versa, your marriage will connect up with the cosmos, which, despite our biases toward manipulable order, is a *chaosmos*; reterritorialize and recode that chaotic cosmos—and welcome home, again.

Whereupon Barth might have asked his phantasmatic visitors the same question he asked himself in his self-introduction to *The Friday Book*, a question—*Can* you go home again?—whose answer—yes and no—implies that there can be no repetition without difference. Barth's model is Odysseus tied to the mast but with his ears wide open, drinking in the sirens' wail of molecular desire that was meant to override the king of Ithaca's molar plans for returning home to Penelope and the conjugal state. Barth's Odysseus is never again the same man he was before hearing that siren call: "It goes without saying that what the original sirens sang to that canny other sailor must have been something like 'You can't go home again,' and that that song ain't so very far from wrong. As with Heraclitus' man standing by the river, into the same which he cannot step twice, it isn't only the Home that changes, but the You, too, and so you can't and you can" (*FB*, 12).

Whereupon Deleuze and Guattari would give our author an A plus and a bon voyage, although they might have preferred a rephrasing that brought the question closer to their home ground: Can I sing our old *refrain* again? In *A Thousand Plateaus*, our homeboys' plateau of the refrain (310–50)—even better in French as *ritournelle*—immediately precedes the plateau on nomadology. Before the reader follows the deterritorializations of these extra-territorial nomad-wanderers over land and sea, he or she must first learn, as Barth obviously did, how a territory is built up and how a couple might occupy it.

In its broad definition, the refrain refers to "any aggregate of matters of expression that draws a territory"; it is the mark that makes the territory, the mark properly of a domain, not of a subject—as an author's "signature" marks a body of work as his refrain-domain, or as a couple with an insider language between them delimits the site of an abode. Originally the whole earth—so our lesson in the nomadic history of geography goes—was smooth space like our present deserts and oceans, a body without organs, a plane of consistency holding together heterogeneities without consolidating or conjugating them, a thousand plateaus of vibrating and volatile intensities in open equilibrium, a chaosmos. In between this chaos and the thick strata that will later belt the earth are the milieus constituted in the periodic repetition of rhythmic components, whose vibrations threaten chaos with order. Rhythm is the milieu's answer to chaos, a difference that is produced by repetition and takes flight as the refrain, its sonority (now in the strict definition) marking in the biological world the first territorial assemblage that establishes the critical distance between two beings of the same species. It is when the milieu components become dimensional rather than directional, when they become expressive and not functional, that there is territory. As rhythm builds a consistency through consolidation and capture of motifs and counterpoints, its melodies are harmonized to draw a circle and organize a space that is home. This is territorialization.

Sabbatical, A Romance is Barth's book of the territorializing refrain of marriage, the hisnher refrain that marks out a domain of two, that captures the sailing motifs from the milieu and makes them consist, that tries out counterpoints and varies them ("It goes without saying"), that consolidates the interior ("In our house, the rule is—"), that thickens the modality and tonality through advantageous conjugation (dialogue and duet, the dual)—until marriage as a domain is brought from mark to signature to style, and becomes the sign of the natal, of all that is native to this exclusive distribution of space called home (Deleuze and Guattari 1987, 318–19).

The refrain, however, is not dogmatic, as Deleuze and Guattari are quick to point out. It neither codes nor controls milieus, but rather changes them by taking them as it found them. And the refrain itself can be laid hold of and deterritorialized, swept away by the abstract machine of music or voice itself; it is not only the listener who can be carried away by music, but also the songbird himself (331). When this happens, the refrain becomes a strong *de*territorializing force, putting the assemblage of two into connection *with* an outside rather than conjugating it *against* an Outside. Wherever there is passage, there is rhythm, but now the refrain's "matters of expression" are superseded for a functional "material of capture," as densities, intensities, tensors, and traits are seized from the plateaus of continuous variation and held at the highest level of relativity, opening the assemblage all the way up to chaosmos, which is the great deterritorialized refrain itself (326–27). Every passage through rhythm is a transcoding that carries the surplus value of a new plane of consistency, and when all localization is left behind, the assemblage will *re*territorialize itself on the cosmos ("to wed the cosmos") and make of that "marriage" something that carries the valence of home.

The Tidewater Tales is Barth's book of the deterritorializing refrain, his rewrite of that same old song, his going home again to a duet that now opens itself to the outside. Only now is the claustrophobia of *co*-recognized; *Sabbatical*'s Fenn and Susan truly had no outside, except as it brought to the *co*llaboration of the *co*uple, in metaphorical match-up, everything that could make them even *co*zier in their *co*habitation. For all the flexibility they built into the we-ness of their first-person plural, there was none that would allow for evolving and experimenting with an outside; and one could perhaps predict that, five years later, this fictionally perfected couple would sail into the doldrums and horse latitudes of a steady future short on becomings. Barth was not wrong in *Sabbatical* about marriage: It *is* a territory for two that has to be won and held and continually "adroited up" by a couple as spirited and intelligent as Fenn and Susan. But he does seem to have been wrong about what's outside a good marriage: It is not a map on which a stabilized stratification is already articulated, but rather an expanse of smooth space that must be followed and its quanta of deterritorialization explored, by a couple who keep their equilibrium open to conjunctive and disjunctive becomings.

In *Tidewater* there's a new ship called *Story*, and over its side goes all that *co*-cargo meant to enhance the couple in their isolation, which made the *Pokey* such a heavy-laden vessel: no more twins and doubles, no more dual narration, no more Jewish Stecklers and WASP Turners, no more convenient coincidences of sea monsters and ghosts and returning *boinas*, no more allegory and metaphor for their own sake and the couple's. Barth has traded in the copula for the heterogeneous rhythms of a marital future that is not all sewn up but sailing into the winds of chance and change—a copula barely to be discerned, *sous rature*, between *Tidewater*'s two subtitles: "Our House's Increase"

"Where the Wind Listeth." This is to inflect conjugality through its temporal tenses, to modulate from noun to verb, from a state of being to the ongoing of becoming, where repetition and difference are caught up with each other in the asignifying breaks and flows that consist in smooth space. Marriage, then, on the flow model.

Nor does the critic have to call upon intuition and inference to render visible the implicit in these matters; a very pragmatic Barth has written *Sabbatical* into *Tidewater* as an object of explicitly adverse literary criticism. Barth has recycled Fenn and Susan, with all their history intact, as Franklin and Leah Talbott, one of the several satellite couples in *Tidewater*, whose good ship *Reprise* ties up to the *Story* of our new couple, Katherine Sherritt and Peter Sagamore. The Sagamores and Talbotts agree: Frank/Fenn's first novel of the couple was "long-faced confessional melodrama," the very kind of inclined-to-whine auto-biographical realism that John Barth deplores. An ex-CIA agent like Fenn, Frank is great at real-life exposé but woefully incapable of artistic invention. His book—entitled *Reprise*, but sounding *Sabbatical*—was unconstrainedly mimetic and political; so appalled was he by the Company's covert operations that, in Peter's words, he committed "that apprentice error of allowing the Agency to appear in his story because it seemed to have appeared in his life" (414).

Even though the heavy reality of CIA intrigue is going also to intrude in this book of Barth's reinvention of the couple—it is largely responsible for Peter's abject silence as a writer and the couple's fears about bringing children into such a world—Barth immediately gets busy plugging up any holes of autobiographical entry that might lead back to Jack and Shelly Barth. There are no easy autobiographical doubles of that couple in *Tidewater*. When Kathy directly introduces her handsome husband to the reader—"He wears no moustache, beard, or eyeglasses"—she is denying him the three identifying characteristics of John Barth, there for all to see in the contemporary photograph on the back cover of his 1984 *Friday Book*. In fact, some of the book's funniest comedy lies in the stark opposition between the author and his hero on the matter of writer's block. Unlike Barth himself, who with the best of resolutions can't ever make it short and simple, Peter Sagamore is suffering from "prolific superminimalism," so cursed by his "happy fits of abbreviation," practiced as the "art of everdiminishing fiction" under the slogan "Less is More," that his latest work has been reduced to the "ultimate kenosis": He has eliminated all of it, even its already stripped-clean title, $B\flat$. Moreover, there is to be no tragic pathos or pathetic self-pity for the childlessness of a June/September marriage. The Sagamores are of an age: Peter is 39 years and eight-and-a-half months old, Katherine is thirty-nine years old and eight-

and-a-half months pregnant. The poetic task that she sets for her husband is clearly corrective of *Sabbatical*: "Tell me a story of women and men like us . . . (that ends in) a rhyme less discouraging, more pregnant so to speak with hope, than *lost*." And her accommodating husband responds in prose with "Our Ordinary Point Delivery Story" that ends comically and happily, 638 pages later, with the birth of their little Adam and Eve.

What Barth has done, anadiplosively, to his territorializing couple of the Turner-Talbotts is to consign them to an estuary somewhere during much of *Tidewater*, while setting his Sagamores out for the exploration of smooth space. In Arthur Quinn's little delight of a book, *Figures of Speech, 60 ways to Turn a Phrase* (1982), *anadiplosis* figures in one of the two chapters (out of eight) that define and exemplify the ways that rhetoric repeats. The following basic definition of the trope eminently suits Barth's tactics in *Tidewater* with his couples, and will be seen to be even more appropriate in his literary dealings with the repetition and beginnings of the figures out of myth which we have yet to bring on board. Anadiplosis is "the repetition of the end (the Turners of *Sabbatical* as the Talbotts of *Tidewater*) at the next beginning" (as the Sagamores sail away from them). Seconding our encomiums to the Deleuzean outside, anadiplosis in Quinn's presentation is a corrective of *epanalepsis*, which ends a sentence or clause with the same word or phrase that began it, in a way that makes the statement "stand apart from its surroundings": for example, "Rejoice in the Lord always: and again I say, Rejoice"; "Nothing can be created out of nothing" (Quinn 1982, 87). Anadiplosis, on the other hand, aspiring to neither emphasis nor aphorism, ties the statement to its surroundings by having its last word or phrase repeated in the first word or phrase of the subsequent sentence. Anadiplosis rings in the new through a repetition from the old, collaborating with the outside to bring on novel adventures, as in these examples: "All men that are ruined are ruined on the side of their natural propensities"; "Who has not the spirit of his age, of his age has all the unhappiness"; "Talent is an adornment; an adornment is also a concealment" (Quinn 1982, 89–90). The beauty of anadiplosis is that, while belonging to the territory that it consolidates through its repetition, it sequentially deterritorializes itself.

Which is precisely what the Sagamores are doing out there exploring the geography of Deleuze and Guattari's smooth space, "where one no longer goes from one point to another, but rather holds space beginning from any point; instead of striating space, one occupies it with a vector of deterritorialization in perpetual motion" (1987, 387). Better even than the nomads' desert, Peter and Katherine have before them the sea, perhaps principal among smooth spaces, the hydraulic model per se. State science, our Frenchmen inform us, treats the fluid as a special outside case for its theory of solids, but nomad science follows its flows and fluxes as the real plane of consistency, which opposes the stable, the eternal, the identical, and the constant (361). The protected waters of the Chesapeake Bay offer a "ubiquitous horizontality" and "slick calm," and its low landfall of sand bars, mud flats, salt marshes, and tidelands are almost wholly without any vertical supports for stable identification (read: smooth space is inimical to metaphor and allegory). "Where the boundary between land and sea is never prominent and always negotiable" (*FB*, 126), the Chesapeake Bay is a giant holding tank for free and inconsistent singularities in contiguity—a prebiotic soup awaiting some *ad lib*, *ad hoc* voyagers. Man/woman/boat/story is an assemblage on the cutting edges of deterritorialization, a nomadic war machine that seeks not war with the State, but its evasion.

And boyoboy, do the Sagamores know how to do it, especially that ballooning mother-to-be! Every "block" on the stratum's maps of marriage and pregnancy, of reading and writing, can be demolished through the nomad sailors' method of diagramming with their wake; all "points" vanish before wave and wind, flux and flow. Unblocking the strata (of significance, subjectification, the organism) is so easy once you get the hang of it, exclaims Kathy, that even her parents' cook can do it: "What's afoot is the simple though heroic and anyhow ineluctable matter of driving through the Vanishing Point and coming out on the farther side. The sand in Olive Treadway's egg-timer does it every morning" (401). So Katherine makes a war machine of her pregnant body. Her silhouette has become the mark of a domain that is being rapidly reterritorialized by the "overextended generosity" of her very rich and loving parents, who are hammering and wiring that body into the dense stratum of Sherritt's Point. Irma and Henry Sherritt have remodeled their old guest cottage, striated its space into a nursery with twin beds and a nanny's room, and are presently testing out a newly installed video intercom, with all eyes upon the territorialized belly of their pregnant daughter. Whereupon cheeky Katherine deterritorializes their monitor, with a bellyful of striptease and cheesecake and a nonstop recital of the gay gang-bang slang which proliferates in places of confinement (54–55). Get it, Mom and Dad?

Screens quickly click off all over Sherritt's Point, and Kathy seizes the chance to snatch Pete away from the territory for their last "duetude of sailing" before the twins arrive. When the anxious grandparents-to-be pursue them in their *Katydid IV* with its arsenal of formidable electronic hardware, Kathy once again does her "privacy or privates" act and drives her discreet Episcopalian father away when she "beavers his bowsprit" (131). Henry is no match for his daughter's deterritorializing impudence, and thus the Sagamores get themselves free of landside entanglements.

It is in the library, of all unlikely places, that Katherine has picked up these cut-and-run nomad tactics. As a cataloguer, she learned early what a demon of disorder can be just one saucy book that refuses to huddle nicely under a steady-State identity; such a book forces one to reach out for it, enter into a dialogue that shifts slightly each time, always resisting inclusion and classification. Currently, as an oral story-teller, Katherine is deterritorializing the Enoch Pratt Library (this "book museum" of the written word) with her community-service out-reach program, sending her storymobiles out into the smooth space of Baltimore's nonliterates. This is one smart nomad of a librarian. She has also learned how to *re*territorialize upon the public's *de*territorializations of her library: When a tampon wrapper is left by a borrower in Burton's *Anatomy of Melancholy* and a secondhand condom turns up in *Little Women*, Katherine solicits other "bookmarks" from her library colleagues and mounts them in a traveling exhibit of "The Public's Gifts to the Public Library." What do all these items have in common with one another: a Mason-jar ring, a broken drive belt, a black lace garter, a 500-lire note, a whole fried egg (332)? Absolutely nothing, until Katherine makes a "block" and "point" of them as "bookmarks" and "gifts"; left alone, they would merely consist in unsorted hetero-geneity on a nonhierarchical plane of consistency.

Like her bookmarks, Katherine Sherritt Sagamore is now "out of Circulation and into circulation" (333), and once aboard the *Story*, she sets about reterritorializing the womb of her deterritorialized tummy. The womb gets peopled with a population of two, whose names shift according to parental whim (Nice and Easy, Chick n Little, Pomp and Circumstance, Spit and Image), but always promote that nomadic increase that deters a metaphor or reanimates a cliché. Alert and Locate acquire the proper sense apparatus to do so, and soon Lo and Behold are checking out and responding to everything that circulates on and through their mom's body. They develop motor responses to Kather-ine's exercises and Peter's peter; they cultivate, or fail to cultivate, a taste for pita bread, tournedos Rossini, and tuna salad; they lend an avid ear to the bedtime stories which it is the bound duty of their father to tell them each evening. (Katherine's second task, beyond womb lib, is to unblock her word-gagged writer-husband.) Soon enough, you betcha, Toil and Trouble begin to sing their own territorializing refrain, mark-ing out the womb as that warm and lively place that is home.

Revved up by all this oral storytelling, Peter's narrative machine begins to purr, and he carries off the refrain of their twins-to-be to his own home territory of fiction writing. From cannisters mysteriously

floating around the bay, the Sagamores have retrieved the first two acts
of an anonymous script entitled "Sex Education, a Play" (scenes we
have read before in *Sabbatical*), and they are severely critical of this
amateurish allegory of egg and sperm hooking up despite ordeal (an
allegory, we recall, that was the mapper's "find" of *Sabbatical*). When a
desperately blocked Frank Talbott owns up to its authorship, Peter has
some pretty inspired ideas for a third act that would abort the allegory
and deterritorialize its striated space. Peter's first imperatively dismis-
sive remark indicates how far he has traveled from Fenn Turner's
enthusiasm for the matchings of metaphor:

> Never mind that it's a kink in somebody's uterus. If I were a playwright, I'd
> plant that place with cattails and honey locust trees and throw in some blue
> herons and crabs and oysters. Then I'd fetch a full moon up behind those
> honey locusts and fly a few Canada geese in front of that moon while June and
> her pal are making out on the beach. I'd hold the camera right on the moon
> and freeze frame and fade right there: Smack in the crotch of the Y. But what
> do I know. (425)

The fact is, Peter knows a lot. He knows how to deterritorialize an
already mapped uterine allegory, and reterritorialize upon its barren
land other worlds from the outside; he knows that enough narrative
detail will always decode any existent schema of metaphor or allegory.
Neither storytelling mother nor writer-father of this nomadic couple is
going to settle for an untenanted womb. And when Peter writes Frank's
third act for him (Peter's ultimate tuning up before writing *The Tidewater Tales*), he gives his uterine lovers just the right line, as they
fearsomely cancel themselves out in copulation, a line that just might
ensure them some immortality through a storytelling child: "Once
upon a time . . ." (632).

Peter also has some advice for Frank on the matter of coincidence.
Frank loves the magical return of his Spanish beret (the *boina* that
convinces Fenn to hang at Wye's Point and await further chiasmic
coincidences) because it was the single incident he invented in his
dismally mimetic novel. Not this round, pal, says Peter Sagamore:
Coincidence is old hat; just as you can't go home again, so also "the hat
that comes back is not the hat you threw away." Sometimes a *boina* is just
an old hat bunched in a discarded cannister of failed script, and about
all it's very good for is being passed, anadiplosively, to whoever's turn at
storytelling is next. In Barth's recycling of deterritorialized metaphor
in *Tidewater*, even the belly wears the hat as it tells its story. Metaphor
can never be story's map, for story has a wayward trajectory of its own.
Metaphor as coincidence may provide an initial *point* of contact, or in
its terminal summation of meaning may form a *block* of what's gone

down; but in the middle is a plateau of variable vibrations without beginning or end, what's up for grabs is story. For example, the paisley scarf enclosed in Cannister Two doesn't have to be matched up with John Arthur Paisley's murder by the CIA; one way that Frank might neutralize the CIA in his writing, so that he is neither silenced nor outraged, would be to note the similarity of paisley to sperm and then write himself a free-standing fiction of floaters and swimmers. Story is always going to deterritorialize, decode, and deschematize metaphor; it's the nomad's way of walking away from the State's mimetic contract.

But Peter was a nomad reader long before he learned the knack of nomad writing. Peter reads as Katherine circulates, intensively and independently. With a book before him, Pete is what Deleuze and Guattari would call a "numbering number": an autonomous subject, rhythmic and directional and movable, a cipher (the reader as war machine) which is the necessary consequence of the nomads' arithmetic and algebraic organization. Most citizens, confined within the geometrics of striated space, are the subjected "numbered numbers" of the State, which gains mastery over its human population through metric power, overcoding even lineages and territories with the statistical element, submitting the variations and movements of the people to a numerical organization that will bind them to the stratum's spatio-temporal frameworks (387–94). But when Peter reads, he occupies the domain of the book with absolute speed and autonomy: a nomad pragmatist on the make for his own writing, and reading beyond the author's intentions for the stray detail or loose end or plot incongruity that might just have a story in it. For the nomad, whatever is anomalous is probably fertile.

Presently, Peter and Kathy's little brother Chip (after "micro chip": the kid is a math whiz and numbers cruncher) have a number of nomad questions pending about literary numbers: How come the boy in Joyce's "Araby" didn't do his arithmetic down the road, since it's clear that the single florin he has copped isn't going to get him both a gift for Mangan's sister and a ride home on the trolley? What's the story behind the odd, but certainly nonrandom, number of nights in the 1,001 of Scheherazade? And what does Don Quixote think he's doing, in Cervantes' Cave of Montesinos episode, lending four real *reales* to enchanted princesses, when everyone knows that money plays no part in lands of enchantment?

We recall that John Barth, way back in 1966 with *Giles Goat-Boy*, was asking the same kind of questions of Sophocles' *Oedipus Rex*, and his own answers became the parodic set-piece at the center of that book. Barth has never used myth the way modernism did—to trivialize and mock the present or mourn a golden past; for him, myth is dead if it isn't living in the present. Still, he has come a long way since *Taliped Decannus*, and the nomad's way with the *de-*'s and *re-*'s of revolutionary territorializations (as well as anadiplosis) have taught Barth what's wrong with parody: The parodist doesn't *de*territorialize story, open it to its surroundings and the drift of a smooth plane of consistency, before he *re*territorializes on it; and any telling that does not introject this nomadic outside into its repetition will sing only a domesticated refrain that returns it to the local, natal territory.

Someone aiming for chaosmos would do better to follow received stories with numbering attention, as Peter does, seeking the openings and exits that disperse the characters, set them wandering, and thereby map new and supple segments of story. This is how anadiplosis gets escalated from Quinn's sentences and *Tidewater*'s *Sabbatical* couple to Barth's plot, where it functions narratively as the schizophrenic *sequel*. Set myth afloat on the Bay of Story and then see what happens: a lot of fictional folk bumping into us on our own Chesapeake. The three longest, deterritorializing refrains that Barth sings in *Tidewater* are sequels to myth, whose endings are openers to new and more story, to the unending story of myth's non sequiturs. Released from their myths, mythic characters become nomads, and (reason the Sagamores) if we can figure out where they might have been as extraterritorial wanderers since their stories, then Don Quixote, Odysseus and Nausicaa, and Scheherazade might help us Sagamores to get a tack on where we might be going.

This, then, is the tropological exit-through-repetition by means of which Barth fabricates the three central nomad stories of his *Tidewater Tales*: Release your mythic figures from their stories, put them out to sea, and see where the tides have taken them. How might we account for this present material reality (ask the Sagamores) of a strange, black boat anchored near us, with a winking eye and *Rocinante IV* on its bow, skippered by that curious Cap'n Don Quicksoat? What tides dragged the Knight of the Doleful Countenance from land to sea and changed him into this dirty old salt who is winking his lustful eye at both Carla B. Silver and her daughter Mims? Peter thinks that the old coot's exit point must have been from the Cave of Montesinos, the only enchanted caper not disproved by Cervantes' fictional reality. However, the enchanted Don Quixote that stayed down there would have had to wait for Cervantes' exhaustion and the disenchanted Don Quixote's death before he climbed out and discovered his first beat-up skiff, *Rocinante II*. *Différance* is about to defer to anadiplosis.

Moreover, just as the Don who went down the hundred-fathom rope could not have been the one who re-emerged from the cave, so also the river he retraced could not have been the river he came down. Another gift of a bigger boat, sail craft having been learned, and the *Rocinante III* might have gotten him to Portugal, at the tip of Europe and facing the open sea. Peter gets this far with his story, when Cap'n Dee Kew himself finishes it for him up to the present. Having turned in Amadis de Gaul for Columbus, having cashed in on those initial *reales* multiplying over the centuries in the Bank of Portugal, and having decided to become "his own goshdarn Cervantes . . . the passenger who is also the skipper," our nomad Quixote simply gave *Rocinante IV* her head across the Atlantic, and here he is on our dock—Popeye the sailor man.

Ditto Odysseus and Nausicaa. They had to get lost from the *Odyssey*, which finished them off forever in an early chapter, if they were to tie their Phoenician ship up to *Story* and, as the gorgeous, chiton-clad couple of Ted and Diana Dimitri, swap favorite parts of the *Odyssey* with the Sagamores. Of course, a deal had to be made with Homer: your silence about our getaway, and you can return to Penelope, your first love. A nice sequel indeed, which eschews themes of adultery and abandonment, and lets even the stay-at-home couple participate in the benefits of uncharted space. Ever since they became unstriated, Odysseus and Nausicaa have been mapping the chaosmos in the world's fastest boat, ever rediscovering the "magic escape velocity"—by literally whistling up a breeze, singing up a storm—that will keep them on a graceful line of flight forever as eternal lovers.

Peter leaves Chip and Carla B. to figure out the 1001 nights in their "Story of Scheherazade's Second Menstruation." What he's interested in is what happened after Scher's long, happy marriage that got her unstuck from her own PTOR (place, time, order of reality) and now unhappily stuck in ours. The problem is that, in crossing between stories, you can't count on symmetry: "The magic words in one story aren't magical in the next." Metaphoric substitution and simultaneity—even a duplicate couple of the genie Djeann and his Schmah, even a whole congress of oral storytellers—cannot get this "prisoner of dramaturgy" back to her Sharyhar: "The lock on the door of the prison of dramaturgy is not to be picked with Technicolorful gizmos and distractions. Babies don't come from storks, and dénouements don't come from automatic timers" (611). But perhaps the password might come from a story next door to Scher's, on the outside chance and the outside slant, as a molecular flash that hits but for a moment and then is gone. Sure enough, this is the case with Scheherazade, who is suddenly jerked up and out into her own dimension when Cap'n Don, telling his own story of the lost rope to the storytellers assembled at Kitty Hawk, halts in mid-sentence . . . and it is this "dangling line," de-metaphorized out of language into life, that gets Scher home.

Indeed, Barth has crafted all his stories in *Tidewater* along the figure of the *rhizome*, that decentered and decentering root system that De-leuze and Guattari deploy from their nomad arsenal of metaphor to deterritorialize the solid trunk and centered arborescence of the State's Tree-thought and Tree-organizations (3–25). Barth's stories form rhizomes with one another, and their rhizomatic structure—their enchainment that relays, through buds and knots and grafts, other supple segments of story—ensures that Kathy Sagamore can't deliver until her husband does. Katherine is more than ready, and so are Rough and Ready; but the new More-is-More Sagamore is below deck, pregnant with stories, in labor with stories, and until *his* water breaks, Kathy is as blocked as Scher was. Luckily for her, Peter's narrative touch is back, and within a flash of the next-to-last chapter, he logs in all the stories of their real and fictional friends that will be the book we have read. Then, Lo and Behold—now re-christened Adam and Eve—enter the world, their garden, to the sights and sounds of sea flags waving, conches trumpeting, and a whole flotilla of well-wishers.

Story—both the ship and the narrative practice—is thus the greatly mobile pick-me-up for a marriage whose sails are luffing. Katherine's favorite scene from Homer's epic is the reunion of the long-separated couple, which depends upon Odysseus' correct answer "to an intimate marital question rich in sexual suggestion: the secret construction of the couple's immovable marriage-bed, its stout chief post a living olive-trunk" (167). Despite this conjugal sentimentality, Barth in *The Tidewater Tales* has put that stable marriage out to sea and decentered its trunk with the rhizomatics of story, deterritorializing in the process also the phallic genitality that is adultery's bane and reproduction's boon. The conjugal eroticism of our sailing couple is the molecular, diffused sexuality proper to bodies that merely consist and do not lend themselves to the official worship of the phallus or to the State's organization of sexuality along the paranoid, molar line of totem and taboo. Contrary to the sexual impotence that plagued the long marriages of Odysseus and Scheherazade, the Sagamores exude a sexual shimmer that vibrates with that of the other couples they encounter, without that chemistry pulling them into any adulterous action.

Of course, the Sagamores have their own sexual histories—Peter's "Month of Mondays" with Scher, Katherine's "Forest-Green Crayoning" at the hands of her sadistic ex-husband, their own steamy first and second meets. Mostly, however, in this decentering for the people, sexuality is fun along the rhizome—old Don Quicksoat hopping from mother to daughter below deck, May Jump (vivacious lesbian story-teller) looking to jump Kath a second time, our eight-and-a-half months pregnant couple contenting themselves with the buss on the head or belly, the penis tuck-in at night, the sleepy morning roll in the hay. The most erotic moment for the Sagamores customarily occurs with the mutual opening of their hands and spreading of their fingers, hand to hand with fingertips touching, point for point (117). With such rhizomatic decenterings of genital sexuality ever on the move, sexual impotence can afflict only the sedentary landlubbers captive to the shore and to the State's all-or-nothing centered genitality. What Barth has written, in the purely additive multiplicities of rhizomatic sexuality, is the becoming-flotilla of the sexual houseboat.

Peter Sagamore's opinion is that "a chief value of realizing what's pushing you, and how, and why and where, is that it enables you to push back, or to use that push to go off in some other direction" (316). But "pushing back" is not a nomad strategy—indeed, directly oppositional confrontation is the primary *verboten* of the nomad's war machine—and Barth's tragic view of everything tilts all his choices toward "pushing off in another direction," the direction of comic deterritorialization. We should not confuse this very smart stance with cowardice, indecision, romantic individualism, wishy-washy liberalism, or any of the other charges hurled by politicized intellectuals against those individuals who positively affirm the nomad alternative to marching behind the groupie banners of party, class, and the movement. Like the CIA and other terrorist, guerrilla assemblages, the nomad's success depends upon covert operations, and Barth knows maybe more about these things than do most of us. He will not be counted among the determinedly ignorant chickens pecking around on the python's back, nor will he settle into the cheerful nihilism of black comedy that early critics credited him with.

Still, Barth is the steadiest skipper of deterritorialization, heeding Deleuze and Guattari's advice that one must experiment with caution, tentatively try out sub-molar lines and smooth-space directions, avoid falling into black holes. When it all comes down, Barth is essentially a man of the territory, one who is willing to compromise and negotiate with the shore in order to push off from it. The Sagamores push off for only fourteen days, during which they periodically call home to relieve grandparental anxieties, pipe aboard Sherritt chafing dishes of gourmet delicacies to acknowledge parental bestowing virtues, hang a little engine on *Story* their last day just in case. A few of the bad guys are blown out of the sky, but the rest are just as hellbent for Doomsday as ever. Barth has got the goods to justify an apocalyptic paranoia, but he prefers to be rhizomatically distributed across his own PTOR, always subtracting the bad constant through n-minus-one stories.

As book after book becomes a solid section of "The House That Jack Built," we risk missing the chaosmic cartography that informs each blueprint. In his rhizomatic machining of story, Jack Barth has ever been the alert *bricoleur*, picking up the bits and pieces of story that nobody else wanted and cording them into supple structures that are never duplicate re-cordings. He is the ultimate post-Romantic that Coleridge warned us against, the man of fancy and player with "counters and fixities," whose books are nevertheless signed with the craftsman's signature, "Made by the hand of John Barth," just like the fishing crafts made by old Fritz Sagamore. It's a delicate balancing act, this one that fabricates the new from the old and recirculates the brightest literary coin of the realm, while heeding at every moment the exemplary schizzes that might serve to carry us off the map—a covert operation perhaps best undertaken by an undercover agent posing as a man of the territory. Barth's personal brand of nomadism, announced forthrightly in *The End of the Road*, has been securely in place since his second novel at age twenty-six:

> The greatest radical in any society is the man who sees all the arbitrariness of the rules and social conventions, but who has such a great scorn or disregard for the society he lives in that he embraces the whole wagonload of nonsense with a smile. The greatest rebel is the man who wouldn't change society for anything in the world. (*ER*, 129–30)

So there we leave him—at the helm of story, the storyteller's old hat firmly in place, an undercover rebel in cut-offs and deck shoes. And we can bet that the next time the coin is flipped, it will come up, as always—Tales, you win!

Chapter 10
The Last Voyage of Somebody the Sailor (1991): Reflowering the Deflorated Virgin

Image	Trope	Defense	Ratio
Camera obscura	Defamiliarization	Serendipity	Zahir

In the medieval Islam of Sinbad the Sailor, as told by Scheherazade in the tenth volume according to Barth, it is done all the time: The virgin girl—upon whose sexual purity much of the socio-economics of the Orient depends, yet who is uncommonly liable to premarital liaisons and the sexual ravagings of pirates and familial males—can have her wâhât outfitted with a new maidenhead guaranteed to pass the visual and tactile inspections of the most conscientious of dowry negotiators, all without compromising her value on the bride market. This mundane practice of the exotic Orient has a hopeful, metaphorical appeal for our marathon teller of hand-me-down tales, who, at the tale-end of a long career of telling refitted tales for the reflowering of literature, has at least one more to tell. Male lust and male impotency may yet be pervasive concerns in *The Last Voyage of Somebody the Sailor*—there are zabbs that force, zabbs that won't stand, zabbs that contain the future—but the zabb cannot compete with the wâhât, which is the female locus (the "oasis") of love and life. This book is going to be Barth's summational defense of a personal and professional lifetime, of all the repetitions that have been good, including the ultimate repetition of all, the rebirth that follows the return to the womb.

To share his narrative duties from the other side of innocence, Barth calls upon Islam's "aptest, sweetest, hauntingest, hopefulest" storyteller (*FB*, 56) and its most celebrated virgin, Scheherazade. The young Scheherazade of *The Thousand and One Arabian Nights*, we recall, presented herself as a volunteer virgin to his sultan Shahryar, whose sour practice of deflowering a virgin every night and murdering her the morning after was rapidly depopulating his kingdom of marriageable females. Scheherazade, however, so beguiled the shah with her artfully contrived and compounded tales-within-tales that not only were the country's women spared, but the heroic vizier's daughter was rewarded with her life, three sons, and official marriage to the king.

The Scheherazade of this book is an ancient crone with sparkling eyes who, long eager to be done with life, rises one final time to the narrative challenge, and tells her last virgin story to her ultimate auditor, Death. Her task is to be shared with the similarly bedridden Simon Wheeler Behler, who is hospitalized in an asylum and must tell his story to prove his sanity, to a young woman doctor with blazing green eyes who looks to Simon very much like Love. Thus the initial twin chapters set up the double frame that will reverse the ascendancy of death over love. With its singular fidelity to this difficult affirmation, *The Last Voyage of Somebody the Sailor* is Barth's apologia for a life and career that have been steered by this star.

Barth's love affair with Scheherazade began in the Oriental Seminary of the Classics Library at Johns Hopkins University, where as a student book-stacker he began reading through the collections of great tale-cycles and in the process discovered his personal and technical muse of a lifetime. At age thirty-five, having recently given Scheherazade her own book in his oeuvre, Barth pledged his troth to her for the duration: "When I think of my condition and my hope, in the time between now and when I shall run out of ink or otherwise expire, it is Scheherazade who comes to mind, for many reasons" (*FB*, 57). These reasons include Scheherazade's sense of apocalypse as "ultimately personal," her persistence because of and despite her "publish or perish" situation, her nonetheless erotic relation to her listener, the "opportunity for counterrealism" that she maximizes in her avoidance of contemporary material, her magical and light touch on the passionate, dark mysteries of myth, and the narrative complexities she introduces with the device of the frame-tale (*FB*, 57–59). Yarning through a lifetime with love and death as her most familiar strangers, Scheherazade was destined to become Barth's most familiar stranger, the heart and head of his harem of beloved women to, for, and about whom his stories have been told.

Thus Scheherazade has her own history within Barth's literary career. It began with his corner-turning sixth volume, *Chimera*, where Barth-as-Genie dropped in on her PTOR to talk narrative technique and gender relations. Omitted from the seventh book, I would now suggest, because she was meant to be the muse, mistress, wife and best friend of Late Barth, Scheherazade opened up an ocean of story that could not be navigated by such backwater marshlanders as Mensch, Cook, Bray, and Company. In the love affair of muse and poet, therefore, *Chimera* is followed by *Sabbatical, A Romance*, where Barth's life asserts itself for the first time in Barth's literature, as the loverly narrators Susan and Fenn Turner literalize the dream of gender equality that was the "as if" philosophy of Scheherazade's younger sister and her shah. In *The Tidewater Tales* Scheherazade returns Barth's first visit by dropping in on the Peter Sagamores as a champion oral storyteller, her torrid affair with Peter now long in the past. In Barth's ninth, it is Scheherazade who gets seriously stuck in his PTOR until she finds herself serendipitously catapulted back into her own; in Barth's tenth, it is Simon Behler (alias Baylor the Taler, alias Somebody the Still-Stranded) who has landed in Scheherazade's Baghdad and is looking for a way home.

The fictional present is 1980, and Behler, a successful New Journalist, has been washed overboard off the coast of Sri Lanka (formerly known as Serendib) while attempting with his mistress to retrace the voyages of Sinbad the Sailor. Unaccountably, shipwrecked Behler finds himself aboard Sinbad's own *Zahir* and is now in the very home of Sinbad, who is trying to interest investors in his projected seventh voyage back to Serendib. Over six evenings at his host's sumptuous table, Somebody alternates with Sinbad in their mutual accounts of their first six voyages, stories that begin and end in complete divergence one from the other, but exhibit much convergence and semi-convergence in their in-between. It is around this table, where East meets West in imaginary time-space, that Barth commences his encroachments on the bogus boundary between the familiar and the strange—by giving a full hearing to Islamic literary criticism. Sinbad's first four voyages are the fantastic stuff of myth—Whale Island, the Valley of Diamonds and Serpents, Ape Island, Swine Island, the Peppercornians; whereas Somebody's first four are the domestic markers of autobiography—on his seventh birthday, Simon Behler of East Dorset, Maryland, receives his first watch and his first airplane ride; on his fourteenth, he receives his sexual initiation from an older woman of sixteen, Crazy Daisy Moore, and his first moral dilemma from a can of Bon Ami cleanser; for his forty-second, on the last land-legs of his marriage, Simon cruises the Caribbean with wife and family; for his fiftieth, he is resailing Sinbad's voyages with his photographic collaborator and new lover, Crazy Daisy's little sister Julia.

Sinbad's guests and household warm to the familiarly fantastic tales of their host and master, but (with the exception of Sinbad's gorgeous, refitted virgin of a daughter, Yasmin) they are completely put off by

Somebody's improbable, boring, vulgar, and morally unedifying stories from his own biography. Yasmin's tomato-faced suitor speaks for the majority of the diners when, as a defender of "homely Islamic realism," he critiques Somebody's first two narrative voyages:

The high ground of traditional realism, brothers, is where I stand! Give me familiar, substantial stuff: rocs and rhinoceri, ifrits and genies and flying carpets, such as we drank in with out mother's milk and shall drink—Inshallah!—till our final swallow. Let no outlander imagine that such crazed fabrications as machines that mark the hour or roll themselves down the road will ever take the place of our homely Islamic realism, the very capital of narrative. . . .

And may not the same be said for a story's action? Speak to us from our everyday experience: shipwreck and sole-survivorhood, the retrieval of diamonds by means of mutton-sides and giant eagles, the artful deployment of turbans for aerial transport, buzzard dispersal, shore-to-ship signaling, and suicide (Allah forfend) as necessary. Above all, sing the loss of fortunes and their fortuitous re-doubling: the very stuff of story! Do not attempt to distract us from these ground-verities with such profitless sideshows as human copulation, which is no more agreeable to hear about in detail than are our visitor's other narrative concerns: urination, masturbation, and—your pardon, Sayyid Sinbad—regurgitation. (*SS*, 136)

That one man's real may be another man's imaginary is Somebody's first lesson in boundary negotiation, and there is going to have to be a lot of willing suspension of disbelief around this table if East and West are to swallow each other's stories. With the ease of an old expert, Barth sees to it that the rapprochement proceeds with a minimum of fuss at the levels of allegory and structure. Asks Somebody of his Arabic audience: Isn't the human condition, after all, the "classic Sinbad situation?" Aren't all of us in our everyday lives lost at sea and floundering in the waters, until we somehow find ourselves again on the other side of drowning? And doesn't that "somehow" bring into ordinary reality all that is fanciful and fortuitous in Sinbad's Oriental mythmaking? Having refitted East and West into a virgin commonality with this governing metaphor, the practiced pro of plots then skillfully structures his voyage-tales to promote the defamiliarization of the familiar and the refamiliarization of the strange. Our sailors' fifth narrative voyages are, in fact, mutual border-crossing experiences, as the autobiographical realist drowns in Sinbad's exotic Orient, and Sinbad's need for personal revenge takes over his scheduled flight into the fanciful. By their sixth voyages, they are thoroughly entangled in the knots of a single riddle that appears to violate both Oriental and Occidental logics, while their seventh voyages find Somebody sailing into Sinbad's familiar fantastic, and an everyday Sinbad taking an autobiographical trek into the desert.

Clearly, Barth has not relinquished his critical task of surmounting the old war between realism and irrealism, aboutness and metafiction, metonymy and metaphor; yet with this book, Barth folds these ancient eggs of contention into his narrative batter more smoothly than ever before, and the cake that he bakes has no taste of the rational, prepared determinations of the Hegelian synthesis. In the convergence and crossings of Simon's familiar and Sinbad's strange, Barth gives his most graceful answer yet to the arbitrary dualisms that limit our perspectival thinking. It's an answer that likewise surprises, for it demonstrates that the transcension of contraries is a consequence mostly of lucky happenstance.

In the autobiographical content of Somebody's tales, the quotidian goes more than halfway to meet the fantastic. It seems that Simon has always been "a castaway from the Here and Now," has always already known the technique for border crossing—a technique that we might call the "rocking back and forth into black space." The practice began early. At age seven Simon was already living his young life with "Voice Over," narrating it as it happened to his imaginary playmate and deceased twin sister Bijou (from Bee Gee, from Baby Girl Behler), who exited the womb before Simon did and didn't make it into his world. It was between sleep and waking, rocking himself into the unfamiliar, that Bijou's storytelling kid brother got himself beyond the border: "It was not long before I reached that state between two worlds where distances go strange and the familiar is no more. I was in black space, suspended, or as it were with one eye open above some surface, one below" (59). The practice continued into Simon's adolescence, when it was rocking, and not his sexual climaxes with Daisy, that brought him to true ecstasy: "charged suspension, vertiginous, electrically humming, in which the ceiling, the walls, the frames of the doors and windows, and the very bed beneath me were at once their familiar selves and unspeakably alien, their distance and configuration fluid, and I myself was no longer or not merely I but as it were the very lens of the cosmos: a sentient star of light-years, more compass than anything named Simon William Behler" (107).

On his third voyage the Islamic Middle Ages falls through the black hole between two worlds into Simon's adult life, by means of the rocking this time of the nearly drowned. Having through his long marriage to plain-Jane Price adulterously experienced the "elasticity of hashished time and space" in Tangiers with Teri-from-Teaneck and the "as if" joys of personal and professional collaboration with Theresa-from-Last-Semester, Simon is left to drown by his fed-up wife, tangled in the anchor of their rented cruise-boat *So Far*. Rocking himself to and fro, he frees himself from those dark waters and rises to buy a new watch in the tourist town of Charlotte Amalie, port of St. Thomas, the

Virgin Islands—which suddenly materializes defamiliarized as a Marrakesh marketplace, where a Third World salesperson with striking green eyes is cutting out the extra links of Simon's new Seiko and refitting it on his wrist.

Barth's first fascination with the defamiliarizations of black space took the form of that "lens of the cosmos," the *camera obscura*. In his 1960 lecture on "How to Make a Universe," Barth generalized the photographic effect to include the literary effects of the novelist's own "dark chamber":

> There is on the coast of California, or used to be, or I wish there had been, a big *camera obscura*, of the sort that once fascinated Leonardo da Vinci. A long-focus lens on the roof of the building receives the image of the ocean and projects it by means of mirrors into a large ground-glass plate inside the darkened room. You can stand outside and see the ocean firsthand for free, but people pay money to step inside and see it on the screen. I quite understand them: It's not the same thing at all. There is something about the dark chamber and the luminous plate that makes the commonplace enchanting. Things that may scarcely merit notice when seen directly—a tree, a rock, a seagull—these things are magically displaced, recomposed, represented. Like the drowned man Ariel sings of in *The Tempest*, the scene is familiar yet transfigured: things shine serene by their inner lights and are intensely interesting.
>
> A novel works like the *camera obscura*. The arbitrary facts that make the world—devoid of ultimate meaning and so familiar to us that we can't really see them any longer, like the furniture of our living room—these facts are passed through the dark chamber of the novelist's imagination, and we *see* them, perhaps for the first time. More, we hang upon them, often with a passion—characters and events that in real life might bore us or simply escape our notice. We stand before them rapt, entranced, like the spectators at the panther's cage in Kafka's "Hunger Artist" story; we do not want ever to go away. (*FB*, 21)

Barth's metaphorical deployment of the *camera obscura* suggests that all art is a "making it strange," a magical dislocation that refurbishes the commonplace and replenishes the humdrum, stunning the reader/viewer into aesthetic bliss. But in *Somebody the Sailor* Barth's metaphor for poetry becomes the characters' reality: Simon's and Sinbad's lives are studded with little black holes, entrances into another vivid and wondrous world that is always yet this one, exits through which one slips into the rapturous recognition of a virgin universe right before one's eyes, and thick with the extraordinary and the unpredictable. This is the holey space of opportunity, through which all the cosmos comes flooding in to maximalize our miniaturized lives. The black hole is the "Open, Sesame!" of Barth's one thousand and second night.

To arrive at the luminous, numinous ecstasy of black holes, one must redeem them from their customary threatening connotations, by which the absence of light signifies the absence of life and activates our never very latent fear of death. (Indeed, we must suppress an infamous historical incidence of a black hole, which has its specific locale in the Orient: The Black Hole of Calcutta was the horrific name given to a small Indian prison, where 123 of the 146 British soldiers interned there died of suffocation on the infamous night of June 30, 1756.) Barth, just now thinking like a cosmologist, gets support for his redemption of black holes from the physicists, who must become poets when they approach the reality of black holes, for they lay at the very limit of scientific knowledge.

Initially, the physicists' description seems to answer to Sinbad's greatest terror of being devoured, swallowed up, drowned: Their black hole is "a great star-swallower in the heart of a galaxy . . . a perfect trap, a turnstile to oblivion" for any body that gets sucked into its heavy gravitational pull (Calder 1979, 5, 40). However, both a popularizer of science like Nigel Calder (*Einstein's Universe*, 1979) and our leading theoretical physicist Stephen Hawking (*A Brief History of Time*, 1990) aim their own poetic cameras upon the black hole, and imagine what it would be like for an imaginary astronaut (or an argonaut like Somebody the Sailor) in black-hole space-time. Because no light and therefore no information can escape from a black hole, both writers must resort to an imaginary explanation, which Hawking interestingly refers to as "the realistic solution."

Contrary to our expectations, the singular defamiliarizations of the black hole, they conclude, would make the astronaut's experience one of ecstatic rebirth rather than dark oblivion. He would not feel sucked "like water approaching a plug-hole," or stuck "like a fly struggling against flypaper"; he would not in fact feel compelled by any force whatsoever, but would experience a free fall from one "timeshell" to another. This is because the black hole that traps all outward-bound light also stops time at its edge, and there would be no present time, no "passing moment" for our astronaut (Calder, 40–42). "The singularities would always lie in the future (like the singularities of gravitational collapse) or entirely in the past (like the big bang)," affirms Hawking (89). Moreover, the fact that space and therefore light are curved indicates to Hawking that the astronaut would discover that "black holes ain't so black," that instead "they glow like a hot body, and the smaller they are, the more they glow" (97). Calder's description is even closer to the argonaut's navigation of the *camera obscuras* strewn about Barth's fictional landscape: "Close to a black hole the curving of the path of light is much more marked, and you can see around corners. Objects judged in the ordinary way to be behind the black hole, and eclipsed by it, will be visible out to one side" (45).

It is this "sidewise" illumination of the physicist's *camera obscura* in the sky that we want to retain, for it is how as drowning Everybodys we may retrieve our sea-legs; and we don't need to worry overmuch about Hawking's judgment of the astronaut's necessary "recycling" ("All that would survive of him is his mass and energy") as "a poor sort of immortality" (112). Barth's *Jaws II* theory of recycling is much more hopeful, yet we might expect it nevertheless to encounter its own limit at the very boundary where post-Einsteinian science goes poetic. The post-Bloomian "tropes" of Barth's Recommencement have been tending precisely in this direction, toward the literalization and materialization of rhetoric within Einsteinian space-time. In the first voyage out, the couple lateralized their doubled origin and thereby opened up space to synergetic cooperations; then to this spatial smoothing were added the deterritorializations of time-travel through anadiplosis; and now both synchronicity and sequel are to be superseded by the privatized plunge, "like a genie through the neck of an hourglass" (*SS*, 63), into no-time/all-light black space. A quarter of a century after and light-years beyond *Giles Goat-Boy*, Barth is beaming back his messages from inside the *Axis Mundi*, informing us that black holes, taken to be the ultimate killing power in the universe, are sites of illumination and regenerative terminals that effectuate re-entry after exit. Barth's potent play with the "reflowering" potential within the cosmos is his poetic circumnavigation of postmodern science's farthest parameter, at which he converges with the poetic physicist.

As one reads *Somebody the Sailor*, one is reminded of another, metafictional cosmos in which a queer and unexpected world appears through a hole in the familiar, in which life is like a dream where time forks and lost space reappears. With that shock of recognition, one realizes that Borges is back!—Barth's much admired "*dernier cri* modernist," whose fascination with *Las mil y una noches* rivals Barth's own. One of Borges' fictions, in fact, is the black hole through which Barth drops back in for postmodern replenishment. Since virtually all of Borges' short stories collected in his translated *Ficciones* (1962) and *Labyrinths* (1964) answer the general description above, and since Barth doesn't make his debt to Borges explicit until more than halfway through his book, the reader is free to pick and choose "which Borges?" My own hunch was the last tale of *Ficciones*, "The South" (167–74). I liked it, not solely for the similarities of content, but because it would cast doubts upon the sanity of Barth's narrator Simon Behler, while concurring with the flower power of Barth's black holes even to the point of death. A brief summary of this not-yet-it story, as a prelude to the just-perfect story that was Barth's actual Argentinian connection, will reveal how much cannier Barth was than this critic, and how much greater in this book is the range of his ambition than she had first imagined.

Juan Dahlmann is Borges' Argentine librarian who, having just purchased a copy of *The Thousand and One Nights*, falls into a black hole on a fatal day in February of 1939. What sucks him in is an unknown something that brushes by his forehead and draws blood, and he has to be brought back from the point of death-by-septicemia through the humiliating curative rituals of a local sanitarium. Now, Scheherazade once again in hand, he is traveling south from Buenos Aires by train for a season of convalescence at a family ranch he has inherited, long dreamed of, but never seen. The objects of the rural countryside in his view from the train seem "accidental, casual, like dreams of the plain," and Dahlmann feels "as if he was two men at a time: the man who traveled through the autumn day across the geography of the fatherland, and the other one, locked up in a sanitarium and subject to methodical servitude" (170).

Disembarking, Juan Dahlmann discovers that he has also traveled back in time, as he enters a cafe with a horse-drawn shay parked out front and finds inside some gauchos drinking beneath the dim light of a kerosene lamp. When one of them in mockery throws a spitball of breadcrumb at his forehead, and another throws him a naked dagger, the librarian goes out to avenge his honor and meet his fate on the open plain. The story ends with Dahlmann's two contradictory thoughts, of which the second cancels the first: (1) "*They would not have allowed such things to happen to me in the sanitarium*"; (2) "To die in a knife fight, under the open sky, and going forward to the attack, would have been a liberation, a joy, and a festive occasion, on the first night in the sanitarium when they stuck him with a needle. He felt that if he had been able to choose then, or dream his death, this would have been the death he would have chosen or dreamt" (174).

Borges' metavision in this story, I thought, would be redemptive enough for Barth—that, retroactively, one can be seen as actively choosing the black hole, that the sea-change is for the better, and that in the doubled event (flying bird or bat, and flying breadcrumb) at the "event-horizon" (the physicists' term for the black hole's outer rim), one's loss in the world of light is one's gain in black space. Barth's sights are set much higher, however. In what may be his last voyage out (though one wouldn't count on it), he boldly sets out to reflower Freud: What marvelous, virgin garden might bloom with the refitting of Freud's death-drive and repetition-compulsion, his neurotics' obsessions and his psychotics' uncanny doubles, to the actively chosen fascinations of robust psychic health? Might not one expose to the light of day that ultimate black hole of Freud's theory, the grotto of the unconscious—fragment and multiply it, make it proliferate, and spread it out over ordinary reality, making it available to any properly obsessive

perception that has eyes to look sideways, alert to peripheral opportunity? And in these life-enhancing plunges into black holes, might not
a comic postmodernist discern a jim-dandy defense of the literary
repetitions that he has chosen throughout an entire career? As its most
outside parameter, *The Last Voyage of Somebody the Sailor* exuberantly
converts all of holy psychoanalysis into holey space, and it is because of
this secret and hidden aim, I am arguing, that of all his stories to choose
from, Barth fixed upon Borges' specific parable of psychotic obsession.

It is announced in Somebody's fourth voyage, when Simon and his
ready-for-anything Julia, who has just been diagnosed as cancer-posi-
tive, are shopping for a ship in which to re-sail Sinbad's voyages. They
come upon one that bears a name which Barth's readers already know
to have been that of Sinbad's original ship, and which Borges' readers
would recognize as the title of a short story in *Labyrinths* (156–64), the
Zahir:

> "It's an Arabic term for an Arabic legend," Simon explained to Julia Moore.
> "Imagine some unobtrusive object—it may take different forms in different
> epochs—that has the power once your eye falls innocently upon it to gradually
> take possession of your mind, the way a computer virus gradually takes over
> the computer's memory bank. Finally you can think of nothing else except that
> one thing, and you freak out altogether. It might be a paper clip or the ashtray
> on your desk, or one particular pine tree in a pine forest, or one brick no
> different from all the other bricks in the building, or an incidental face in a
> crowd shot. But if it happens to be the zahir, then bingo!"
> . . . . *Cancer*, we both said to ourselves. "Serendib!" offered smiling Julia
> Moore, her head cocked. "Sold." (*SS*, 328)

A huge task of regenerative defamiliarization is demanded here, but
Barth and his protagonist couple are up to it. Just as Julia and Simon
ignore the dark metaphor of obsession as a cancerlike growth and look
to the bright light at the side of that black hole, thus informing dire
coincidence with positive auspiciousness, so will Barth take the repetition of one's beloved obsessions as a portent of good health, against
Borges' dark tale of severe mental derangement and long-term disaster.
For "Borges" the insane narrator, his zahir has become the black hole as
theorized by the physicists from the outside; his whole world has
collapsed on itself and contracted to the zahir, "as though my eyesight
were spherical, with the Zahir in the middle" (Borges 1964, 163). His
zahir is a common twenty-centavo coin received in change at a bar, and
his obsession with it sucks up all the narrative content, in the pedant's
crazed pursuit of all the recondite scholarship on zahirs: the mythical,
historical, and fictional representations of coins as zahirs, the prolifera-
tions through culture of a single zahir, the "repertory of possible
futures" in the zahir. Because the impeccably correct "Borges" went to

the bar immediately following his ex-sweetheart's funeral, the reader could follow Freud and diagnose his obsession as the result of grossly exaggerated feelings of guilt, but the Oriental aura of Borges' magical explanation absolutely overshadows the Western authority of psychoanalysis.

It is better to follow the lead of Gene Bell-Villada (1981), the kind of sleuth-critic that Borges' metafiction demands. Bell-Villada's extensive bibliographic researches have turned up no such object as the zahir in the history of the Orient. As a power-word, however, the "zahir" does exist as one of the ninety-nine attributes of Allah, meaning "visible" and "notorious" (213). He also reports (215), much to our present delight, that the "Zahirites" were a medieval religious sect, who "believed in a strict, unmetaphorical interpretation of the Koran. (The group was named after its founder Daud uz-Zahiri, 'David the Literal')." Bell-Villada's disinclination toward a Freudian interpretation of the obsessional object is Barth's own, and his alternative recourse to etymology and religious history both resolves a minor quandary and reveals a major strategy in Barth's book. We can understand now that the Muslims' negative critique of Somebody's tales had a religious basis in the generalized taboo on Arabic autobiography: That one must not add anything to the Koran is a Zahirite prohibition.

But Barth has himself been working at becoming a literary Zahirite ever since he rechristened himself as Late Barth, and as "Jack the Literal" he has been busy defamiliarizing metaphor into real action and actual objects within his holey fictional worlds. Think of the overboard *boina*, in Novel #8 a marvelous coincidence, but in Novel #9 strictly old hat. In Barth's tenth, the obsessive object that keeps turning up—a watchband with missing links, an identification bracelet, a discarded can of cleanser, for example—is neither fantastic nor ordinary, but rather a defamiliarized object that has survived black-hole navigations. From such objects one learns faith in the unpredictable and a respect for incalculability, for when the cosmos comes pouring into one's life, the grossest unlikelihood will materialize as a magical singularity that cannot be attributed to metaphor or symptom.

Nevertheless, Barth does give Freudian guilt its place in his book, as it impinges upon the sooty unconscious of Sinbad the patriarch who, in his incest with his daughter Yasmin and in his attempted murder of his adopted son Umar, has committed two oedipal crimes against the family. Barth's Sinbad, then, is much more than a mythic hero defamiliarized as a shrewd con-man. Unlike Somebody of the clear conscience, for whom the unconscious and its phantasies are black holes of the marvelous, Sinbad's trip down his own black hole on his fifth voyage puts him inside the befouled mirror of his monstrous desires.

This experience of filth and fury that makes him his own toilet is a repetition of the self, harshly divided between cruel superego and insistent id, which we have already seen in the Siamese twins of *Lost in the Funhouse* and in the Eierkopf/Croaker duo of *Giles Goat-Boy*. Sinbad must wrest the truth of his unconscious from the Old Man of the Sea, and when his dirty secrets are made known to the caliph, he receives the punishment of exile traditionally meted out to the criminal Oedipus.

But it is because Sinbad's obsessions proceed from lust and guilt that his end is so psychoanalytically deterministic. The moral in this quarter is that life is deterministic only if we make it so; otherwise, it's serendipitous. Even in the midst of his career as a voyager-hero, Sinbad was so busy capitalizing on the past that he lost any future except that of an obsessive repeater. Assuming that what happens in the past will happen in the future, and therefore with each voyage preparing for shipwreck, Sinbad substitutes ever rattier ships for his *Zahir*, shuns his soon-to-be-gone human shipmates, and scrambles posthaste into his Tub of Last Resort to await his own inevitable drowning. Furthermore, Sinbad has lied about his sixth voyage to Serendib: He never reached "that elusive island," and cannot sail back to it per his caliph's orders on his seventh voyage, for the very good reason that Serendib can be reached only through indirection. Despite its actual existence as the ancient name of Ceylon, "Serendib" in the narratives of both Sinbad and Somebody functions only as a code word. For Sinbad, it's a cover-up for his breakout into piracy, murder, and revenge, the predictable consequence of his evil obsessions; for a serene Somebody narrating his autobiography, Serendib is "where we came from and that to which we would return"—the "several Serendibs" of late maturity, mid-manhood, adolescence, childhood, and ultimately, the womb (23).

A serendipitous life requires the psychic faculty for making desirable discoveries by accident, for responding to objects and persons as they turn up, especially when the found object is inevitably the love-object which, in Freud's oedipal theory of sexuality, has been lost and is now refound. It is Simon Behler's obsession with his first love-object of Bijou that ultimately gets him home, as he refinds his twin sister in Daisy, in Julia, in Yasmin, and after the shipwreck of their seventh voyage, as Yasmin pushes off first—in the familiar stranger listening to his tale in the hospital room. Thus does Barth draw the teeth from Freud's definition of the death-drive, by putting love into death's position of insistence: It is love that "seeks to restore us to an earlier state," and it is through Love that each of us "chooses to die in his own fashion." And with love as his zahir, Barth also milks the poison from Freud's repetition-compulsion: Repetition is not the fatal return of the repressed, but rather the unprepared for and fortunate find which usually appears for Somebody as "the next thing I knew after I knew nothing," a refinding of oneself on the other side of lostness.

Somebody and the steadfast friends of his life do well, then, when they fix on the accidental as the serendipitous object, for it is through such quotidian objects that the obsession with love replenishes and repeoples one's life. In Barth's quite lovely phrasing, it is the means by which "a dream long dreamed may grow a real geography, unsuspected by the dreamer" (26)—a formulation that we might take as Barth's replenishment of the "passion never spent" implied by Freud's repressed. With lovers, the bad never repeats itself, or better, it is replayed only in the affirmative: Yasmin replays for Simon all the women he has ever loved, Simon is for Yasmin her lost brother/lover Umar refound, and their month of sexual terrorism aboard the pirate ship is repeated as their month of sexual bliss on shore. This is the way of this whole serendipitous world, if one stays alert to its black-hole potentialities. The PTOR's of Sinbad's world and Somebody's, of East Dorset and Baghdad, are in immediate, although indirect, communication: The incestuous Sam Moore converges with Sinbad, as does Simon's older brother Joe through another black hole; Simon's Caribbean *So Far* communicates with the historical Tim Severin's *Sohar*, and both maintain their unlikely connection with the Arabic *Zahir*. It is like the musical chairs around Sinbad's table—some diners dropping out, but the others moving up to the head, until only the most faithful repeaters remain, lovers and friends all.

The largest question is, How do you handle your time so that your life does not become what Freud said it was, a mere substitute for death? For Barth and Scheherazade, the "Destroyer of Delights" is not Death, but Time, and "who could mistake Time, that great depotentiator, for an aphrodisiac?" (449). But if we are all in the familiar Sinbad fix, waiting on shipwreck and hoping for rebirth, love might be what pulls us through—fixing our gaze on the point of light to the side of the black hole, staying obsessed with it, and letting our zahir carry us the long way round to home. Simon doesn't grow a life by adding up all the wristwatches he has discarded—the Ingersoll, the Bulova, the Omega, the Seiko. Instead, he acknowledges that in the here and now "my watch isn't right. Do I complain? On with the story" (4), and using his watch as a compass, he navigates his life by following up on the missing links of his watchband wherever and whenever they serendipitously reappear.

"To get to Serendib one must plot one's course in good faith elsewhere, and then lose one's bearings—serendipitously." These words are not Somebody's, but Barth's, speaking for himself to the readers of the *New York Times Book Review* of January 21, 1991, just twenty-one days before the book we have been analyzing would come of age in publication. Barth himself, he tells us, is entering the seventh decade of his life. Having this past year retired from his full-time professorship at Johns Hopkins, having used all twenty-one gears of his retirement-gift mountain bike on Maryland's Eastern Shore, and having already aborted two attempts at an eleventh novel, Barth is wondering whether maybe post–*Somebody the Sailor* isn't going to look "disagreeably grave-like." It's of course possible, but his well-wishing readers have cause to doubt it. For Barth has kept one foot in Hopkins with a single graduate-level fiction-writing seminar, he's finding "portentous coincidence" among ancient steno pads and roll books, he's defining *kenosis* as the "emptying out of the spirit's vessel in preparation for a refill," and with his title he has once more pledged his obsessive fidelity to Scheherazade: "Romancing the Muse: Just Wait, and She'll Come Sidling Up." Here's to the white nights of love and tales that recommence for John Barth, serendipitously, with #1003.

Works Cited

Bakhtin, Mikhail
    1987 *The Dialogic Imagination: Four Essays by M. M. Bakhtin*. Ed. Michael Holquist. Trans. Caryl Emerson and Michael Holquist. Austin: University of Texas Press.
Barth, John
    1956 *The Floating Opera*. New York: Bantam, 1972.
    1958 *The End of the Road*. New York: Grosset and Dunlap, 1971.
    1960 *The Sot-Weed Factor*. New York: Doubleday Anchor, 1987.
    1966 *Giles Goat-Boy or, The Revised New Syllabus*. Greenwich, CT.: Fawcett Crest, 1967.
    1968 *Lost in the Funhouse: Fiction for print, tape, live voice*. New York: Doubleday Anchor, 1988.
    1972 *Chimera*. Greenwich, Conn.: Fawcett Crest, 1973.
    1979 *LETTERS*. New York: G. P. Putnam's Sons, 1979.
    1980 "The Literature of Replenishment: Postmodernist Fiction." *Atlantic* 245 (January): 65–71.
    1982 *Sabbatical, A Romance*. New York: Penguin, 1983.
    1984 *The Friday Book: Essays and Other Nonfiction*. New York: G. P. Putnam's Sons, 1984.
    1987 *The Tidewater Tales: A Novel*. New York: Fawcett Columbine, 1987.
    1991 *The Last Voyage of Somebody the Sailor*. Boston: Little, Brown, 1991.
Bellamy, Joe David, ed.
    1974 *The New Fiction: Interviews with Innovative American Writers*. Urbana: University of Illinois Press.
Bell-Villada, Gene H.
    1981 *Borges and His Fictions: A Guide to His Mind and Art*. Chapel Hill: University of North Carolina Press.
Bloom, Harold
    1973 *The Anxiety of Influence: A Theory of Poetry*. New York: Oxford University Press.
    1975 *A Map of Misreading*. New York: Oxford University Press.
    1982 *The Breaking of the Vessels*. Chicago: University of Chicago Press.
    1983 *Agon: Towards a Theory of Revisionism*. New York: Oxford University Press.
    1988 *Poetics of Influence*. Ed. John Hollander. New Haven, Conn.: Henry R. Schwab.

Bluestone, George
1960 "John Wain and John Barth: The Angry and the Accurate." *Massachusetts Review* 1 (May): 582–89.
Borges, Jorge Luis
1962 *Ficciones.* Ed. Anthony Kerrigan. New York: Grove Press.
1964 *Labyrinths: Selected Stories and Other Writings.* Ed. Donald A. Yates and James E. Irby. New York: New Directions.
1984 *Seven Nights.* Trans. Eliot Weinberger. New York: New Directions.
Bruner, Jerome S.
1962 *On Knowing: Essays for the Left Hand.* Cambridge, MA: Harvard University Press.
Bryant, Jerry H.
1980 "The Novel Looks at Itself—Again." In *Critical Essays on John Barth.* Ed. Joseph Waldmeir. Boston: G. K. Hall.
Calder, Nigel
1979 *Einstein's Universe.* New York: Greenwich House.
Calvino, Italo
1978 *Invisible Cities.* Trans. William Weaver. New York: Harcourt Brace Jovanovich.
Campbell, Joseph
1949 *The Hero with a Thousand Faces.* Princeton: Princeton University Press, Bollingen Series XVII.
Dane, Joseph A.
1988 *Critical Concepts versus Literary Practices, Aristophanes to Sterne.* Norman: University of Oklahoma Press.
Deleuze, Gilles
1987 *Dialogues: Gilles Deleuze and Claire Parnet.* Trans. Hugh Tomlinson and Barbara Habberjam. New York: Columbia University Press.
Deleuze, Gilles, and Félix Guattari
1983 *Anti-Oedipus: Capitalism and Schizophrenia.* Trans. Robert Hurley, Mark Seem, and Helen R. Lane. Minneapolis: University of Minnesota Press. [1971]
1987 *A Thousand Plateaus: Capitalism and Schizophrenia.* Trans. Brian Massumi. Minneapolis: University of Minnesota Press. [1980]
Derrida, Jacques
1976 *Of Grammatology.* Trans. Gayatri Chakavorty Spivak. Baltimore, Md.: Johns Hopkins University Press.
1982 *Dissemination.* Chicago: University of Chicago Press.
Eco, Umberto
1985 "Innovation and Repetition: Between Modern and Post-Modern Aesthetics." *Daedalus* 114, no. 4: 164–76.
Eliot, T. S.
1972 "Tradition and the Individual Talent." In *20th Century Literary Criticism.* Ed. David Lodge, 71–77. London: Longman. [1919]
1923 "Ulysses, Order, and Myth." *The Dial* (November): 175–78.
Enck, John
1965 "John Barth: An Interview." *Wisconsin Studies in Contemporary Literature* 6, no. 1: 7–13.
Felman, Shoshana
1983 "Beyond Oedipus: The Specimen Story of Psychoanalysis." In *Lacan and Narration: The Psycho-analytic Difference in Narrative Theory.* Ed.

Robert Con Davis, 1021–53. Baltimore: Johns Hopkins University Press.

Foucault, Michel

1980 *Language, Counter-Memory, Practice.* Ed. Donald F. Bouchard. Trans. Donald F. Bouchard and Sherry Simon. Ithaca, N.Y.: Cornell University Press.

Freud, Anna

1967 *The Ego and the Mechanisms of Defense.* New York: International Universities Press. [1936]

Freud, Sigmund

1961 *Beyond the Pleasure Principle.* Trans. James Strachey. New York: Norton. [1920]

1965 *The Interpretation of Dreams.* Ed. and trans. James Strachey. New York: Avon Books. [1900]

1974 "Mourning and Melancholia." In *The Complete Psychological Works of Sigmund Freud*, Vol. 14. General ed. James Strachey, 239–56. London: Hogarth Press. [1917]

Girard, René

1965 *Deceit, Desire, and the Novel: Self and Other in Literary Structure.* Trans. Yvonne Freccero. Baltimore: Johns Hopkins University Press.

1978 "Perilous Balance: A Comic Hypothesis." In *"To double business bound": Essays on Literature, Mimesis, and Anthropology*, 121–35. Baltimore: Johns Hopkins Univ. Press.

1990 "Innovation and Repetition." *SubStance* no. 62/63: 7–20.

Gorak, Jan

1987 *God the Artist: American Novelists in a Post-Realist Age.* Urbana: University of Illinois Press.

Harris, Charles B.

1983 *Passionate Virtuosity: The Fiction of John Barth.* Urbana: University of Illinois Press.

Hassan, Ihab

1984 *Paracriticisms: Seven Speculations of the Times.* Urbana: University of Illinois Press.

Hawkes, John, and John Barth

1979 "Hawkes and Barth Talk about Fiction." *New York Times Book Review* 84 (April 1): 7. Excerpts from the University of Cincinnati Fiction Festival, November 2, 1978.

Hawkes, Terence

1972 *Metaphor.* London: Methuen.

Hawking, Stephen

1990 *A Brief History of Time: From the Big Bang to Black Holes.* New York: Bantam.

Holland, Eugene W.

1986 "The *Anti-Oedipus*: Postmodernism in Theory or, the post-Lacanian historical contextualization of psychoanalysis." *Boundary 2* 214, nos. 1/2: 291–308.

Hutcheon, Linda

1985 *A Theory of Parody: The Teachings of Twentieth-Century Art Forms.* London: Methuen.

Irwin, John T.
  1975 *Doubling and Incest/Repetition and Revenge*. Baltimore: Johns Hopkins
    University Press.
Joyce, James
  1961 *Ulysses*. New York: Random House. [1922]
  1964 *A Portrait of the Artist as a Young Man*. New York: Viking. [1916]
Kerner, David
  1959 "Psychodrama in Eden." *Chicago Review* 13: 59–67.
Klinkowitz, Jerome
  1975 *Literary Disruptions: The Making of a Post-Contemporary American Fiction*.
    Urbana: University of Illinois Press.
Lacan, Jacques
  1977 *Écrits: A Selection*. Trans. Alan Sheridan. London: Tavistock.
  1981 "*Discours de Rome*." In *Speech and Language in Psychoanalysis*. Trans.
    Anthony Wilden, 3–87. Baltimore: Johns Hopkins University Press.
    [1953]
  1988 *The Seminar of Jacques Lacan, 1953–1954: Book 1, Freud's Papers on
    Technique*. Ed. Jacques-Alain Miller. Trans. John Forrester. New York:
    Norton.
Laplanche, Jean
  1976 *Life and Death in Psychoanalysis*. Trans. Jeffrey Mehlman. Baltimore:
    Johns Hopkins University Press. [1970]
Laplanche, Jean, and J. B. Pontalis
  1973 *The Language of Psycho-Analysis*. Trans. Donald Nicholson-Smith. New
    York: Norton.
LeClair, Thomas (Tom)
  1973 "John Barth's *The Floating Opera*: Death and the Craft of Fiction."
    Texas Studies in Literature and Language 14, no. 4: 711–30.
  1989 *The Art of Excess: Mastery in Contemporary American Fiction*. Urbana:
    University of Illinois Press.
Leclaire, Serge
  1980 "Jerome, or Death in the Life of the Obsessional." In *Returning to
    Freud: Clinical Psychoanalysis in the School of Lacan*. Ed. and trans. Stuart
    Schneiderman, 94–113. New Haven, Conn.: Yale University Press.
Lipking, Lawrence
  1981 *The Life of the Poet: Beginning and Ending Poetic Careers*. Chicago: Uni-
    versity of Chicago Press.
Lloyd, Geoffrey
  1973 "Right and Left in Greek Philosophy." In *Right and Left: Essays on Dual
    Symbolic Classification*. Ed. Rodney Needham, 167–86. Chicago: Uni-
    versity of Chicago Press.
Lodge, David
  1980 "Barth's Folly." *Times Literary Supplement* (May 30): 607–608.
Morrell, David
  1976 *John Barth: An Introduction*. University Park: Pennsylvania State Uni-
    versity Press.
Needham, Rodney
  1973 "The Left Hand of the Mugwe." In *Right and Left: Essays on Dual
    Symbolic Classification*, Ed. Rodney Needham, 109–26. Chicago: Uni-
    versity of Chicago Press.

Newell, Allan
  1985 "SOAR: An Architecture for General Intelligence." Lecture. Cognitive Studies Colloquium, Princeton University, March 25.
O'Donnell, Patrick
  1986 *Passionate Doubts: Designs of Interpretation in Contemporary American Fiction*. Iowa City: University of Iowa Press.
  1979 "PW Interview: John Barth." *Publishers Weekly*, October 22: 6–8.
Piaget, Jean
  1976 *The Child's Construction of Reality*. Trans. Margaret Cook. London: Routledge and Kegan Paul.
Prince, Alan
  1968 "An Interview with John Barth." *Prism* (Spring): 44–49.
Quinn, Arthur
  1982 *Figures of Speech: 60 ways to turn a phrase*. Salt Lake City, Utah: Gibbs M. Smith.
Reilly, Charlie
  1981 "An Interview with John Barth." *Contemporary Literature* 22: 1–23.
Rovit, Earl
  1963 "The Novel as Parody: John Barth." *Critique* 6, no. 2: 77–85.
Safer, Elaine B.
  1989 *The Contemporary American Comic Epic*. Detroit, Mich.: Wayne State University Press.
Said, Edward W.
  1975 *Beginnings: Intention and Method*. New York: Basic Books.
Schneiderman, Stuart, ed. and trans.
  1980 *Returning to Freud: Clinical Analysis in the School of Lacan*. New Haven: Yale University Press.
Scholes, Robert
  1967 *The Fabulators*. New York: Oxford University Press.
Schulz, Max F.
  1990 *The Muses of John Barth*. Baltimore: Johns Hopkins University Press.
Serres, Michel
  1982 *Hermes: Literature, Science, Philosophy*. Eds. Josué V. Harari and David F. Bell. Baltimore: Johns Hopkins University Press.
Stark, John
  1974 *The Literature of Exhaustion: Borges, Nabokov, and Barth*. Durham, N.C.: Duke University Press.
Stonum, Gary Lee
  1979 *Faulkner's Career: An Internal Literary History*. Ithaca, N.Y.: Cornell University Press.
Tharpe, Jac
  1974 *John Barth: The Comic Sublimity of Paradox*. Carbondale: Southern Illinois University Press.
White, Allon, and Peter Stallybrass
  1986 *The Politics and Poetics of Transgression*. Ithaca, N.Y.: Cornell University Press.
Wilden, Anthony
  1981 "Lacan and the Discourse of the Other." In *Speech and Language in Psychoanalysis*, 157–311. Baltimore: Johns Hopkins University Press. [1968]

Woolf, Virginia
  1972 "Modern Fiction." In *20th Century Literary Criticism*. Ed. David Lodge,
        86–91. London: Longman. [1919]
Wyatt, David
  1980 *Prodigal Sons: A Study in Authorship and Authority*. Baltimore: Johns
        Hopkins University Press.
Ziegler, Heide
  1987 *John Barth*. London: Methuen.

Index

Penn Studies in Contemporary American Fiction

A Series Edited by Emory Elliott, University of California at Riverside

Alan Wilde, *Middle Grounds: Studies in Contemporary American Fiction*. 1987

Brian Stonehill, *The Self-Conscious Novel: Artifice in Fiction from Joyce to Pynchon*. 1988

Silvio Gaggi, *Modern/Postmodern: A Study in Twentieth-Century Arts and Ideas*. 1989

John Johnston, *Carnival of Repetition: Gaddis's* The Recognitions *and Postmodern Theory*. 1990

Ellen Pifer, *Saul Bellow Against the Grain*. 1990

Arthur M. Saltzman, *Designs of Darkness in Contemporary American Fiction*. 1990

Paul Maltby, *Dissident Postmodernists: Barthelme, Coover, Pynchon*. 1991

Patricia Tobin, *John Barth and the Anxiety of Continuance*. 1992

This book was set in Baskerville and Eras typefaces. Baskerville was designed by John Baskerville at his private press in Birmingham, England, in the eighteenth century. The first typeface to depart from oldstyle typeface design, Baskerville has more variation between thick and thin strokes. In an effort to insure that the thick and thin strokes of his typeface reproduced well on paper, John Baskerville developed the first wove paper, the surface of which was much smoother than the laid paper of the time. The development of wove paper was partly responsible for the introduction of typefaces classified as modern, which have even more contrast between thick and thin strokes.

Eras was designed in 1969 by Studio Hollenstein in Paris for the Wagner Typefoundry. A contemporary script-like version of a sans-serif typeface, the letters of Eras have a monotone stroke and are slightly inclined.

Printed on acid-free paper.